HAMAS
VS.
FATAH

ALSO BY JONATHAN SCHANZER

Al-Qaeda's Armies: Middle East Affiliate Groups &
the Next Generation of Terror

HAMAS VS. FATAH

THE STRUGGLE FOR PALESTINE

Jonathan Schanzer

palgrave
macmillan

in memory of
David Schanzer

HAMAS VS. FATAH
Copyright © Jonathan Schanzer, 2008.
Foreword copyright © Daniel Pipes, 2008.
All rights reserved.

First published in 2008 by PALGRAVE MACMILLAN® in the US-a division of St.
Martin's Press LLC, 175 Fifth Avenue, New York, NY 10010.

Where this book is distributed in the UK, Europe and the rest of the world, this is by
Palgrave Macmillan, a division of Macmillan Publishers Limited, registered in England,
company number 785998, of Houndmills, Basingstoke, Hampshire RG21 6XS.

Palgrave Macmillan is the global academic imprint of the above companies and has
companies and representatives throughout the world.

Palgrave® and Macmillan® are registered trademarks in the United States, the United
Kingdom, Europe and other countries.

ISBN-13: 978–0–230–60905–1
ISBN-10: 0–230–60905–8

Library of Congress Cataloging-in-Publication Data
Schanzer, Jonathan.
    Hamas vs. Fatah : the struggle for Palestine / by Jonathan Schanzer.
       p.   cm.
    ISBN 0–230–60905–8
    1. Palestinian Arabs—Politics and government—1993–   2. Harakat al-
Muqawamah al-Islamiyah.   3. Fatah (Organization).   4. Israel—Politics and
government—1993–   5. Arab-Israeli conflict—1993——Peace.   I. Title.
DS119.76.S34   2008
956.95'3044—dc22
              2008009959

A catalogue record of the book is available from the British Library.

Design by Letra Libre, Inc.

First edition: November 2008.
10   9   8   7   6   5   4   3   2   1
Printed in the United States of America.

CONTENTS

ACKNOWLEDGMENTS

Writing this book, particularly in its last weeks, became an all-consuming project. Accordingly, I thank the Jewish Policy Center, particularly Matthew Brooks and Dick Fox, for understanding the importance of this work and for providing me with the time to complete it.

For excellent editing of my previously published works, I acknowledge Martin Kramer (*Middle East Quarterly*), Gary Gambill (*Middle East Intelligence Bulletin*), Kathryn Jean Lopez (*National Review Online*), and Mark Cunningham (*New York Post*). These fine editors made my work unquestionably stronger the first time around and helped me understand how to improve it and refine it for the purposes of this book. In fact, their edits often helped me refine my view of the Fatah-Hamas conflict over the years.

I also wish to thank my good friends and colleagues Khairi Abaza, Jonathan Calt Harris, Avi Jorisch, and Asaf Romirowsky for accommodating my need for fast yet substantive critique and for filling in some very important gaps in this book. While these readers helped me identify some errors, any remaining ones are mine alone.

Maryann Karinch, my agent, deserves special mention too. We made our connection by chance years ago, but I went out of my way to reconnect with her on this project. Her workmanlike determination to find this book a home at Palgrave gave me the wonderful opportunity to work with my editor, Alessandra Bastagli, and her patient assistant, Emma Hamilton.

A final professional thank-you goes to Dr. Daniel Pipes, the man who gave me my first real break in this business and then gave me another break nearly a decade later when he agreed to take time out of his incredibly busy schedule to write the foreword to this book.

On a more personal note, I would like to acknowledge my mother, Sharon Schanzer, not only for reading the first draft of this book with a critical eye but for imbuing me with a passion for the Middle East.

Finally, I want to thank my chief copy editor and loving wife, Elana. We spent our first date discussing her edits of my last book between bites of gourmet pizza. The rest, as they say, is history.

Jonathan Schanzer
Washington, D.C.
August 2008

GLOSSARY

Al-Mujamma' al-Islami—An Islamic movement founded by the late Hamas leader Ahmed Yassin, and the precursor to Hamas in the Gaza Strip.

Al-Aqsa Martyrs Brigades—The Islamist armed wing of the Fatah organization, responsible for suicide bombings and other attacks against Israeli civilians.

Fatah—A secular Palestinian terrorist organization founded in the late 1950s by Yasir Arafat. It is now a political faction, but has not broken completely from its terrorist past.

Gaza Strip—The disputed territory captured by Israel in the 1967 Six-Day War, bordering the Sinai Peninsula and the Mediterranean Sea.

Green Line—Israel's borders after the 1948 war of independence, which do not include the West Bank or Gaza Strip.

Hamas—Also known as the Islamic Resistance Movement. This group is the primary Islamic opposition to Fatah in the West Bank and Gaza.

IDF—The Israel Defense Forces, or the Israeli army.

Izz al-Din al-Qassam Brigades—The arm of Hamas that typically claims credit for suicide bombings and other acts of violence.

Intifada—The term Palestinians use to describe uprisings or campaigns of violence against Israel. It literally means "shaking off."

PA—The Palestinian Authority, which is the governing body of the Palestinians, pursuant to the Olso diplomatic process of the 1990s.

PIJ—Palestinian Islamic Jihad, an organization that predates Hamas, carries out similar acts of violence against Israel, and is largely funded by Iran.

PLO—Palestine Liberation Organization, an umbrella organization of Palestinian factions that came under the control of Yasir Arafat following the 1967 Six-Day War.

UNLU—Unified National Leadership of the Uprising, a grassroots organization during the intifada of 1987, which directed protests and violence against Israel.

West Bank—The disputed territory captured by Israel in the 1967 Six-Day War, located on the west side of the Jordan River.

Credit to Andrea R. Cohen

FOREWORD

Divisions among Palestinians generally do not receive their due attention, Jonathan Schanzer correctly points out, in the immense academic and journalistic coverage of the Arab-Israeli conflict. Instead, an official, propagandistic, and inaccurate party line holds sway. To quote Rashid Khalidi, a former Palestine Liberation Organization employee now teaching at Columbia University,[1] a "uniform Palestinian identity" exists. The Palestinians are one—full stop, end of story.

This simplistic and ahistorical understanding largely dominates how outsiders see the Palestinians, to the near exclusion of other, more nuanced analyses, and the party line afflicts the whole history of the conflict—the period before 1948,[2] the heyday of pan-Arabism, the emergence of the Palestine Liberation Organization, and especially the 20-year period, 1987 to 2007, that Schanzer studies in the following pages. As he puts it, "While the mainstream American media overreported the violence between the Palestinians and Israelis, the 'other struggle for Palestine,' which began to play out between Fatah and Hamas, received little to no coverage in America."

Many differences divide Palestinians—Muslim and Christian, urban and rural, sedentary and nomadic, rich and poor, regional—but Schanzer, a highly talented historian of the modern Middle East, establishes here the nature, extent, and significance of two specific intra-Palestinian tensions: primarily that fight between Fatah and Hamas, for this has the most acute and immediate political importance, and secondarily the dichotomy between the West Bank and Gaza.

Hamas vs. Fatah traces the history of the two groups' relations from the emergence of Hamas in late 1987 to the Hamas conquest of Gaza in June 2007, then surveys the implications of this hostile but subtle relationship. In summary, Schanzer traces the simultaneous weakening of Fatah and strengthening of Hamas over this period. By 2008, Fatah's leader, Mahmoud Abbas, is enfeebled, "no more than the president of the Muqata compound in Ramallah," while Hamas rules the roost in Gaza, threatens to seize power on the West Bank, sends hundreds of rockets into Israel,[3] and even challenges the government of Egypt.[4]

This dramatic shift in fortunes can be attributed to many factors, but perhaps most of all to the fact that whereas Yasir Arafat's Fatah was all things to all Palestinians, Hamas represents a coherent movement, with a fixed outlook and specific goals. Time and again Schanzer demonstrates how the discipline and purpose of Hamas has given it the edge over the corrupt and amorphous Fatah.

Palestinian self-destruction, neglected or not, ranks as a major U.S. foreign policy concern, especially since 1993, when Washington cast its lot with Yasir Arafat, Fatah, the Palestine Liberation Organization, and the Palestinian Authority, hoping against hope that Western backing would transform a revolutionary movement long allied with the Soviet Union into an agency of good government and status quo aspirations.

Among its many conceptual mistakes, this hope implied devoting too little attention to the competition raging between Fatah and Hamas since 1987 for the backing of the Palestinian street, a competition that impelled Fatah not to be seen as going easy on Israel but as aggressively anti-Zionist as Hamas. Given that Fatah was in negotiations with successive Israeli governments and it had to make gentle noises to the Israeli and Western media, the organization had to take a particularly ferocious stance on the ground. What American (and Israeli) policy makers tended to dismiss as incidental turned out to have deep and abiding consequences; suffice it to say that the Palestinian constituency for accepting Israel as a Jewish state has steadily decreased since the heady days of late 1993, to the point that it now represents only about a fifth of the body politic.

Schanzer also documents the cost for U.S. foreign policy of inattention to the Fatah-Hamas *fitna* (Arabic for "internal strife"). For one thing, it led to a misreading of the Palestinian mood in the period leading up to the January 2006 elections, causing Washington to keep promoting them in the happy expectation that its favorite, Fatah, would win; when elections came, the crushing victory by Hamas over Fatah came as a shock. For another, in early 2007, what Schanzer calls "relatively weak mainstream media coverage" of Fatah-Hamas fighting meant that the June conquest of Gaza by Hamas came as another surprise to the Bush administration. In brief, those responsible for American interests neither anticipated nor prepared for the two climatic events in Hamas's rise to power, a situation as embarrassing as it is revealing. So limited an understanding of the issues almost guarantees severe policy mistakes.

Why, given the extent of intra-Palestinian differences and their importance, has this subject been so rudely ignored? Schanzer prudently stays away from this sensitive topic, but what keeps researchers away in droves should at least be mentioned. I believe it reflects the fact that few academics have a genuine interest in the Palestinians. Rather, they devote outsized attention to this otherwise small and obscure population because it represents a convenient and potent tool with which to malign Israel.

Organizations intent on criticizing Israel's every move by default become masters of tiny Palestinian grievances.[5] They document in loving detail residential and transportation patterns in the West Bank, water and electricity grids in Gaza, and impediments to reaching holy places in Jerusalem. Those intent on showing Israel in a bad light must champion the Palestinians with allegations of mass executions, torture, denial of hospital services—but this should not be confused with genuine concern for the Palestinians. Nor does it lead to an understanding of Palestinian life.

It particularly pleases me that the author undertook some of his initial research for this study while at the Middle East Forum, the research institute I direct, notably his studies on Fatah versus Hamas,[6] on comparative Palestinian uprisings,[7] and on the Gaza–West Bank split.[8] This last discussion, elaborated here in chapter 11, offers a particularly valuable review of the many and growing differences between the "two Palestines," a subject on which there is hardly anything in English but the writings by Jonathan Schanzer.

Most books on the Arab-Israeli conflict tread well-worn ground. *Hamas vs. Fatah* offers an original analysis of a key topic.

Daniel Pipes
Director, Middle East Forum
www.DanielPipes.org

INTRODUCTION

ISLAMISM VS. PALESTINIAN NATIONALISM

On January 26, 2006, an estimated 3,000 Palestinians aligned with Hamas marched through the West Bank town of Ramallah, chanting Hamas slogans and waving green flags emblazoned with the Hamas logo. Onlookers from the Fatah organization, the longtime ruling party, watched in disbelief. Only the night before, Fatah's supporters had driven through Manarah Square and fired celebratory gunshots into the air. According to polling data, Fatah would win the Palestinian legislative elections by a comfortable margin.

The following morning, however, it was Hamas that was celebrating. The polls had been wrong. Indeed, Hamas had won an overwhelming electoral victory. Frenzied supporters of the group, most known for its headline-grabbing suicide bombing tactics against Israel, chanted euphorically outside the Palestinian Legislative Council building. In a move that was seen as both disrespectful and audacious, the revelers raised the green Hamas flag over the building. Infuriated, Fatah supporters tried to lower the banner. A 30-minute struggle ensued, with the two sides throwing stones and breaking windows until Palestinian security fired warning shots into the air.

For months following the election, tensions between the two groups remained high. Fatah, the longtime power broker in the Palestinian territories—the West Bank and Gaza—refused to hand over the reins of power. Hamas, for its part, insisted that its landslide electoral victory had granted it legitimate control over the Palestinian Authority (PA), the governing structure for the territories. A conflict had been set in motion.

More than one year later, on June 7, 2007, forces loyal to the Hamas terrorist organization launched a military offensive against Fatah in Gaza, taking command of major arteries, commandeering the media, and assuming control over PA government buildings and installations. Four days into the fighting, after a series of pitched battles, Hamas gunmen clad in black ski masks controlled the dusty streets. It would not be long before the fall of the PA's fortress-like security compound, al-Suraya. Indeed, Hamas fighters had burrowed a tunnel beneath the building, detonated deadly explosives, and breached it. After just six days of fighting, all of the Gaza Strip was under Hamas control.

The violence between Hamas and Fatah came as a surprise to many observers. Innumerable news reports out of the Middle East over the years focused only on the conflict between Israelis and Palestinians. The Palestinians have traditionally been viewed as maintaining a united front and, in the words of Rashid Khalidi, a professor of Middle Eastern studies at Columbia University, a "uniform Palestinian identity."[1]

Khalidi and many other sympathetic observers of Palestinian politics could not have been more wrong. A critical view of Palestinian history, particularly over the last two decades, reveals that the Palestinians are a house divided, marked by sharp political differences and sporadic political violence. While many analysts have dismissed these differences as minor or insignificant over the years, the June 2007 violence was an unmistakable milestone. It was a clear and outward manifestation of a civil war that had gone undeclared for years. The battle between Fatah and Hamas was not simply a territorial conflict. It was not a misunderstanding. It was a bitter battle in a wider power struggle between two rival Palestinian factions known to hold two diametrically different ideological positions with regard to the role of religion and politics in what is commonly referred to as the struggle for Palestine.

The June violence was not a milestone simply because it was the first time that the Palestinians engaged in open warfare against one another. It also changed the way Middle East observers would interpret events that took place within the context of the Arab-Israeli conflict. Indeed, responsible decisions about the conflict or prescriptions for its settlement cannot be issued without taking into account the internal violence between the Palestinians.

In fact, conflict between the two most influential Palestinian factions must be, and always should have been, a critical component to understanding the Arab-Israeli conflict. As this book demonstrates, the Fatah and Hamas factions have been locked in a power struggle since 1987. However, this crucial facet of the "struggle for Palestine" has gone drastically underreported.

The internal Palestinian power struggle has been downplayed for a number of reasons. Some might blame America's intelligence services for failing to recognize this important subplot to the Palestinian-Israeli conflict. However, even if U.S. intelligence had a good handle on this issue, such information would likely remain classified. Similarly, the Israelis could be expected to keep their intelligence closely guarded.

The blame might fall, in part, on the shoulders of the myriad journalists covering the conflict over the years. The mainstream media should unquestionably accept some responsibility for missing this story. America's television networks, newspapers, and magazines have spent countless man-hours sensationalizing the acrimonious fight between Palestinians and Israelis. The story sells. But how often did intra-Arab fighting make front-page headlines in the *New York Times?* The genocide in the Darfur region of Sudan beginning in 2003 is a telling example of how important stories can become journalistic backwaters if they fail to capture the imagination of American consumers or advertisers.

In all fairness to the journalists, perhaps they did not have access. In 2006, free press watchdog Reporters Without Frontiers ranked the Palestinian Authority 134 of a total of 169 countries or territories surveyed, with number 169 having the worst freedom of the press.[2] As a result of draconian Palestinian press measures, most foreign and local reporters in the West Bank and the Gaza Strip do not enjoy access to unsavory aspects of Palestinian politics, but are provided ample opportunity to report on purported Israeli abuses of Palestinian rights throughout the disputed territories. Only a few journalists found ways to report on this conflict with color and clarity. Of them, Khaled Abu Toameh of the *Jerusalem Post* and Sarah El Deeb of the Associated Press deserve special mention for consistently finding stories that few others did.

In academia, hundreds of Arabic-speaking professors and researchers have spent millions of dollars in fellowship funds to travel to the West Bank and Gaza over the years. Only a handful chose to analyze the potential for a Palestinian civil war. Notably, Mahmood Monshipouri, of little-known Alma College in Michigan, published an article in 1996 entitled "The PLO Rivalry with Hamas."[3] Don Peretz of the State University of New York in Binghamton also predicted a clash between Hamas and Fatah, noting that "internecine conflict will very likely erupt among them when the time comes for the Palestinians to determine their political future."[4]

Unfortunately, most of the professorate has produced streams of anti-Israel diatribe but very little critical work on the internal Palestinian dynamic. Some critics charged that professors of Middle Eastern studies had an ax to grind and that their research had a naked political agenda. One noted Middle East scholar, Martin Kramer, wrote an entire book about the problem, entitled *Ivory Towers on Sand: The Failure of Middle Eastern Studies in America*, which documents the shortcomings of many of America's Middle East scholars. Kramer notes that the political agenda of these professors caused them to commit a litany of crucial errors in recent years. Among their recent failings, he believes, the academy consistently downplayed the deadly impact of Islamism and minimized the dangers of terrorism coming out of the Arab world.[5]

Tellingly, after the Hamas conquest of Gaza in June 2007, several Middle East studies professors argued that the Gaza coup was a positive development. They argued that the violence was a signal that it was time to start a dialogue with Hamas, which they viewed as a force for Palestinian democracy. Notably, Harvard University's Sara Roy and Boston University's Augustus Richard Norton wrote a piece in the *Christian Science Monitor* entitled "Yes, You Can Work with Hamas."[6]

These professors, and scores of others, seem to ignore that Hamas is a violent, totalitarian organization that has taken the lives of hundreds of Israelis and Palestinians over the years and vows to continue down that same path. Similarly, in the early 1990s, many Middle Eastern studies professors insisted that Fatah and the Palestine Liberation Organization (PLO) were prepared to renounce violence, even as these groups continued to openly call for Israel's destruction.

What the professors did not grasp then, and do not grasp now, is that radical Islam and the modern incarnation of Palestinian nationalism are both dangerous ideologies. These two worldviews were behind countless acts of violence against Israelis in recent decades. By 2007, they were also responsible for many acts of violence against Palestinians. According to B'tselem, an Israeli human rights group, more than 330 Palestinians were killed in internecine fighting between Hamas and Fatah in 2007, with thousands more wounded.[7] Scores of additional casualties were reported in 2008, although numbers were not readily available at the time of this writing.

The driving ideological force behind Hamas (which is an acronym for *Harakat al-Muqawamma al-Islamiyya,* meaning "Islamic Resistance Movement") is radical Islam. Radical Islam, as Americans have learned since September 11, 2001, is an expansionist and utopian ideology that often justifies violence in the name of what is commonly recognized as a peaceful religion. Those who embrace this ideology seek to implement a strict interpretation of the Quran (Islam's holy book) and *shari'a* (Islamic law) in all Muslim lands. This can include interpretations of laws that stipulate the subjugation of women, poor treatment of minorities, as well as a strong disdain for non-Muslim cultures. Islamists also seek a united Muslim polity, spearheaded by the leadership of a caliph, that would one day dominate the globe. *Jihad,* or holy war, is often seen as the means to achieve these objectives.

It is commonly asserted that the Islamist movement today comprises a minority of the estimated 1.5 billion Muslims in the world. While estimates vary and numbers are hazy, Islamists could account for as much as 15 percent of the Muslim world.[8] But even if only 10 percent embrace Islamism, some 150 million people seek a world dominated by a radical interpretation of the faith and harbor a deep hatred for the principles upon which the West was built, including capitalism, egalitarianism, individualism, and democracy.

The fact that radical Islam appears to be proliferating at an alarmingly rapid rate led America to invade Afghanistan in late 2001 for providing safe haven to the al-Qaeda terrorist network and to increase counterterrorism operations around the world. It has prompted the U.S. Department of State to launch what is now called the "War of Ideas," a public relations campaign to persuade the Muslim world that liberalism and democracy are on the march. To be sure, the Hamas election victory in 2006 and subsequent takeover of Gaza did little to support that notion.

Unfortunately, the United States and its allies have hard work ahead. The modern Islamist movement has been adding adherents steadily since at least the seventeenth century. The movement's growth coincided with the decline of the Ottoman Empire. Until the Ottoman decline, the Muslim world had enjoyed the most vibrant culture on earth, with territory encompassing the Middle East and parts of Africa, Asia, and southeastern Europe. Soon, however, the West achieved military superiority and began to hand the Muslim world one defeat after the next. The West also eclipsed the Muslim world in the practical and physical sciences, modern weaponry and military tactics, mass communication, law, and political science.

This startling change to the status quo sparked a range of responses. Although many adapted, some Muslims sought refuge in a totalitarian interpretation of Islam that reminded adherents of an era when the religion was the reigning world force. The ideology rejected the West and its new ways of viewing the world. Rather than simply seeing the West as "the other," this new breed of Islamic fundamentalist perceived the West as its enemy.

Over time, several seminal thinkers shaped and molded the Islamist view of the world.[9] Under the sway of these figures, Islamists often rejected the influence of the West and even the legitimacy of their own secular governments for being subservient to the West. The overthrow of these pro-West regimes soon became an integral part of the Islamist agenda.

This negative view of secular governments was undoubtedly the way in which Hamas viewed Fatah and the Palestinian Authority. After all, both the PA and Fatah had long engaged in diplomacy with the United States and even negotiated with Israel for a peaceful settlement to the Palestinian-Israeli conflict. The very thought of negotiating with Israel, a Jewish state that Hamas sees as usurping Muslim lands, has earned Fatah and the PA the wrath of Hamas. The Islamist group's covenant of 1988 is a vitriolic, revolutionary document that glorifies violence in the name of Islam. The Hamas covenant declares that "Allah is its target, the Prophet is its model, the Quran its constitution: Jihad is its path and death for the sake of Allah is the loftiest of its wishes."[10]

Inside the West Bank and Gaza, the only ideology that can compete with Hamas's Islamist ideology is secular Palestinian nationalism. This ideology is fueled by the legitimate and understandable desire of the Palestinian people to create a state with permanent and recognized borders. Although there is certainly nothing inherently dangerous about a people who seek to inhabit the land they view as their historic homeland, nationalism has been responsible for numerous wars and conflicts around the globe. Combined with xenophobia, chauvinism, and/or irredentism, nationalism can become as dangerous as any other radical ideology.[11] In its current incarnation, as commonly expressed by Fatah and the PLO, the ideology of Palestinian nationalism often meets these criteria.

Despite the fact that the Palestinian Authority, a quasi-government staffed primarily by Fatah faction members, is commonly identified as a moderate faction within the Palestinian political spectrum, both Fatah and the PA have sponsored numerous acts of violence over the years. In fact, a persuasive argument can be made that since the very inception of the movement, there has never been a noteworthy nonviolent Palestinian nationalist stream. Dating back to the British mandate (1923–1948), Palestinian nationalism has been based more on destruction (of a Jewish state) than creation (of its own state).

Haj Amin al-Husseini, the *mufti* (religious authority) of Jerusalem from 1921 to 1948, was the first prominent leader of the Palestinian nationalist movement. An ardent anti-Zionist, Husseini whipped up Arab hatred in August 1929 by accusing the Jews of endangering the al-Aqsa Mosque and other Muslim holy sites in Jerusalem. In 1936, he led a terrorism campaign against Jewish and British targets, prompting the British to exile him in 1937 (although the Arab revolt he sparked continued through 1939). While in exile during World War II, Husseini established close ties with Nazis, including SS chief Heinrich Himmler, earning the early Palestinian nationalist movement an ignominious place in world history.[12] If Hitler won the war, Husseini reportedly hoped to rule over a vast territory in the Middle East.

French historian Gilles Kepel adds that Husseini helped create the "Handjar (Dagger) SS Battalion that was raised among the Bosnian Muslims" for the Third Reich in the Balkans.[13]

Husseini was not the only leader to soil the name of the Palestinian nationalist movement. Guerrilla leader Yasir Arafat catapulted Palestinian nationalism back onto the world stage in the 1960s and 1970s with spectacular terrorist attacks against Israeli targets, both in Israel and abroad. With perennial facial stubble, olive fatigues, and a *keffiyeh* (the traditional checkered Palestinian headscarf), Arafat was a self-styled revolutionary who directed violence against Israel while also lobbying against it through various diplomatic channels. Arafat's Palestinian Liberation Organization, an umbrella group for a cornucopia of guerrilla squads, became the preeminent model for terrorism in the modern era. Thanks mostly to PLO violence in the 1970s, the West came to view the entire Palestinian people (not just the violent groups) as bloodthirsty and vengeful, and most commonly identified with headline-grabbing terrorist assaults.

The spate of violence carried out by Palestinians against civilians in the 1960s and 1970s was unprecedented. Beginning in 1968, Palestinian terrorists initiated 35 airplane hijackings.[14] Other acts of terror included the 1972 massacre of Israeli athletes at the Munich Olympic games; the 1973 attack on the Saudi embassy in Khartoum, Sudan, that led to the murder of the U.S. embassy's chief of mission; and the 1985 attack on the cruise ship *Achille Lauro,* in which a wheelchair-bound American Jew was shot dead and dumped into the water.

It can also be argued that violence in the name of Palestinian nationalism has led to death and destruction in nearly every territory that the Palestinians have inhabited in their quest for a nation. In the early 1970s, for example, the Fatah-backed PLO attempted to hijack the kingdom of Jordan. The result was Black September, a bloody war that resulted in thousands of Palestinian casualties and the reemergence of a free Jordan. Fatah and the PLO then attempted to create a mini-state inside Lebanon in late 1970s and early 1980s, which contributed in no small part to an anarchic civil war. Unable to control the violence launched against it from the north, Israel invaded Lebanon and the Palestinians were forced to flee once again, leaving a decimated Lebanon in their wake. Finally, following a decade of exile in Tunisia, the PLO descended on the West Bank and Gaza after the signing of the Oslo Accords between Israel and the Palestinians in 1993. Since then, the two territories have plummeted into utter disarray, culminating in the 2007 civil war and the violent Hamas takeover of the Gaza Strip. Thus, with the exception of Tunisia, every home base of the PLO, and subsequently the Palestinian Authority, has been destroyed by the tragic blight of the Palestinian mini-state.

In an attempt to redress the demands of the Palestinians to create a homeland, the international community has floated numerous plans for negotiated settlements over the years. However, the Palestinian leaders have rejected each one. This refusal to compromise, coupled with the adoption of violence as a strategy, has only alienated the Palestinians from the world powers that might have helped them achieve their nationalist aspirations.

In 1947, the United Nations put forth a plan that afforded the Palestinian people half of what is today Israel, with significantly more land than what is now called the Gaza Strip and the West Bank. When the Palestinians rejected this plan, war erupted, leading to a free-for-all Arab land grab. The Egyptians usurped Gaza. The Jordanians occupied the West Bank. The Israelis took everything else in a victorious military campaign. The Palestinians were left with nothing.

A disastrous series of Palestinian choices in 2000 and 2001 demonstrated that, more than a half-century later, obstinacy still trumped the desire for a viable state. Specifically, Yasir Arafat's rejection of the 2001 Taba plan, a last-ditch effort by U.S. president Bill Clinton to save the Oslo peace process, was an unmitigated disaster for the Palestinians. This plan, drafted in the coastal Egypt town of Taba, afforded the Palestinians a state under U.S. guidance, including nearly all lands pursuant to United Nations Resolution 242 (the pre-1967 borders), including small parts of Jerusalem, and permission for a symbolic number of refugees to return to their historic homeland. Seeking to regain lost popularity on the Palestinian street, which put a premium on attacking Israel in both word and deed, Arafat rejected the offer. In so doing, he plunged the Palestinians deeper into a violent uprising and internal upheaval that eventually led to civil war.

While Hamas and Fatah, representing radical Islam and Palestinian nationalism respectively, are at odds, it is interesting to note that their ideologies are not entirely antithetical. Hamas, for example, does not embrace the secular ideology of nationalism as its guiding principle, but it certainly champions the movement's history of rejecting compromise with Israel and fighting for its historic homeland. The very fact that Hamas embraces Palestinian nationalism is what invited many non-Islamist Palestinians to support its platform when it won the votes of more than 45 percent of the Palestinian electorate in early 2006.

Fatah, for its part, was founded in the late 1950s by a number of practicing Muslims, some with ties to the Muslim Brotherhood. Over its 50-year history, Fatah has embraced Islamist symbols when convenient. The al-Aqsa Martyrs Brigade, for example, which Yasir Arafat founded after the launch of the 2000 intifada (uprising), was the way in which Fatah and its umbrella organization, the PLO, competed with Hamas in the Islamist arena.

Some observers view the fact that both Hamas and Fatah borrow from the other's ideology, when convenient, as common ground between the two warring factions. However, this is likely not the case. Both groups are engaged in a struggle whereby neither is ashamed to adopt the rhetoric or tactics of the other to gain an edge. Both factions know that Palestinian nationalism and Islamism are equally useful tools that can be wielded to generate support from the Palestinian street, depending on the political circumstances.

Thus, although the amorphous ideologies of these two factions are important to understanding the motivation of Hamas and Fatah, they are not the focal point of this book. Rather, this book endeavors to provide a useful history of the Fatah-Hamas struggle. Framing the bulk of discussion between the launch of the first intifada in 1987 and the June 2007 civil war, this book seeks to bring the antagonistic relationship between Hamas and Fatah into sharp relief.

In early 2008, Palestinian negotiators insisted that Israel's intransigence was the primary impediment to Palestinian statehood. Meanwhile, the "other struggle for Palestine" raged. The West Bank and the Gaza Strip were two separate nonstates, ruled by two nongovernments. Violence between Fatah and Hamas continued with no end in sight.

America may yet devise an effective peace plan to finally end the Palestinian-Israeli conflict. Israel might even make painful concessions at the negotiating table. However, the Palestinians must first reconcile their internal conflicts and make critical decisions about the use of violence against Palestinians and Israelis alike. In the current political climate, however, this kind of internal review will likely not happen. Real reform will be possible only with the rise of new parties and new leaders who eschew the violent tactics, strategies, and ideologies of the factions that represent most Palestinians today: Hamas and Fatah. In other words, only by rejecting the platforms of both parties will the Palestinian people begin to break the self-destructive cycle described in the pages that follow.

CHAPTER ONE

THE ROOTS OF HAMAS AND FATAH

Founded in Egypt in 1928, the Muslim Brotherhood (*al-Ikhwan al-Muslimun*) blazed a trail that other Islamist groups have only imitated or built on since. The Brotherhood's ideology has inspired, to one extent or another, many of today's radical movements, including al-Qaeda. Hamas was a splinter faction of the Palestinian Muslim Brotherhood. Fatah had nominal ties with the Palestinian and Egyptian branches of the organization but emulated some of its activities. Indeed, it would be difficult to fully comprehend the intra-Palestinian rivalry, which began in the late 1980s, without first understanding the history of the Muslim Brotherhood, which was founded a full seven decades earlier.

Founded by a bearded religious schoolteacher and watch repairman named Hassan al-Banna, the Brotherhood sought to inculcate and spread fundamentalist Islamic beliefs and values in Egypt and throughout the Muslim world. Born in 1928 of frustration with British (more broadly, Western) influence in Egypt, the movement envisioned the return to a time marked by a global Islamist order (the caliphate) in which Islam reigned supreme through one devout Muslim ruler (the caliph). Al-Banna's fiery orations captured the imagination of many Egyptians growing restless under British rule. He identified the primary ills affecting Muslims as "orientations to apostasy and nihilism" and the "non-Islamic" or "secular" currents that were growing stronger. Al-Banna was also a talented networker; he made connections throughout Egypt with Muslims who identified with his religious outlook. Inevitably, frustration over a lack of progress on the part of his network of advocates led him to determine that the "time for action" had arrived. Al-Banna and his followers soon developed armed cells that attacked Egyptian officials and supporters of the secularism that had taken control of Egypt. It is believed that in an attempt to quell the movement, elements within the Egyptian government killed al-Banna in Cairo in 1949.[1]

Al-Banna's death did not prevent the rapid spread of the movement he founded. The Brotherhood found further inspiration in Sayyid Qutb, a captivating Egyptian speaker and writer who declared the era in which he lived (the twentieth century) to be one of *jahiliyya* (ignorance and darkness) due to the Muslim world's lack of adherence to shari'a law. Qutb, a gaunt figure with a mustache and protruding eyes, spent two years studying in Colorado but left unimpressed. His skewering of permissive U.S. culture in his writings captured the imagination of his Brotherhood followers, who were already seeking reasons to hate the West. He also provided Quranic justifications for attacking Muslim leaders whose governments were not in accordance with shari'a. The Egyptian regime executed Qutb in 1966 for his incendiary politics, but his legacy, like al-Banna's, survived. His most famous book, *Ma'alim fil Tariq* (Milestones), is considered to be on the must-read list of today's Islamist thinkers and is even said to have influenced Usama bin Laden.[2]

Soon after Qutb's death, following the shocking Arab loss to Israel in the 1967 Six-Day War, the Muslim Brotherhood received a surprising boost in support. Moderate Muslims began to look for meaning in these seemingly inexplicable events. The Arab armies of Egypt, Jordan, and Syria had lost a war to the Jews, a people many Islamists regard as inferior. True, Jews are sometimes referred to as "people of the book" (*Ahl al-Kitaab*) among Muslims, due to a shared belief in one God as well as shared religious heritage rooted in the teachings of the Old Testament. However, Jews have also been treated as second-class citizens within Islam, or "*dhimmis.*" This meant that they were allowed to practice their religion but had to pay a tax to Muslims and recognize the supremacy of Islam. This led to a commonly held belief that Israel was inferior to the Muslim states.[3]

Moreover, Muslims were in shock over the fact that Israel had conquered Jerusalem, often described as Islam's third holiest city after Mecca and Medina in Saudi Arabia. This holy ground, like Israel itself, was considered to be *waqf,* or land endowed to Muslims by Allah. It was therefore unacceptable that it would be under the political and military control of non-Muslims.

Thus, an increasing number of Muslims returned to their Islamic roots and joined the Muslim Brotherhood, which believed that the loss of this land was Allah's punishment for Muslim sinners. The goal, then, was for Palestinian and other Muslims to return to their faith. Only then could they reclaim what they believed to be Palestine, including Jerusalem. This liberation theology remains the immutable cornerstone of the Hamas belief system today.

Throughout the twentieth century, the Muslim Brotherhood expanded rapidly, despite periods of government repression in several countries, to become one of the largest (if not the largest) Islamist organizations in the world. Experts often haggle over the exact membership of the worldwide movement, but the Brotherhood has penetrated every Muslim country, with predictably strong membership in the Arab world but also surprisingly large numbers in the West. The secretive society maintains strong chapters in the United States and western Europe. The movement's Egypt-based chairman, Dr. Mohammed Mahdi Akef (who continues to come under pressure from the Egyptian government) reaches out to his followers through the Brotherhood's English Web site (www.ikhwanweb.net), which charts the news and progress of the organization in Egypt and around the world.

———

The British mandate of Palestine was one of the first territories to be influenced by the Muslim Brotherhood movement. In fact, the Brotherhood was believed to be the first religious and political movement of its kind in mandatory Palestine. A handful of branches were founded even before the State of Israel was established in 1948.[4]

The Brotherhood first established branches in the West Bank between 1946 and 1948. The movement created more chapters there after the Hashemite Kingdom of Jordan conquered the territory in the 1948 Arab-Israeli war. The

Islamist organization subsequently extended into the Gaza Strip, where Egypt had taken military control. However, in 1948—when the State of Israel was founded, Jordan occupied the West Bank, and Egypt occupied Gaza—the Palestinian Muslim Brotherhood was forced to split into two separate organizations for geographic reasons.[5]

The Brotherhood grew steadily but separately in the two disputed territories over the next several decades, albeit under the watchful eyes of the Egyptian and Jordanian *mukhabarat* (security services). Indeed, the Brotherhood's Islamist ideology was not particularly welcomed in either state. The religiosity of Islamism posed a threat to the popularity of Pan-Arabism, a brand of secular socialism championed by Egypt's strongman, Gamal Abd al-Nasser, the Alexandria-born son of a postal worker who came to be seen as the leader of the entire Arab world. Islamism's populist appeal threatened the legitimacy of several traditional Arab monarchies, including those of Jordan and Saudi Arabia.

After Israel's conquest of the West Bank and the Gaza Strip in the 1967 Six-Day War, it was not Islamism that won the hearts and minds of Arabs. Rather, revolutionary Palestinian nationalism was seen as the panacea for the Arab world's failings. Yasir Arafat, a zealous engineering student turned activist with vague ties to the Muslim Brotherhood, emerged as the unlikely leader of this movement. Arafat had sought to fight alongside the Arab armies in the 1948 war with Israel but was turned away by the invading Arab regimes that sought to maintain control of the battlefield, and ultimately, the land they expected to conquer.[6] It is believed that this experience served as an awakening for Arafat, who came to believe that the Arab regimes would never defeat Israel. He believed that only a Palestinian revolutionary movement could achieve that goal.

In 1968, Arafat was given control of the Palestine Liberation Organization (PLO), a hitherto ineffectual organization created by the Arab League in 1964 that paid only lip service to "liberating" the lands that Palestinians coveted. Arafat soon positioned the PLO, under the leadership of his own Fatah organization, as the only entity that actively sought to conquer Israel.

As previously noted, Fatah was undoubtedly influenced by Islamism. HATAF, which means "death" in Arabic, might have been a natural Arabic acronym for *Harakat al-Tahrir al-Filastiniya* (the Palestinian Liberation Movement). Arafat's group, however, decided to reverse the order of the letters to give it a quranic meaning; *fatah* means "conquest," "victory," or "triumph."[7] Thus began the Fatah tradition of wielding Islamist words and symbols when expedient without relinquishing the socialist, revolutionary zeal that motivated the movement's thinking and actions.

Fatah was founded in 1958 in Kuwait by Arafat, along with seven other Palestinian activists: Khalil Wazir, Salah Khalaf, Khaled al-Hassan, Adil Abdel Karim, Mohammed Yusuf al-Najar, Khalid al-Amira, and Abdel Fatah Lahmoud. Their dream was to one day defeat Israel by force and raise a Palestinian flag over the land that had been conquered in 1948. Fatah was influenced by Islamic ideology but stood for the establishment of a secular state after the destruction of Israel. Over the course of two or three years, Arafat and the others had laid the foundation for a network of secret cells to launch terrorist attacks against Israel. By 1960, Arafat had a small Middle East network and raised enough money to publish a magazine called *Filasti-nuna: Nida' al-Hayat (Our Palestine: The Call to Life)* to raise consciousness about the Palestinian plight. The magazine's circulation was negligible, but it left the impression that there was an active Palestinian underground.[8]

On January 3, 1965, Fatah launched its first military operation when commandos placed a small explosive in the water system in Israel's Galilee region. A worker for the Israeli Mekorot Water Corporation found the bomb, however, before detonation. When the commandos crossed back over into Jordan, they were arrested by a Jordanian patrol. From a military standpoint, Fatah's subsequent attacks were also unimpressive. Most of its bombs did not explode, and Israel actually captured one Fatah commando when his rifle misfired. Still, Fatah carried out ten raids against Israel in the first three months of 1965.[9]

Early on, Fatah was based in Syria but launched operations from every state bordering Israel. Syria trained Fatah's commandos and even broadcast its military communiqués on its state radio but denied responsibility for the attacks, which increased in number and intensity.[10] Between February and May 1965, Fatah carried out several operations from Gaza, prompting Israeli reprisals against the towns of Qalqilya and Jenin inside the West Bank.[11]

Between May and October 1966, Arafat ordered his Fatah group to exe-cute 15 sabotage operations, 14 of which came from Jordan. Israeli Prime Minister Levi Eshkol, an intense man of Ukrainian background, ordered an antiguerrilla offensive. Israel attacked the Jordanian village of Samu in the West Bank on November 13, killing more than 70 people. The devastating offensive only appeared to legitimize Fatah. By the end of 1966, Arafat's ter-rorist group claimed to have carried out 41 raids into Israeli territories.[12]

In the first half of 1967, the rate of terrorism in Israel doubled. Arafat and his lieutenants ordered 37 attacks against the country in just six months.[13] The Israel Defense Forces (IDF) also clashed with the Syrian mili-tary repeatedly in the Golan Heights, culminating in an air battle over Dam-ascus in which six Syrian MiG fighter planes were shot down, humiliating the Syrian defense minister, Hafiz al-Asad—the man who would wrest con-trol of Syria by coup in 1970 and subsequently maintain authoritarian rule for three decades.

Thanks in part to Fatah, war was on the horizon. Jordan, Syria, and Saudi Arabia made the situation worse by taunting Egypt with claims that it was frightened of a conflict with Israel, choosing instead to hide behind the United Nations (UN) forces that buffered Egypt and Israel. On May 15, 1967, Egyptian President Nasser ordered the UN to withdraw from Sinai and positioned two Egyptian divisions on Israel's southern border. Nasser, who took power by coup in Egypt in 1954, was widely recognized as the leader of the Arab world; he inspired the Arabs with an ideology that synthe-sized Arab nationalism and socialism. The world looked on anxiously as he blocked Israeli ships from accessing the Red Sea port of Eilat. Fatah made the situation worse by carrying out five sabotage missions against Israeli tar-gets between May 15 and May 26.[14]

Seeking to preempt what appeared to be an inevitable war, the Israelis launched a surprise attack on June 5 that decimated the Egyptian, Syrian, and Jordanian armies. In six days, those three Arab states lost East Jerusalem, the West Bank, the Gaza Strip, the Sinai Peninsula, and the Golan Heights. All of the territory that the Arabs had captured in 1948 was now under Is-raeli control.

Egypt's defeat was devastating. Nasser was seen by many, not just in Egypt, as the only figure who could restore Arab power in the region. After his army's abject failure on the battlefield, many Palestinians ceased trusting the Arab regimes to "liberate Palestine." With no one else to turn to, the Palestinians looked to their indigenous freedom fighters for salvation. Fatah had captured the imagination of the Arab world.

"We do not have an ideology," Arafat stated in 1969. "Our goal is the liberation of our fatherland by any means necessary."[15] Those means would soon include shocking acts of violence outside of the territory that Arafat sought to conquer.

Among all the Arab actors, Arafat emerged as the only clear winner of the Six-Day War. The self-styled guerrilla, with his trademark checkered headscarf and sunglasses, assumed control of the Palestinian Liberation Organization and quickly thrust it onto the world stage with spectacular acts of terrorism against Israeli targets around the world. In so doing, Arafat became the de facto leader of the Palestinian people and the military commander in the "struggle for Palestine."

———

As Arafat, Fatah, and the PLO launched a campaign of terror against Israel, the Palestinian revolutionary movement captured the admiration and respect of the Arab world. By 1974, the PLO was recognized as the unquestioned leader of the Palestinian people at an Arab summit. The summit, held in Rabat, Morocco, and attended by 20 heads of state from around the Arab world, officially recognized Arafat and the PLO as the "sole legitimate representative of the Palestinian people."

The Rabat conference rattled Israel. The PLO was an unabashedly violent organization that continued to attack Israeli civilian targets worldwide. Thus, Israel sought to find strategies that would undermine the guerrilla movement, particularly among the Palestinians of the West Bank and Gaza Strip. By the late 1970s, the Israelis believed they had found Fatah's Achilles' heel. Indeed, Fatah had become anxious over the growing influence of the Muslim Brotherhood in Gaza. In fact, arguments there between Fatah and the Gaza Brotherhood sometimes turned violent, spilling over into the streets.[16] Israeli officials correctly determined that the Muslim Brotherhood was Fatah's primary competition. Seeking to undermine the terrorist group, the Israelis made the ill-fated decision to permit the Brotherhood to operate with relatively little oversight.

This flawed and dangerous plan stemmed from the fact that the Brotherhood maintained a rather strict policy of refraining from armed struggle against Israel. Faced with unprecedented guerrilla violence, the Jewish state was relieved to find groups that opposed Israel in word rather than deed. In retrospect, had Israel cracked down on the Brotherhood, there might have been less support for Hamas after its founding in 1988.

The Brotherhood received an unexpected boost after the 1967 war; once Israel took administrative control over both Palestinian territories, the Gaza and West Bank Brotherhood chapters united.[17] Both groups also established ties with the Islamist movement among Arabs inside Israel's Green Line, (the internationally recognized borders following the 1948–1949 war). The biggest boost for the Brotherhood came in 1973, however, when the Israeli military provided Ahmed Yassin, the eventual founder of Hamas, with a license to establish al-Mujamma' al-Islami (the Islamic Center). For the next 15 years, his center served as a political and cultural center for most Brotherhood activities in the Gaza Strip. More important, it provided a vehicle through which Yassin could reach out to all Palestinians. The center boasted an aggressive network of health services, day care, youth activities, and even food services that won the support and loyalty of the destitute Palestinians living in Gaza's refugee camps. These services were part of a long-term strategy of *dawa,* or outreach, to the Palestinian people. They gained Yassin many supporters and laid the foundation for a powerful movement that even he likely could never have foreseen.

Born to a middle-class family in 1938 under the British mandate of Palestine, Yassin came of age as the early failures of Palestinian nationalism became increasingly apparent. When Israel defeated the invading Arab armies in 1948 and 1949, leading to the subsequent creation of the State of Israel, Yassin and his family were relocated to al-Shati refugee camp in the Gaza Strip. After a childhood sports accident left him crippled, he devoted his life to Islamic scholarship and activism. The future Hamas founder studied at al-Azhar University in Cairo, Egypt, a breeding ground for the early members of the Muslim Brotherhood.

Yassin's Brotherhood activism was not popular with Nasser's Pan-Arabist regime. Many of Yassin's cohorts were deported, arrested, or even killed. Egyptian authorities reportedly were more lenient with Yassin due to his health problems. Thus, he was detained for only a short period and then returned to Gaza, where he found work as a teacher and continued to preach the sanctity of Palestinian land and other Brotherhood precepts. He saw his role as one of a cultural and educational mentor, preparing future generations of Palestinians to wage jihad, or holy war, against Israel.[18] This was the foundation for his center's network, which would in turn become the infrastructure of Hamas by 1988.

There is no denying that the Israeli strategy of allowing Yassin to build his *mujamma'* network in the 1970s and 1980s was shortsighted. The decision makers at the time must not have fully grasped the powerful allure of his message. According to one account, the Israelis arrested Yassin in 1984, but released him in 1985. By the mid-1980s, his network included numerous mosques, charities, and schools that later served as Islamist recruiting grounds for Palestinians throughout the territories. These institutions also became meetings points for Hamas operations, fundraising centers, and even safe houses.

While Yassin built the foundations of Hamas, another violent Islamist organization was born of a fissure that developed among Islamists in the territories. The fissure emerged between the young guard and the old guard of the Muslim Brotherhood. The younger, more zealous Islamists believed that Israel had to be conquered (and become Palestine) before the larger spiritual transformation could take place in every Muslim. The old guard, which represented the longstanding Brotherhood approach, held that nonviolent outreach (*dawa*) was the way to slowly retake Palestine in what they viewed would be a long and protracted battle of wills.

This fissure was the impetus for the founding of the Palestinian Islamic Jihad (PIJ) in 1979. PIJ was founded by two Gaza Strip–based Islamists, Sheikh Abd al-Aziz Awda and Fathi Shiqaqi, who sought to leverage the momentum of Ayatollah Ruhollah Khomeini's Iranian revolution of that year. Khomeini, the stern and scowling founder of the modern Iranian regime, had inspired Islamists around the world to embrace revolutionary Islam. PIJ was among them. The new Palestinian group advocated immediate confrontation with Israel as part of its commitment to changing the existing world order and replacing it with one dominated by Islam. PIJ's Khomeini-inspired views also stipulated a complete and total rejection of the existence of the State of Israel, with the ultimate goal of destroying it through jihad.[19] Within a decade, Hamas would embrace these ideas as its own.

PIJ, operating under a variety of names (including the Islamic Vanguard, the Revolutionary Islamic Current, and the Independents Movement), carried out a spate of guerrilla attacks against Israeli targets, particularly military ones in the Gaza Strip. Despite numerous successful Israeli counterterrorism operations against the group, in the 14 months prior to the Palestinian uprising of 1987, PIJ carried out a wave of unparalleled violence. On October 15, 1986, PIJ perpetrated its most famous attack, known as Operation al-Buraq. In this attack, PIJ hurled grenades at the IDF's elite Givati Brigade, which had gathered at Jerusalem's Western Wall (known as *al-Buraq* in the Quran). A string of other PIJ attacks followed, as well as a jailbreak by group members from a Gaza Strip prison in May 1987.

Heading into the Palestinian uprising, or intifada, later that year, many Palestinians viewed PIJ as the most prominent Islamist guerrilla movement in the territories. Indeed, when the Palestinian intifada erupted in December 1987, PIJ was given credit for infusing it with a distinct Islamist character. For this very reason, IDF operations systematically weakened PIJ within several months. The intifada's Islamist overtones had thoroughly alarmed the Israelis, prompting them to deport several PIJ leaders and to assassinate others. Additionally, Israel made sweeping arrests of suspected lower-ranking members throughout the West Bank and Gaza Strip. Successful operations notwithstanding, the intifada had an unmistakably Islamic identity as it gained momentum.

While PIJ was decimated by Israeli arrests and operations, it must be credited with forging a path that encouraged Palestinians to confront Israel in the name of Islam. PIJ's ideological rupture with the Muslim Brotherhood leadership also had lasting implications. Thanks to PIJ, more elements from within the Palestinian's Muslim Brotherhood called for active participation in "resistance" activities against Israel.[20]

Thus, the stage was set for yet another splinter organization of the Muslim Brotherhood to explode onto the Palestinian political scene. While PIJ influence steadily eroded, Hamas emerged to challenge both the Fatah-backed PLO and Israel. Neither Israel nor the PLO appeared to be prepared.

CHAPTER TWO

HAMAS, FATAH, AND THE FIRST INTIFADA

On December 8, 1987, an Israel Defense Forces truck crashed into a car filled with tired Gazans returning home from work in Israel, killing four and injuring others. That night, the funerals turned into angry demonstrations, which quickly spread. This was the start of the intifada, a spontaneous campaign of violence and protest against the Israeli presence in the territories.[1]

Soon after the violence began, leaders from various Palestinian political factions in the West Bank created the Unified National Leadership of the Uprising (UNLU) to promote planned violence against Israel. The West Bankers were soon joined by Gazans. Together, they created an underground organization with anonymous leaders who printed leaflets, or *bayanat*, designed to inform Palestinians in both territories of the developments surrounding the uprising.[2]

From their exile in Tunis, Arafat and the rest of the Fatah and Palestine Liberation Organization (PLO) leadership were caught off guard. But they quickly moved to take control of the UNLU, asserting Fatah/PLO as the established, leading faction in the "struggle for Palestine." Still, a broad spectrum of political factions in the territories participated in the UNLU, including the Palestinian Islamic Jihad (PIJ) and several others. Local committees were also established in neighborhoods throughout the territories to provide social services and coordinate the mostly violent protest activities.

At the outbreak of the intifada, the Palestinian Muslim Brotherhood was a house divided. Not unlike the PIJ debate of the late 1970s, there were those who sought to join the fray and attack Israel, while others maintained that the Brotherhood's tradition of nonviolent radicalization through teaching and outreach was the proper course of action. Those who embraced nonviolence supported the protest activity and produced propaganda emphasizing the Islamic nature of the intifada. They continued to work via the strong network of social services established by Ahmed Yassin's Islamic Center.

Those who sought a guerrilla war against Israel, specifically Yassin's cadre of younger Muslim Brotherhood members in Gaza, elected in December 1987 or January 1988 to create an umbrella organization. The group was called *Harakat al-Muqawamma al-Islamiyya,* meaning the "Islamic Resistance Movement," whose acronym was HAMAS, meaning "zeal" in Arabic. As was the case with PIJ, a generation of younger, more revolutionary Muslim Brothers broke from their elders. While the older generation still believed that *tarbiyeh* (education) and *dawa* (outreach) were the answer, the younger generation advocated jihad. This was not a clean break, however. Hamas still claimed it was a wing of the Brotherhood and venerated its long history of Islamist activism, education, and *dawa.*

This new splinter faction immediately asserted itself. Though it was an unknown entity, Hamas began to distribute leaflets like the PLO. While some historians assert that the first *bayan* bearing Hamas's name appeared on February 11, 1988, calling itself the "powerful arm of the Association of Muslim Brothers,"[3] the movement's leaders insist that the first leaflet was dropped on the streets of Gaza on December 14, 1987, just five days after the start of the uprising.[4] Regardless of when the movement truly was launched, Hamas's pamphlets dealt with issues ranging from ideology to logistics surrounding civil strikes. It is at this point that the struggle between Hamas and Fatah/PLO begins.

By imitating the PLO's leafleting tactics and trying to harness popular support on the Palestinian street, the nascent Hamas was openly challenging the faction that claimed to be the "sole legitimate representative" of the Palestinian people. The Hamas leaflets and grassroots protest activities played a significant role in the mobilization of violence, imbuing the uprising with a zealous Islamist flare.

Of course, in 1988, Hamas did not yet pose a serious political challenge to the PLO. Although it is estimated that Hamas, through Yassin's *mujamma'* network, controlled some 40 percent of all mosques in Gaza,[5] and although the Islamists continued to win the support of Palestinians by providing crucial social services, Hamas had only minimal influence over the politics of the territories. Indeed, Yassin and the other Hamas leaders insisted that they did not view their new faction as a challenger to Fatah or the PLO. They acknowledged those groups' long history of attacking Israel and expressed support and respect for that approach.

Still, Hamas did not join the UNLU.[6] It had its own decision-making apparatus, comprised of several wings that operated independently but in concert with the larger movement. The political wing dealt with decisions concerning interactions with the Palestinian community. Hamas's communications wing was responsible for disseminating leaflets and other information about Hamas to the broader Palestinian public. The internal security wing punished so-called collaborators who endangered Hamas fighters or those who refused to join in the Hamas-sponsored strikes and demonstrations. The fighters belonged to the intifada wing of Hamas, while the youth wing was responsible for coordinating the intifada's demonstrations and rock-throwing. Hamas leaders oversaw the operations of these wings, but much of the activity was done at the grassroots level. In this way, Hamas was a well-oiled machine that almost instantly posed a challenge to the PLO's primacy on the street.[7]

Ties between Hamas and Fatah quickly became strained. Arafat's men increasingly saw Hamas as entering into competition with them. Indeed, Hamas was winning over many Fatah supporters on the Palestinian street. It was not long before conflicts arose between Hamas and Fatah supporters in cities across the territories.[8] In a speech in Yemen soon after the outbreak of the intifada, Arafat reportedly described Hamas members as ants that his forces could crush.[9] However, over time it became clear that the veteran Palestinian guerrilla leader was concerned.

Despite the tension that arose, the two sides attempted to pretend that the Palestinians were still united under one flag. One Hamas member claimed that Israel tried to exploit this rift by publishing statements in the name of Hamas against the UNLU and Fatah.[10] Hamas, however, continued to challenge Fatah on university campuses and other political power centers throughout the West Bank and Gaza.[11]

The Fatah-backed PLO leadership recognized that because it was in exile, and not side by side with the rock-throwing masses, it was losing organic support on the Palestinian street to Hamas, PIJ, and other groups. Yasir Arafat quickly sought to solidify his position of leadership among the Palestinians.

With seemingly uncontrollable violence raging in the territories, U.S. president George H. W. Bush, recognizing America's new role as sole superpower after the downfall of the Soviet Union, desperately sought a government that could control the Palestinians and perhaps even attempt to tend to their needs. Arafat smelled an opportunity. He tacitly recognized Israel by accepting the November 1947 UN General Assembly Resolution 181 that called for a partition of Palestine into a Jewish and an Arab state. The United States and Israel immediately viewed this as an opening for peace and a means to quell the intifada. Bush and Secretary of State James Baker began to work with Arafat and a team of Palestinian negotiators.

However, the administration faced a Herculean task. Fatah was a terrorist organization founded with the primary purpose of "liberating Palestine," which essentially amounted to the destruction of Israel. Fatah took control of the PLO in 1968 and launched a paramilitary campaign that resulted in dozens of attacks against Israeli civilian targets. Now Washington was working to find common ground between Israel and an organization whose stated goal, according to its 1964 charter, was the "eradication" of Israel's "economic, political, military, and cultural existence."[12]

While Arafat set out to demonstrate the legitimacy of the Fatah-backed PLO as a viable governing body for the Palestinian people, Hamas began to exploit the general frustration in the Gaza Strip and West Bank, where many Palestinians were losing confidence in Arafat's leadership. Some Palestinians interpreted his recognition of Israel as a sign of weakness or even unwillingness to fight. Some questioned why Fatah and the PLO had not succeeded in ousting Israel from the territories, particularly if both groups had been leading the uprising, as they had claimed. The Muslim Brotherhood, Hamas, and other Islamist groups portrayed these failures as stemming from the

PLO's secular and nationalist ideology and sought to persuade West Bankers and Gazans that Islamism was the solution.

Hamas soon extended its influence in both the Gaza Strip and the West Bank, and became the only recognized alternative to the Fatah-dominated UNLU in the intifada.[13] This was a significant achievement. For years Fatah had been the lone voice of the Palestinians; now there were two.

The Palestinians were not alone in recognizing Hamas as an important alternative to Fatah. Deep-pocket donors in oil-rich Saudi Arabia and other Gulf countries recognized the zeal of Hamas and sought to reward it. Money began to pour in from shadowy figures who sought simultaneously to attack Israel and to spread Islamist influence throughout the Middle East.[14]

On August 18, 1988, Hamas published its covenant, a document of 36 articles calling for a synthesis of Islamism and Palestinian nationalism. Unlike its PLO counterpart, the Hamas covenant appeared to have been embraced by the organization without debate, which granted it instant legitimacy.[15] The charter envisioned Palestine as a state run according to Islamic law, or shari'a, and declared that when "enemies usurp some Islamic lands, jihad becomes a duty binding to all Muslims."[16] Further, it stated that Palestinians should not cede one inch of land because Palestine is *waqf* (land endowed by Allah). This, in effect, made jihad in the name of redeeming lost land a religious duty. The organization asked Arab states to open their borders to Hamas mujahideen (jihad fighters) and to provide the necessary support to liberate Palestine. By releasing this covenant, Hamas broadcast an Islamist vision that openly challenged the Fatah constitution and PLO charter, both of which took a more nationalist and secular approach but had always been viewed as the guiding documents in the Palestinian quest for self-determination. Less than one year into the uprising, Hamas and the Fatah-led PLO were in open opposition.

The intifada continued to gain momentum in 1988, marked by large demonstrations and a seemingly endless Palestinian enthusiasm for violence against Israel. It was also fueled in part by King Hussein's July 31 declaration that Jordan officially relinquished its claim to the West Bank. Jordan had occupied the territory during the 1948 war, held it until 1967, and continued to invest in the Israeli-controlled infrastructure, hoping to one day reclaim it. Fearing a spillover of Palestinian violence into Jordan, the king declared that "the independent Palestinian state will be established on the occupied Palestinian land, after it is liberated, God willing."[17] This gesture gave hope to those Palestinians who had been involved in the intifada that at least the West Bank could one day be theirs.

As the PLO sought to demonstrate to the world that it could run a transitional government, it relinquished its traditional role as a guerrilla fighting squad, which had always been its source of popular support. Hamas appeared to understand this dynamic and quickly filled the vacancy. The more the PLO removed itself from the uprising, the more Hamas continued to direct aspects of the intifada and to gain members. By the end of 1988, analysts speculated that Hamas was on the verge of replacing Fatah and the PLO as the leading power in the territories.

The perception that Hamas was on the verge of becoming the most influential actor in the West Bank and Gaza continued to spread. Swelling the ranks of Hamas supporters, to the surprise of Fatah, was the Palestinian intelligentsia, including teachers, students, doctors, lawyers, and accountants. Observers soon suggested that if free elections were held in the territories, Hamas might have won more seats than the PLO.[18]

On November 12, 1988, Arafat declared Palestinian independence in Algiers at an emergency meeting of the Palestine National Council (PNC). In a communiqué released a few days later, the PLO called for a peace conference based on UN resolutions 242 and 338, which called for Israel to withdraw from territories it had conquered during the Six-Day War. Arafat's recognition of Israel's 1948 borders was a historic moment. Within two weeks, at least 55 nations recognized the Palestinians' call for independence,[19] thereby making the PLO an instant, makeshift quasi-government with Arafat at the helm. No longer was the PLO merely the official radical guerrilla faction representing the Palestinian cause. Recognizing a vacuum, Hamas quickly filled that vacancy.

———————

The intifada brought about several fundamental changes within existing Palestinian Islamist circles. It widened the ideological gap between the

Brotherhood's old guard and the younger generation. In this way, the intifada pushed the Muslim Brotherhood to more clearly define its approach to violence against Israel or other means to opposing the Jewish state.[20] But, without question, the most important by-product of the intifada was Hamas. The group's growth in popularity was unparalleled, both in the Palestinian territories and in the Arab diaspora. Within a few short years, Hamas found further financial, material, and logistical support throughout the Middle East, with special assistance from the Islamic Republic of Iran as well as Islamist benefactors and illegal charities in the United States and Europe that siphoned the donations they collected to terrorist causes abroad.

Finally, Hamas leaders learned during the first years of the intifada that their new group had the potential to expand its appeal among Palestinians in both the West Bank and Gaza. Hamas, they realized, even posed a challenge to the ruling Fatah party. Indeed, Hamas leaders appeared to understand that the rejection of Israel was critical to gaining popular support on the Palestinian street. However, this would also serve as a potential liability for the longevity of the organization, particularly as Israel gained a better understanding of its new enemy, and devised ways to weaken it.

CHAPTER THREE

HAMAS UNDER FIRE

In 1989, at the height of the intifada, Hamas took credit for the spread of Islam and violence on the Palestinian street. Between 1986 and 1989, the number of mosques in the Gaza Strip jumped from 150 to 200.[1] Hamas also bombarded Palestinians with leaflets designed to "use theology to galvanize the entire society."[2] Hamas gained support by underscoring its commitment to morality and family values. This message was important, given the common perception among Palestinians at the time that these issues were largely neglected by Arafat and the Palestine Liberation Organization (PLO). The influence of Hamas was soon noticeable; Palestinian women increasingly took to wearing the hijab (traditional head covering).[3]

"What is happening today in this blessed land," read a Hamas leaflet on February 25, "is but a new creation of the Islamic *Umma* [nation] and of the Muslim generation that carries the banner of Islam."[4]

It was soon clear that Ahmed Yassin and his nascent Hamas organization were gaining clout vis-à-vis the PLO. In January 1989, Hamas and the Popular Front for the Liberation of Palestine circulated a leaflet calling for an alternative to the UNLU.[5] By the summer, Hamas openly and unabashedly challenged the authority of the Unified Leadership. Indeed, Hamas leaders refused to allow its schools and universities to become staging grounds of Fatah-led civil disobedience and protest, insisting instead that studies continue as planned.[6]

The year 1989 was also significant in that Hamas began to carry out new and grisly acts of violence against Israel, a foreshadowing of the bloodshed to

come. In February, Hamas for the first time took credit for kidnapping Israeli soldiers, beginning what the group called "the development of the
movement's methods of resistance." In May, a Hamas fighter stabbed an Israeli soldier to death. On July 8, another Hamas terrorist took control of a
bus on the Tel Aviv–Jerusalem highway and crashed it, killing 16 people. In
October and November, Hamas fighters killed five IDF soldiers.[7] Hamas' use
of violence was increasing in intensity and audacity.

By May 1989, the organization's popularity and violence had caused
such alarm among Israelis that the IDF arrested hundreds of Hamas members. The arrested included Yassin, the group's founder, who was reportedly held on nine separate charges. According to one account, while in
detention in June 1989, the paraplegic mastermind of Hamas admitted
under duress to being the organization's founder and leader.[8] This revela-
tion did little to commute his sentence but had far-reaching ramifications
for the larger organization.

Initially it appeared that the way in which Israel was methodically picking off Hamas leaders would weaken the organization significantly. The
crackdown created a vacuum at the senior and middle leadership levels.
Faced with difficult choices in a difficult operating environment, Hamas
leaders who survived the security sweep realized they had little choice but to
restructure their ranks to ensure that additional arrests or assassinations
would not further debilitate the movement.

According to the testimony of Sufian Abu Samara, a Hamas activist arrested by Israeli security in 1991 after the wave of arrests, Hamas leader
Musa Abu Marzook "initiated approaching many people to fill up the vacuum." Marzook, who had studied engineering in the United States for several years and served as Hamas's senior operative in America, "warned of the
collapse of the movement if no new infrastructure is established."[9]

As the crackdown continued, more members fled the country. These
fugitives, or *mutaradun*,[10] established diaspora footholds in Amman, Jordan,
and Springfield, Virginia, where Marzook directed operations and raised
funds. He commanded critical aspects of Hamas for six years from his Virginia base until he was designated by the U.S. government as a terrorist in
1995 and deported in 1997. Through the Holy Land Foundation for Relief
and Development and the Islamic Association of Palestine, two charities

Marzook helped to establish in the 1990s, Hamas was able to raise millions of dollars in America.

Marzook's operation was critical to the group's survival. Hamas was getting hit from all sides in the Palestinian territories. In addition to Israeli counterterrorism efforts that continued to hobble the organization, the Fatah-backed PLO also tried to co-opt the group by "turning" some of the lower-ranking Hamas members through intimidation or even bribes.[11]

In an attempt to ensure the survival of Hamas, upon Marzook's direction, the Islamist group ironically created a cell structure similar to that of its rival, Fatah, when Arafat and his colleagues first began attacking Israel in the 1960s. Again Hamas appeared to be emulating its secular predecessor. Since the movement could no longer run on a centralized command system, Hamas deliberately split itself into small and independent cells, some of which consisted of no more than three men.[12] Each cell was given the tools (funds and materiel) to run with minimal guidance from the Hamas leadership.

As one Israeli terrorism expert confirms, the institutionalizing stage came in 1989, when Hamas "worked on strengthening its infrastructure while establishing low-level ranks of command on the regional level."[13] This investment had two important ramifications. Hamas reportedly took this opportunity to instruct its new command structure on how to challenge the primacy of the PLO.[14] The new structure also led to junior operatives working on the ground in the West Bank and Gaza Strip while senior decision makers operated far from the field. This structure enabled the perpetuation of a campaign of terror and violence against Israel that continued for decades, eventually earning Hamas terrorist designations from the United States and other Western nations.

On September 28, 1989, Israel declared Hamas an illegal organization. Ironically, this designation was pivotal for the group's legitimacy on the Palestinian street. Prior to this time, Palestinians reportedly distrusted Hamas due to the fact that Israel had previously supported Yassin's Islamic Center, the very foundation of Hamas, in its efforts to undermine Arafat,

Fatah, and the PLO. Now outlawed, Hamas clearly was in direct conflict with Israel. In this way, Israel inadvertently helped Hamas come of age as a jihad organization.

Hamas's standing was further elevated as IDF crackdowns revealed the fruits of its restructuring. Every time Israel tried to destroy Hamas, a pair of Israeli journalists noted, the group sprouted "new shoots, again and again, prompting more violence each time." In just months, Hamas had become an important factor in the Palestinian arena, due largely to its "impressive infrastructure." In fact, it was believed that in two short years, Hamas held the "power to ease or impede progress toward a political solution" between Israel and the Palestinians.[15] This remained the case for years to come; one act of Palestinian violence against Israel could always be counted on to derail dialogue, prompting Israel to demand better security before agreeing to get back to the negotiating table with Arafat and the PLO.

The year 1989 was also an important one for Hamas's foreign relations with sympathetic Islamist communities worldwide. After Israel's crackdown, Hamas leaders in exile and in the Palestinian territories recognized the need to strengthen the movement's support structure among sympathizers abroad.[16] Hamas set about creating a network of financial support that would be crucial to its long-term fiscal viability.

More important, unquestionably, was the announcement on November 16 that the terrorist group had formed an alliance with the Islamic Republic of Iran. Despite the theological enmity that commonly prevents Shi'ites and Sunnis from cooperating (Iran is a Shi'ite country and Hamas is almost entirely Sunni), the two sides agreed to an alliance in the "War to Liberate Palestine."[17] Of course, the Islamic Republic devoted most of its resources to its Lebanese client, Hizbullah, and to a lesser extent Palestinian Islamic Jihad (PIJ), a predominantly Sunni group that carried out attacks against Israel with Iranian support. But this was the beginning of a long-standing patron-client relationship that served Hamas well for years. Iran infused Hamas with the ideology and financing it needed to mount a challenge to the Fatah party and Israel alike. According to James Woolsey, former director of the

Central Intelligence Agency, Iran provided more than $100 million to Hamas from 1988 to 1994.[18]

Hamas also forged stronger ties with governments of Sunni Arab states and deep-pocket Sunni donors. Unlike Iran, these donors appeared to be natural supporters of the Sunni group. Funds to Hamas began to flow from wealthy individuals in Algeria, Egypt, Jordan, Qatar, Saudi Arabia, Sudan, and Tunisia.[19] The notion of supporting an Islamist group that was inflicting damage on Israel, the common enemy of the Arab world, was particularly attractive to these Arab states and individual financiers during the excitement of the intifada.

<hr>

By the end of 1989, Hamas appeared to command the respect of nearly all Palestinians, Muslim and Christian. Its strength was perhaps best demonstrated by the fact that, when it called for a general strike in the Palestinian territories on Christmas Day in 1989, despite the protests of Palestinian Christians, the strike was obeyed. Whether the Christians obeyed out of fear or respect cannot be known for certain, but it is commonly held that Hamas was the leading force of the intifada in its second year.

The year 1989 also brought with it several key lessons that Hamas carried into the future. The ability to restructure and adapt to Israeli strategies and tactics became an important Hamas asset. This flexibility proved to be critically important during subsequent years, particularly as the IDF undertook repeated efforts to arrest or neutralize Hamas fighters, masterminds, and spokesmen.

Perhaps the most important lesson for Hamas was that Fatah's transition away from violence and toward the role of governing represented an opportunity for exponential growth. Hamas leaders understood that their campaign of violence and their ardent rejection of Israel was the best path to winning the support of the Palestinian people, who were still riding a wave of anger, violence, and protest from the intifada. Even as the uprising lost steam in the wake of the 1991 Gulf War, the coming decade would provide Hamas with an excellent opportunity to demonstrate its steadfastness (*sumud*) against the U.S.-backed Palestinian-Israeli peace process and afford it an edge over its political rival, Fatah.

CHAPTER FOUR

HAMAS, FATAH, AND THE OSLO YEARS

The intifada began to subside after Saddam Hussein's crushing defeat in the Gulf War of 1991 at the hands of the U.S.-backed coalition. Both Hamas and Fatah appeared to be united in their hope that when Saddam lobbed SCUD missiles into Israel, a wider war might lead to Israel's defeat. The Israelis, however, were content to watch their enemy fall to the forces of other armies. Indeed, the Iraqi leader's overwhelming defeat sapped the Palestinians of their zeal.

Hamas, however, was not deterred. In 1991, the organization formed its official military wing, the Izz al-Din Al-Qassam Brigades, named after the famous Muslim guerrilla fighter who was killed fighting the British in 1935.[1] The Brigades' attacks brought Hamas increased notoriety for violence and also for the Israeli crackdowns that its new fighting squad elicited.

Yasir Arafat and Fatah were aware of Hamas's growing strength. In both the West Bank and Gaza, Hamas now presided over an impressive network of social service institutions to help fund the organization, recruit new members, and otherwise generate support on the Palestinian street. Yassin's hospitals, mosques, schools, orphanages, libraries, and welfare institutions continued to pay dividends. These services effectively bought the support of the Palestinian people, regardless of whether they backed the Hamas Islamist agenda.

Noting the dangers that Hamas posed, Arafat called for a meeting in July 1990 between his Palestine Liberation Organization and Hamas to discuss their war of leaflets and to invite Hamas officially to join the PLO. The two groups agreed to work together in their fight against Israel, but the tension between them continued.[2] Months later, in fact, reports emerged that Hamas met in November with members of PIJ in Saudi Arabia to devise a strategy on how to best counter the PLO.[3]

Hamas and the PLO met several times but their talks achieved little. The more Hamas threatened Fatah, the more Arafat saw the need for international legitimacy as the sole representative of the Palestinian people. Thus he agreed to participate in the Jordanian delegation to the Madrid Conference for peace with Israel on October 29, 1991. Predictably, Arafat received the backing of dozens of countries worldwide. His overtures led to the PLO's engagement with the Israelis in what became known as the Oslo process, designed to foster Middle East peace. Publicly, Hamas emerged as the foremost opponent of these talks. Leaflets boldly attacked the talks as the "conference of selling the land."[4] Ahmed Yassin reportedly stated that he was "saddened and angry" about the negotiations. From his wheelchair, the Hamas leader said it was "impossible" to sit with Arafat, or for the Palestinians to "remain a united people."[5] In December 1991, Hamas carried out its first attack against an Israeli civilian in a settlement in the Gaza Strip, marking a new policy that encouraged the group's followers to attack noncombatants.

Arafat's plan to consolidate strength backfired in the West Bank and Gaza Strip. A significant portion of the population supported Hamas's violent agenda and its efforts to block peace. It is difficult to determine the number of Palestinians who supported Hamas in the early 1990s. According to poll data in 1993, Hamas popularity stood at less than 15 percent.[6] However, the PLO began to adjust the figure to somewhere around 30 percent, which may have been more realistic.[7] Other observers placed the group's popularity at 40 to 45 percent.[8]

International support also helped Hamas grow. The Islamic Republic of Iran increasingly viewed Hamas as a client that would help it develop into a regional power, particularly after the allied defeat of Iraq, Iran's primary enemy, in the 1991 Gulf War. The mullahs—the ruling Iranian clergy—invited Hamas to attend a conference with other Iranian clients on the "Islamic intifada" in December 1991. Two months later, Hamas attended a conference with PIJ and other anti-PLO factions in Damascus, which produced a communiqué opposing the PLO's peace talks with Israel.[9] In October 1992, a Hamas delegation led by Musa Abu Marzook visited Tehran for meetings with key Iranian figures, including the Islamic Republic's supreme leader, Ayatollah Ali Khameinei. According to PLO allegations, Iran pledged an annual $30 million subsidy to Hamas.[10] Hamas also announced its increased ties to the Iran-backed Hizbullah.[11] This flurry of political activity prompted the organization to create a political bureau *(Maktab al-Siyasi)*, which again paralleled the structure of the Fatah-backed PLO.[12]

By December 1992, due to mounting Hamas violence and fear surrounding the popularity of Islamists in the Palestinian territories, Israel deported more than 400 Islamists, most of whom were Hamas members, to Lebanon. But the Israeli move did little to weaken Hamas. In fact, many of these Hamas members established ties with Hizbullah and built a relationship that would flourish for years.

Moreover, the Hamas members regrouped in their new environment, creating an infrastructure in the Lebanese diaspora that rivaled Fatah's formidable Lebanese presence in the refugee camps through an ever-expanding network of social programs and religious organizations.[13] This Lebanese network mirrored the existing Palestinian network of Yassin's mosques, schools, and charitable committees, and was designed to garner support for Hamas in the diaspora. As one Arab journalist noted, "With the ascendancy of Hamas in the Occupied Territories, Fatah's negotiations with Washington and Tel Aviv, and the siege of Nahr al-Bared [a Lebanese refugee camp] . . . Fatah's support in the camps of Lebanon [sank to] an all-time low."[14] Hamas eventually took over much of the Muslim Brotherhood's infrastructure in the Lebanese camps, which added to its strength.[15]

In the Middle East, 1993 was largely viewed as a year of hope. After Israeli prime minister Yitzhak Rabin and Yasir Arafat agreed to a basis for Palestinian autonomy in the West Bank and Gaza Strip, they signed the Declaration of Principles (commonly known as Oslo I) on September 13, 1993. Oslo I led to the creation in 1994 of the Palestinian Authority *(Sulta al-Wataniyya al-Filastiniyya),* an interim administrative organization, staffed primarily by

Fatah and the PLO, to govern parts of the West Bank and the Gaza Strip. While world leaders lauded Arafat's Fatah-backed PLO for taking brave steps toward peace and statehood, Hamas was steadfastly opposed to the agreement and likened it to sacrilege.

The dividing line was clear from the start. According to reports from the Federal Bureau of Investigation, during a 1993 meeting in Philadelphia, Pennsylvania, Hamas leaders determined that "most or almost all of the funds collected in the future should be directed to enhance the Islamic Resistance Movement [Hamas] and to weaken the self-rule government [the PA]."[16] Subsequent meetings between Hamas and the PA were marked by heightened tensions. Notably, one meeting designed to foster an agreement between the two factions resulted in a hostile shouting match. According to one attendee, "Fatah leaders issued threats and ultimatums against anyone who stood in the way of their attempts to turn an (imperfect) peace process into state-building. Hamas members voiced their doubts and their defiance of an unfair diplomatic process."[17]

To be sure, the new Palestinian political system did not invite diversity. Most of the legislators were also members of Fatah who marched in step with Arafat's dictates. Political opponents came to be perceived as enemies. Those who challenged Arafat often endured threats and arrests. Even nongovernmental organizations were pressured by Arafat's regime when he made it mandatory for international donors to funnel their funds through the PA's financial system.[18]

Despite its unwillingness to legitimize this new political entity, Hamas was reportedly divided internally over its approach to taking part in the Palestinian political and governmental institutions that would be created as a result of the Oslo process. Hamas leaders appeared to understand that these institutions would provide a powerful vehicle to reach out to the Palestinian people. Thus they were of potential use to the Islamists. In the end, however, Hamas declared that it would not take part in such institutions. Rather, it joined the "Democratic and Islamic National Front" with PIJ and several other rejectionist groups, dedicated to thwarting the peace process.[19]

Still, Hamas was careful not to cut itself off entirely from a possible future role in Palestinian politics, in the event that the Oslo process eventually succeeded. Some observers claimed that Hamas was considering the creation of its own political party in preparation for upcoming elections.[20] But except for a few defections to Fatah, Hamas remained defiant. It restated its vow to carry out terrorist attacks as long as Palestinians negotiated with Israel. This approach resonated with many Palestinians, earning the group continued support. After all, some 35 percent of the Palestinian people were opposed to the peace talks.[21]

What was particularly striking about this period was not the PLO's loss of support based on its engagement with the Israelis, or even Hamas's increasing strength. During the period between the announcement of the peace process and the signing of the declaration of principles in September 1993, Hamas rapidly transformed its military capabilities. Egyptian intelligence reported that Iran, under President Akbar Hashemi Rafsanjani, was training up to 3,000 Hamas militants and that Hamas would soon open an office in Tehran.[22]

Ironically, Rafsanjani was seen as something of a moderate in Iran. He earned the nickname *Kuseh,* which means "shark," on account of his cunning as well as his lack of facial hair.[23] He occasionally tested the waters with Washington in an attempt to determine whether a thaw in relations was possible after 14 years of isolation following the 1979 Islamic Revolution. Yet Rafsanjani met regularly with Hizbullah and even hosted an October 1991 conference with Hizbullah, Hamas, and other terrorist groups that slammed the Madrid peace conference between Israel and the Palestinians. "We must endeavor to defeat this conference," he said. "And we know this conference [Madrid] is a sham."[24]

Within just months of the signing of the declaration of principles, Hamas began its wave of suicide bombing attacks against Israel, in part with Iranian financial and material support. The first successful bombing of this kind took place in April 1994, when a suicide bomber killed himself in a car positioned near a bus in the northern Israeli town of Afula, killing eight and wounding many others. By October, Hamas had launched three such attacks inside Israel.

This new tactic was shockingly violent, and represented a drastic change from the Fatah tactics to which Israel had adapted over the years. Indeed, the Hamas approach of "resistance" was virtually unstoppable. There was little

Israel could do to prevent this kind of attack, particularly if the attacker was willing to take his own life.

To date, it is still unclear whether Iran introduced or encouraged the Hamas tactic of suicide bombing. At this point in history, taking one's life in order to claim the lives of others was commonly associated with the Iranian-backed terrorist group Hizbullah and was seen as strictly a Shi'ite tactic. Hizbullah cleric Mohammed Hussein Fadlallah even issued a public statement legitimizing it: "If an oppressed people does not have the means to confront . . . . Israel with the weapons in which they are superior, then they possess unfamiliar weapons. . . . Oppression makes the oppressed discover new weapons and new strength every day."[25]

Fadlallah's black turban, sunken eyes, and white beard quickly became familiar to intelligence analysts in the United States. Iran and elements within Hizbullah were responsible for America's first experience with a suicide bombing. That attack was carried out against the United States Embassy in Beirut, Lebanon, on April 18, 1983, killing 60 people, mostly embassy staff members. This was followed by another attack on the morning of October 23, when a Shi'ite bomber detonated a large truck bomb destroying a U.S. marine barracks and killing 241 American servicemen in Lebanon.

Regardless of its inspiration, Hamas terror, including the use of suicide bombings, intensified in 1994. Hamas claimed that the violence was a response in part to Israeli settler Baruch Goldstein's massacre of 29 Muslims in Hebron's Cave of the Patriarchs in February. However, it was commonly recognized that the violence would have taken place with or without Goldstein's acts. Indeed, violence became the official Hamas response to continued Palestinian-Israeli negotiations. One week after the aforementioned Afula bus bombing, on April 13, another Hamas suicide attack killed five in Hadera, halfway between the cities of Haifa and Tel Aviv. Israel responded by arresting several hundred Hamas suspects and called on the newly formed Palestinian Authority to crack down on Hamas as a precondition for continuing negotiations.

To be sure, the violence was destabilizing for both the Israelis and the PA. But, as Palestinian author Marwan Bishara notes, the violence particularly affected Arafat. His "legitimacy became more uncertain and his position precarious. His attempts to suppress Hamas weakened his popularity, and his reluctance to confront it directly weakened his authority."[26]

Arafat attempted to wield inflammatory Islamist rhetoric as a means to garner support from Palestinians who had switched their allegiance to Hamas. Increasingly, he wove Quranic references into his public speeches, and even borrowed from the Hamas narrative when he stated that "fighters in this revolution . . . are the sons of Izz al-Din al-Qassam," the guerrilla fighter from the 1930s for which the Hamas military wing was named. In one famous speech Arafat delivered in South Africa (and which he did not think was being recorded), Arafat likened his peace treaty with Israel to the Treaty of Hudaybiyya, which was concluded and then broken to achieve the military conquest of Mecca by the prophet of Islam.[27]

On July 1, 1994, determined to reclaim his position as the unquestioned ruler of the Palestinian people, Arafat made his official return as *ra'is* (president) by motorcade via Egypt into Gaza, where he was greeted by hundreds of thousands of jubilant Palestinians.[28] What was not widely known, however, was that Arafat reportedly was fearful that Hamas would attempt to disrupt his triumphant "return."[29]

The leaders of Hamas did not prevent Arafat from having his day in the sun. However, soon after Arafat's return, once he began to settle in to the role of PA chairman, the Islamists made it clear that they would challenge his authority. Indeed, Hamas violence continued unabated in an attempt to thwart the peace process, which was the sole basis for Arafat's legitimacy as the leader of the Palestinian people in the eyes of the international community.

While Hamas attempted to punish Arafat for making peace, the West sought to honor him. On October 14, it was officially announced that Israeli Prime Minister Yitzhak Rabin, Israeli Foreign Minister Shimon Peres, and Yasir Arafat would win the Nobel Prize for Peace, in recognition of their efforts to end the Palestinian-Israeli conflict. The announcement came amid a series of Hamas attacks against civilians inside Israel's borders. Indeed, just five days later, a suicide bomber killed himself and 22 Israelis on a Tel Aviv bus. An additional 56 people were wounded in that attack.

Not surprisingly, the violence prompted Israel and the United States to ask Arafat to take further steps to rein in Hamas. Both countries also requested that Jordan crack down on Hamas within its borders, where it had enjoyed political asylum for several years. According to one account, Arafat may have pressured King Hussein, who himself had made peace with Israel in 1994, to expel several non-Jordanian leaders by the next year.[30]

The violence did not stop, however. In March 1995, Hamas attacked a bus in Hebron, killing two settlers. The group then carried a pair of suicide attacks in April and June 1995, killing a total of 14 Israelis and wounding more than 80. On August 21, Hamas carried out a suicide attack on a bus in Jerusalem, killing 5 Israelis and injuring more than 100. Days later, another attack in Ramat Gan, a town outside Tel Aviv, killed 6 Israelis and injured 30.

Hamas had triggered a wave of violence that neither Israel nor America appeared able to stop. The Clinton administration was jarred by these attacks, viewing them as the most formidable threat to its peace initiative. Ironically, the administration might have been able to prevent some of these attacks had it arrested and deported the Virginia-based Marzook sooner.

Arafat realized that to be the legitimate ruler of the Palestinian Authority, he would need to gain control of Hamas. Thus, upon the prodding of Washington and Jerusalem, Fatah and Hamas met in Cairo in an attempt to work out their differences. The two sides devolved into bickering, and the meeting was for naught. As the relationship soured further, Fatah's top Gaza advisor, Mohammed Dahlan, reportedly accused Hamas of playing dirty tricks with the future of the Palestinian people and claimed that Hamas was executing the will of foreign actors—a veiled reference to Iran and Syria—rather than thinking of the people's good.[31]

On January 20, 1996, amid a wave of Hamas violence, the Palestinian Authority held its first elections. The quandary that Hamas faced in 1994 following the Oslo Accords presented itself again: Should Hamas grant legitimacy to the PA, a product of the accords, or refrain from taking part in the political system? In the end, Hamas chose officially to boycott the elections. Lack of political participation, however, would prove to be the least of Hamas's problems in 1996. The Israelis soon launched an offensive designed to deliver a mortal blow to the group's leaders.

On January 5, 1996, Israeli operatives assassinated Yahya Ayyesh, commonly known as the Engineer, who orchestrated numerous Hamas attacks against Israel. He was killed by a small explosive device placed in his mobile phone. The killing of Ayyesh was a blow to Hamas. As the group's Web site notes, "People were crying in the streets, in the cars, in their balconies, in their rooms."[32] The assassination brought tens of thousands of Gazans out to protest and to mourn the man who had so successfully struck at the heart of Israel, killing as many as 90 people, although the numbers are still in dispute. The assassination also prompted revenge attacks by Hamas (two in February and one in March). Determined to salvage the peace process, Clinton summoned top leaders from Arab and Western states to a summit in the coastal Egyptian town of Sharm al-Sheikh, where he called on all regional and international actors to "stop acts of terror." His words were essentially a declaration of war against Hamas, since the group was responsible for most of the terror attacks.[33]

Israel continued to carry out operations against the Hamas infrastructure in the territories, while the PA security forces arrested Hamas members. On September 25, 1997, Israel attempted to assassinate Khaled Meshal, the Jordan-based head of the Hamas politburo. Allegedly on the orders of Israeli prime minister Benjamin Netanyahu, the Israeli equivalent of the CIA, the Mossad, poisoned and nearly killed him. Israel was humiliated, however, when Jordanian authorities arrested two agents involved in the attempted assassination. Netanyahu, a fluent English speaker and polished politician, could not withstand the heavy international pressure, not the least of which came from the United States. Israel's security services provided Meshal's doctors with the antidote to the poison. The whole affair ended poorly for Israel. The Hamas leader lived, and Jordan later released the two agents in exchange for the release of Ahmed Yassin, who was serving a life sentence in an Israeli prison. Yassin returned to Gaza victorious, assuming leadership of his powerful network of mosques and military cells yet again.

Israel was not the only loser in this equation, however. Yassin began openly to criticize Arafat and the Palestinian Authority. In April 1998, he reportedly stated on al-Jazeera television that the PA was subservient to the United States and to Israel and that Arafat did not represent the true wishes of the Palestinian people. He added that Hamas had elected to avoid confrontation with the PA.[34] This was a rare public reference to the rift that had emerged between the two factions. Indeed, while the groups continued to jockey for power, both Hamas and Fatah often downplayed their differences in an attempt to project a united Palestinian front.

Palestinian unity unquestionably suffered during this period. On balance, so did Israeli security. While Fatah had largely refrained from engaging in violence with Israel, Hamas had developed the operational ability to carry out terror attacks inside Israel with relative impunity, and when Israel responded with military force, it was often condemned by the international community. This dynamic did little to improve the stalled peace process with the PA and even less to bolster Arafat's standing as the sole representative of the Palestinian people.

Hamas continued to trade blows with Israel leading up to the October 1998 Wye Plantation Accords, yet another Clinton-sponsored framework designed to promote Middle East peace. In its continued opposition to peace talks, Hamas carried out at least three successful attacks against Israeli targets that month, killing at least 1 Israeli and wounding more than 80. For the next 10 months, however, Hamas carried out very few acts of violence.

Some analysts claim that this low profile had something to do with the rapprochement that was reportedly taking place between the United States and Iran, now under the leadership of President Mohammed Khatami. The new president, elected in 1997, was yet another self-styled reformer who was popular among Iran's women and younger generation. He also reached out to the West by calling for "dialogue of civilizations" instead of a clash. Khatami may have reined in Hamas as a measure of good faith for the Clinton administration, which began to ease restrictions on the Islamic Republic.

Other analysts believe the lull in Hamas violence was intended to help perpetuate the mandate of Netanyahu, commonly viewed as an anti-peace prime minister in Israel, and implicitly, a continued crisis in PA-Israel relations. Others believe Hamas simply agreed to stop carrying out suicide bombings in the name of Palestinian unity.[35] Still others, however, claim that Hamas made a concerted effort to maintain its campaign of violence against Israel but was stymied by the cooperative efforts of the Palestinian Authority's security apparatus, Israel's internal security services, the Shin Bet, and the U.S. Central Intelligence Agency, a collaboration stipulated in the recently signed Wye accords.[36]

As Yassin later explained, the PA clampdown was stifling. Much of it was done at the behest of Arafat, who appeared to be issuing a direct challenge to Yassin. Journalists visiting Yassin's home were arrested, as was one of his bodyguards. When Yassin visited South Africa in 1998 for fundraising and public support, he learned that the PA had arranged for his meetings to fail. It was also reported that members of the venerated Izz al-Din al-Qassam Brigades were persuaded or bribed to join the Palestinian Authority's security agencies.[37] Indeed, it appeared that the PA had cornered Hamas on many fronts.

In the summer of 1999, however, after a ten-month hiatus, Hamas initiated a rash of shootings and ambushes in the West Bank. In September, Hamas recruited Israeli Arabs to bomb two buses in Israel's north, leading some analysts to fear that recruiting Israeli Islamists would become a new Hamas tactic. Islamism, due in no small part to Hamas, was on the rise among the estimated one million Israeli Arabs who lived within the Jewish state's internationally recognized borders, commonly referred to as the Green Line.[38] PA intelligence reports also noted increasing ties between Hamas and the Islamic Movement, the Islamist faction within Israel's borders, with particular concern over Hamas ties with the mayor of Umm al-Fahm, an Arab town in northern Israel known for its Islamist leanings.[39]

Many Palestinians viewed Fatah's measures to weaken Hamas not as undermining a political foe but as doing Israel's dirty work, which according to one Palestinian commentator "contributed to Hamas' popularity as the political underdog and spokesman for the marginalized and forgotten."[40]

Later in 1999, Hamas was faced with a new challenge. Although the organization had been allowed to maintain offices in Amman, Jordan, for a decade, newly crowned King Abdullah II forced Hamas out of his capital soon after he ascended to the throne following the death of his father, King Hussein. Abdullah's move can be attributed to two things. For one, he likely feared the spread of Islamism in his own country, where a Muslim Brotherhood front organization, the Islamic Action Front (IAF), was gaining popularity. Further, the Western-educated king, who sought to establish goodwill with the United States, supported the Clinton peace process by taking public steps to prevent Islamists from sabotaging the prospects of peace between Israel and the PA.[41]

In August 1999, Hamas wounded six people when operatives plowed a car into two different crowds of Israelis at Nahshon Junction, just inside the

Green Line on the border of the West Bank. In November, the terror group planted three pipe bombs that wounded 27 in the coastal town of Netanya. Leading up to the 2000 intifada, Hamas remained in the public eye, as both a powerful grassroots Islamist force on the Palestinian street and a dangerous military force capable of delivering painful blows to Israel through suicide bombings and other terrorist tactics. There was speculation that Hamas could one day become an even stronger military force, thanks to Iranian sponsorship of Izz al-Din al-Qassam Brigades members who received paramilitary training each year in the Islamist states of Sudan and Iran. These fighters often returned to the West Bank and Gaza Strip to be used in Hamas commando or suicide operations.[42]

Concerns also continued to grow over the financial support for Hamas that was pouring in from the Palestinian diaspora. The 1999 terrorism report issued by the U.S. State Department expressed concerns over Hamas funding "from Palestinian expatriates, Iran, and private benefactors in Saudi Arabia and other moderate Arab states."[43] Contributors included oil sheikhs as well as princes who were influenced by the radical strain of Islam known as Wahhabism, and sought to finance attacks against the Jewish state.

In addition to the influx of funds, some analysts posited that Hamas's internal leadership was also gaining strength and had the potential someday to become a regional power.[44] But in order for Yassin and his lieutenants to gain that strength, the U.S.- and Israeli-backed Palestinian political structures built via the Oslo peace process would have to be weakened (if not destroyed). The al-Aqsa intifada of 2000 provided perfect conditions for this to occur.

CHAPTER FIVE

HISTORY REPEATS: THE 2000 INTIFADA

On September 29, 2000, after seemingly endless U.S. efforts to bring the Palestinians and Israelis together for a peace deal that would effectively end their bitter conflict, the al-Aqsa intifada began. The violence was not spontaneous. This was a war that Yasir Arafat launched, after concluding that he would have to make painful concessions to Israel, in the same way that Israel would have to make painful concessions to the Palestinians if peace was to be made.

When Arafat determined that he would not compromise over the stickiest of issues—Jerusalem and the settlement of the refugee problem—he put his war machine in motion. At Friday prayers, the preacher at the al-Aqsa mosque called on Palestinians to "eradicate the Jews." Palestinian Authority television played and replayed video from the intifada of 1987 to 1993 showing young people out in the streets throwing stones. PA radio played PLO war songs. Arafat then cancelled school in the territories and called for a general strike.[1]

The Friday sermons, radio, and television were all under Arafat's control. Indeed, rarely did anything happen in the PA without his nod. Thus, it is commonly believed that Arafat, the Fatah guerrilla turned Nobel laureate, launched the third Palestinians uprising. Some called it "Arafat's War."

The war against Israel was only part of the picture, however. The new uprising soon fit a recurring Palestinian pattern of self-destruction marked by miscalculation, fratricide, religious radicalism, and economic despair. Indeed, the intifada of 2000 was the third time in 70 years that the Palestinians orchestrated a nationalist uprising, and the third time it led them to disaster.

Specifically, the Palestinians fell into old and predictable routines. Dr. Kenneth Stein, Emory University professor of Middle Eastern studies, pointed out in a landmark 1990 study that a number of remarkable similarities existed among the Palestinians during first two uprisings: self-destructive violence, Islamic militancy, rejection of the West, and internal Palestinian rivalries among political leaders over strategy and tactics. Perhaps most important, "a perception existed that the Palestinian Arabs could not be trusted as equals in the future administration of Palestine or portions of it."[2] Remarkably, these observations were also applicable a decade later, when Arafat launched the third Palestinian uprising.

During the first Palestinian uprising, from 1936 to 1939, the Palestinian Arabs revolted against the colonial British and the Jewish community (*Yishuv*, as it was known in Hebrew) in protest against increased Jewish immigration to the British mandate of Palestine. With a new sense of nationalism, the Palestinian Arabs staged boycotts, strikes, and demonstrations. Thousands of workers left their jobs, causing scores of businesses to shut down. As a result, the Palestinian Arab economy was in shambles.

But the economic cost to the Arab Palestinians was only a small part of the larger picture. Violent clashes with the British and the local Jews left some 5,000 Palestinians dead, 15,000 wounded, and 5,600 in prison.[3] Orchestrating a great deal of this violence was the vitriolic Palestinian Grand Mufti (the top Islamic figure) and head of the Higher Arab Committee, Haj Amin al-Husseini. This now-famous bearded cleric viewed violence as the most effective answer to Jewish immigration and British imperial rule.

As the uprising continued, a rift developed between Husseini's radical faction and the moderate Nashishibi family, a family with historic ties to Jerusalem.[4] The Nashishibis sought a diplomatic solution that would partition the mandate of Palestine into Jewish and Arab states, as the United Nations would later recommend. This division, however, was unacceptable to the Husseini clan; they launched a campaign of murder and intimidation against the Jews of Palestine as well as moderate Arab mayors and officials who did not hold the Husseini view.

The result was a devastating Palestinian civil war that tore at the fabric of a society that was still forming a modern identity. According to historians, a terrible blood feud erupted between the two Palestinian camps, which "resulted in a mutual hatred and dissidence so intense" that reconciliation eventually "became impossible."[5] As a result of the Husseini-Nashishibi civil feud, Nashishibi henchmen abducted a number of *mukhtars* (tribal patriarchs) who were believed to be on the British payroll.[6] In fact, the bitter rift sparked the beginning of a historic trend among Palestinians still observable today: collaborator killings. Palestinians killed their kinsmen for suspected collaboration with the enemy (the British or the Jews). All told, collaboration killings accounted for 494 deaths, or about 10 percent of all Palestinian Arabs killed during the Arab revolt.[7]

Historians also observe that some Palestinians began to allege "collaboration" as a pretext to settle old scores. Some simply killed those for whom they had long-held grudges for reasons having nothing to do with the current conflict, a situation that reportedly created a host of new grievances and exacerbated inter-clan rivalries.[8] As Palestinian society deteriorated into utter lawlessness, allegiances to family, clan, and tribe began to overshadow the very cause that inspired the revolt: Palestinian nationalism. Indeed, by 1939, the Palestinians were so exhausted by their internecine feuds that they could no longer mount a meaningful offensive against the British and the Jews. Instead, the Palestinians were reduced to acts of retribution against other Palestinians they suspected of being traitors.[9]

Desperate, exhausted, and on the brink of self-destruction, the Husseini camp recruited young Palestinian children to fight for their cause. Youth units, known simply as *shabab* (Arabic for "youth") were formed to enforce Husseini's policies and to prevent moderates from "collaborating" with the enemy. Husseini, however, took things a step further in forming "youth troops" fashioned after the Hitler Youth in Germany. The group operated for a time under the name "Nazi Scouts," complete with Hitler Youth–style shorts and leather belts.[10] This disregard for the lives and welfare of children was yet another indication of how the first uprising tore at Palestinian society.

The Palestinian revolt also prompted a wave of Islamic radicalism. For example, Husseini ordered Palestinian Christian women in many cities to veil themselves with a *hijab*. But Christians and Druze (an offshoot of Islam often looked down upon by traditional Muslims) Palestinians endured much worse: regular and organized attacks by Islamists.[11] In 1936, Islamists called for a boycott of all Christians for allegedly undermining the revolt.

An Islamist guerrilla movement also emerged amid the chaos. In early 1935, radical cleric Izz al-Din al-Qassam (for whom the Hamas armed branch was later named) organized a guerrilla unit known as *al-Kaff al-Aswad* (the Black Hand) to attack the British. He was instantly hailed as a hero in the Palestinian uprising. Ironically, Qassam was Syrian, not Palestinian.[12] Moreover, his first squads of holy warriors were largely ineffectual in battle. Although British forces killed Qassam within a year, he is often credited with beginning a new trend in Palestinian history: organized terror and guerrilla tactics. After Qassam's death, his legacy inspired other Islamist fighters. The battle shifted to the countryside, where bands of Palestinian fighters mined roads and exchanged gunfire with British and Jewish forces. It can even be argued that Qassam's guerrilla fighters were the model for Yasir Arafat's Fatah organization and the PLO.[13]

Qassam's Islamist fighters were not the only guerrillas to emerge from the turmoil of the Palestinian Arab revolt, however. Dozens of other irregular fighting groups and armed bands sprouted up as the uprising dragged on. These gangs were diffuse, disorganized, wracked by internal disagreement, and directed by mutually suspicious leaders who often battled each other. As such, the fighting forces were ineffectual, which left the Palestinians vulnerable to defeat at the hands of more organized Jewish and British militaries.

There can be little doubt that the Arab revolt was detrimental to the Palestinian cause. The uprising prompted the local Jews living under the British mandate to rethink their long-term strategy. Indeed, the Palestinian violence forced them to shift their focus and prepare for military struggle against the Palestinians rather than the British. This adjustment in strategy was critical to achieving victory against the Palestinians in the first Arab-Israeli war of 1948, a victory that ultimately led to Israeli independence.[14]

The Arab revolt infuriated the British, who ultimately determined the fate of Palestinians. Rather than forcing the British to make concessions, the uprising pushed the British into a de facto alliance with the Jews of Palestine. In their efforts to neutralize the uprising, British authorities strangled the budding pillars of Palestinian civil society. They banned Palestinian political parties, restricted the Palestinian press, and deported Palestinian leaders. It can be argued that Palestinian civil society never fully recovered.

Finally, when the Jews subsequently launched a concerted effort to establish an independent state, one Palestinian noted that his people "proved too exhausted by the efforts of rebellion between 1936 and 1939 to be in any condition to match [them]."[15] This weakness and exhaustion did not go unnoticed by surrounding Arab states. Indeed, it encouraged Egypt, Transjordan, Syria, and Iraq to intervene on behalf of the impotent Palestinian people and invade in 1948.[16] Unfortunately for the Palestinians, the Arab intervention and invasion only contributed to what they called *al-Naqba* (the disaster). The Arab world, along with the majority of Palestinians, rejected the 1947 United Nations General Assembly partition plan, which endowed the Palestinian Arabs with a state that included an expanded Gaza Strip, the West Bank, and much of the northern territory. However, the promise of a Palestinian state was lost when the invading Arab armies failed to crush the new Israeli army on the battlefield. Transjordan and Egypt, however, did manage to advance, occupying what was left of mandatory Palestine (the West Bank and Gaza Strip, respectively), leaving the Palestinian people without territory of their own.

The 1987 Palestinian uprising, or intifada (which literally means "shaking off"), was discussed in earlier chapters, but the deleterious effects of this uprising were remarkably similar to those of the Palestinian Arab uprising in the 1930s and are worth briefly reviewing.

The 1987 intifada crippled the Palestinian economy. As was the case in the first uprising, the Palestinians shuttered many of their shops and businesses in protest of Israel. Various factions dropped leaflets throughout the territories calling for a halt to business as usual. Of course, the strikes were designed to demonstrate that the Palestinians had united in defiance of Israel. However, in retrospect, the people most impacted by the strikes were likely the Palestinians themselves. Even the late scholar-activist Edward Said, noted for his unwavering support for Palestinian "resistance," called these shutdowns "colossally stupid and wasteful," citing an "immense amount of time lost in stupid posturing." [17]

The Palestinians further damaged their own economy when they attacked IDF targets. The Israelis punished the Palestinians by denying West Bank and Gaza residents entrance to Israel, where many worked. Israel also shut down Palestinian schools and universities, denying education to thousands.[18] The universities were hotbeds of political activity for all of the Palestinian factions involved in the intifada. While the universities would soon become battlegrounds between rival factions, they were also popular meeting grounds for Palestinians before committing acts of violence. Thus the Israelis ordered them closed.

In May 1989, Israel also imposed financial sanctions by barring Palestinian products from entering the state. For example, Israelis cut off all citrus imports from Gaza—a move the Gaza-based Citrus Union Association described as a "noose around the Gaza Strip's neck."[19] It should also be noted that Palestinians often boycotted Israeli products too, which added self-inflicted wounds to their moribund economy. Indeed, the Palestinian economy desperately needed (and still needs) Israeli consumers in order to function. With the enforcement of financial sanctions, the territories effectively ground to a halt.

Israel added to the economic devastation by destroying the homes and property of known terrorists as punishment for violence against the state. As Said noted, 1,882 houses were punitively demolished. He also asserted that 112,000 trees were uprooted in the territories.[20] Said, who was predisposed to vilifying Israel, did not cite sources for his figures. Nonetheless, they provide a sense of the economic devastation that resulted from the Palestinian uprising.

The Palestinian economy was also hurt, inadvertently, by Jordan. Fearing a spillover of Palestinian violence into the kingdom (where nearly half of the population was Palestinian), King Hussein dropped claims to the West Bank dating back to 1948, when Jordan occupied that land, until 1967, when Israel conquered it. Palestinians were undoubtedly thrilled by Hussein's stated vision of an independent Palestinian state in the West Bank, but the monarch also effectively announced his intention to cut the purse strings between Jordan and the West Bank. Between 1980 and 1988 alone, the king had pumped millions of dollars into the West Bank economy, including funds for religious officials of the *waqf* (Muslim holy sites), religious foundations, medical clinics, schools, and other crucial social services.

Intra-Palestinian conflicts also reemerged. After the initial enthusiasm surrounding the intifada waned, there came a sharp rise in killings of suspected Palestinian collaborators.[21] Groups called the Black Panthers and Red Eagles carried out some of the violence. Usually each group was aligned with a specific political faction.[22] The human rights group B'tselem notes 121 cases in which Palestinian factions carried out punitive actions against fellow Palestinians for collaboration.[23] One historian observed that a significant portion of the violence had "little or nothing to do with collaborators and much to do with local feuds and blood debts."[24] The Palestinians used the pretext of the uprising to settle scores with personal enemies or to attack foes in rival clans and families. As one writer noted, the uprising was marked by so much intra-Palestinian violence, it could have been dubbed an "intrafada."[25]

Collaborators were often lynched or assassinated. One well-known lynching took place in Kabatiya, a West Bank village, when an angry mob surrounded the home of an alleged collaborator whose desperate cries for help went unanswered. Soon the mob broke into the home, stabbed and mauled the man, and then hung his bloody corpse up from an electricity pole as a warning to other potential collaborators.[26] In the end, Palestinians in the West Bank and Gaza Strip killed at least 800 of their own for allegedly supplying Israel with intelligence that helped the IDF combat the intifada.[27]

Not all suspected collaborators were dealt with violently, however. Some awoke in the morning to find coffins standing outside their homes. Some were forced to take an oath of contrition on the Quran or the Bible.[28] Hundreds of other alleged collaborators were brought to "trial," where they confessed and asked for forgiveness over mosque loudspeakers. In a few cases, suspected collaborators who refused to confess had their homes set afire.[29]

This culture of violence only encouraged the rise of Islamism. Though the Israeli military had hobbled the Palestinian Islamic Jihad (PIJ), Hamas benefited greatly from the intifada. The principled Hamas ideology, marked by its leaders' vows of steadfastness (*sumud*), was wildly appealing to the defiant Palestinians. The adoption of Islamism became an increasingly popular way for Palestinians to express discontent.

As was the case in the 1930s, the spread of Islamism tore at the fabric of Palestinian society. Islamists attacked liquor stores, movie theaters, video stores, and other symbols of westernization. They threatened prostitutes and admonished or even attacked women perceived as immodestly dressed. The more ascetic Islamists even discouraged weddings with Western music and dancing. Although some historians argue that Palestinian Christians willingly joined the orchestrated violence and strikes of the intifada, a convincing argument can be made that their acquiescence was the sign of a frightened minority attempting to protect itself in a hostile and volatile environment.[30]

As society unraveled, the Palestinian people turned their young children into soldiers, just as their forebears did in the 1930s. Thousands of Palestinian children clashed with the IDF on the front lines of the intifada. They came to be known as "Children of the Stones" (*Atfal al-Hajarah*), and numerous poems were written to glorify their deaths.[31]

Child soldiers, assigned tasks according to their age, were deployed by both the UNLU and Hamas. The youngest group, ages seven to ten, rolled tires into streets, doused them with gasoline, and then set them ablaze. The next oldest group, ages 11 to 14, placed large rocks in the middle of thoroughfares to halt traffic. Others made slingshots to fire rocks at the IDF. The "veteran stone throwers," the 15- to 19-year-olds, inflicted the most damage, heaving larger rocks indiscriminately at cars on the road.[32]

Putting children on the front lines of battle was not only a means to boost the number of Palestinian fighters; child fighters encumbered the Israeli military. The Israelis took great pains not to engage the children. Still, when minors were killed or injured, the Israelis were deluged with critical press coverage. Indeed, the Israelis often were portrayed as the sophisticated military that unfairly fired on children armed only with stones. However, many times the Israelis used rubber bullets and riot gear against the Palestinian minors on the front lines.

In retrospect, few journalists stopped to ask how and why the Palestinians allowed their children to stand in the line of fire. Many parents supported and even encouraged their children to join the uprising. As the violence and frustration mounted, parents of children who were killed were elevated to an honored level in Palestinian society. In many ways, they could be considered VIPs. Indeed, grieving parents received leadership positions in the local, grassroots committees that helped to organize the intifada.[33]

Of the estimated 1,100 Palestinians killed in the 1987 uprising, more than 250 were minors.[34] Of those fatalities, according to one source, the average age was ten.[35] Another source estimates that children accounted for as much as 85 percent of the violence during the intifada's first two years.[36]

The most devastating effects of the intifada, however, would become evident only years later, after the establishment of the Palestinian Authority. Indeed, the uprising left in its wake a culture of violence that did little to encourage successful state building. Notably, the culture of internecine violence never dissipated. Moreover, the economy, despite enormous American and European cash infusions, never rebounded.

Finally, the intifada gave rise to the political rivalry between Hamas and Fatah. As noted in previous chapters, the very rise of Hamas represented a challenge to the long-standing Fatah organization. As historian Don Peretz noted, the new Palestinian rivalry would have lasting effects. In 1990, he presciently asserted that "internecine conflict will very likely erupt among them when the time comes for the Palestinians to determine their political future."[37]

While there is little doubt that Arafat launched the third uprising in late 2000, it must be noted that Israel may actually have invited the violence by showing Arafat the IDF's soft underbelly. Indeed, just before the intifada erupted, in May 2000, Israel withdrew its forces unilaterally from the battlefield in southern Lebanon after sustaining years of heavy casualties in a bloody conflict with the Iranian-backed Hizbullah. This retreat, some argue, emboldened the Palestinians. Believing they could get more from Israel through violence than negotiations, they flatly rejected the Camp David II peace plan in the waning days of the Clinton administration—Israel's offer of an independent Palestinian state in nearly all the territory of the West Bank and Gaza Strip. Thus began the "Lebanonization" of the Palestinian-Israeli conflict, in which Palestinians sought to emulate the guerrilla tactics of their Hizbullah counterparts.

Palestinians, for their part, claim that the violence was sparked by the unwelcome visit of Israeli prime minister Ariel Sharon, with a full security entourage, to the Temple Mount in Jerusalem—a site sacred to both Jews and Muslims—on September 20, 2000. The Palestinians insisted that the former IDF general pushed the Palestinians to take up arms. Speaker of the

Palestine Legislative Council Ahmed Qureia said Sharon's visit was a "clear expression of the Israeli designs to eliminate the Islamic and Arab features of the Temple Mount."[38] Dozens of others echoed his sentiments. This explanation for the uprising, however, was ultimately undermined by Imad Faluji, a member of the PA and minister of post and telecommunications. Faluji was quoted as saying that the violence was "planned since Arafat's return from Camp David" when peace talks collapsed in July 2000.[39]

Arafat launched the 2000 intifada when he realized that his stated policy of negotiating with Israel was not winning him Palestinian support. He almost certainly realized that Hamas's popularity had been growing steadily since 1987 due to its image as a "resistance" group, reinforced by tough talk and attacks against Israel. This message resonated on the Palestinian street.

All the while, Arafat, who attempted to gain legitimacy as the sole representative of the Palestinian people, watched his PLO and Fatah faction plummet in popularity. When forced to make a choice between peace and compromise or violence and rejectionism, Arafat chose war.

It can be argued, in fact, that the al-Aqsa intifada was as much Arafat's war to reclaim the hearts of the Palestinian people as it was his war against Israel. For him, popular backing on the streets was of the highest importance. He had lost that support by negotiating with Israel. Attacking the Jewish state was the best way to regain it. In his attempt to reclaim his lost status as the liberator of the Palestinian people, Arafat began to wield more Islamist rhetoric, similar to that of Hamas. He made Jerusalem, perhaps the lowest common denominator among Palestinians, a focal point of the violence. "We are marching, millions of martyrs to Jerusalem," chanted one frenzied crowd at an Arafat rally in December 2001.[40]

Regardless of how or why the uprising was launched, the outcome was strikingly similar to the two uprisings that preceded it. For example, fatalities were staggering. It is estimated that 2,647 Palestinians were killed in the West Bank and Gaza Strip from September 2000 through August 2003, with more than 36,448 injured.[41] One year into the uprising, approximately 161 minors were killed and 6,000 were injured.[42] One study reported a 27 percent increase in the rate of child deaths from the previous uprising.[43] Accounts reported that increasing numbers of Palestinian children sought to be "martyrs." Indeed, 73 percent of children between the ages of 9 and 16 who were interviewed said they hoped to be killed fighting Israel. Nearly 50 percent of those polled stated that they had participated directly in the intifada.[44]

While Hamas was often blamed for encouraging children to fight, the Islamist group was not the only culprit. As mentioned, many of the children on the front lines were encouraged by their families and the PA. Numerous journalist accounts confirm that the Palestinian Authority, flush with U.S. funds provided by the Clinton administration to encourage the peace talks, had been training its youngsters in the use of automatic rifles and other weaponry.[45] In the first months of the uprising, as minors raced to the front lines, the PA offered families incentives of $2,000 per child killed and $300 for each child wounded.[46] But, according to Khairi Abaza, an Egyptian analyst of Arab affairs, the PA may have believed that it had little choice. "If the PA would not pay these families, then Hamas would pay them, it would only enlarge Iran's client base in the territories," he notes.[47]

As violence became a constant factor in Palestinian society, killings of collaborators returned. Moreover, according to one report, as the PA attempted to make the transition away from governance and back to a revolutionary movement, the vacuum forced families to exert more "influence than ever before in solving feuds," some of which included "vigilante killings." In the Gaza Strip, major feuds erupted between families in the Gaza Strip, resulting in the deaths of several Palestinians.[48] Scores of Palestinians in the West Bank and the Gaza Strip were killed or injured by vigilantes in the first years of the uprising.[49]

One particularly gruesome extrajudicial attack involved the killing of three men who had just been convicted by a Palestinian military court. Militants entered the chamber, riddled them with bullets, then threw their bodies out into the street. Although the defendants had been found guilty of killing a member of the PA security forces, the attack was believed to be a revenge killing carried out by members of his clan. Ironically, during the 1987 intifada, one of the victims had himself killed several suspected collaborators.[50]

Collaboration fever soon spread across the West Bank and Gaza. As noted earlier, sometimes the pretext of collaboration was an excuse to settle scores. In one extreme case, a man was nearly killed for a debt of $250.[51] Other killings were the product of political disagreements and even love triangles. The result, according to observers, was "a witch hunt"[52] that created "a huge social crisis."[53]

There were other problems associated with the PA's decision to shift its focus away from governance. Early on, one Palestinian analyst observed that the new uprising had produced an "unknown, faceless generation of leaders, and nobody knows where they are going."[54] These leaders hailed from radical groups including the Palestinian Hizbullah and PIJ (backed by Iran), the Tanzim (associated with Fatah), al-Aqsa Martyrs Brigades (also tied closely to Fatah), and of course, Hamas. Arafat's Fatah became just one faction among many.

Hamas likely understood that Fatah had miscalculated and sought to exploit its rival's mistake. Hamas elected not to join the intifada in its early stages, since Arafat was responsible for launching it.[55] When it did finally join the uprising, Hamas leaders, along with several clan leaders, effectively hijacked it, which tipped the Hamas-Fatah rivalry toward civil war.

As one Palestinian observer noted, Hamas exploited the instability in the West Bank and Gaza with the intent "to weaken the Palestinian old guard and eventually displace it." It chose "not to create new national institutions but rather to work for control of the existing ones." However, Hamas was not necessarily doing this against the will of the Palestinian people. Whereas support for Islamist groups always hovered below 20 percent, West Bankers and Gazans backed Hamas and PIJ more than ever during the uprising, with poll data showing nearly 31 percent support.[56]

Ironically, as the intifada raged, the PA's security forces were jailing Islamists. It was clear, however, that Arafat was not arresting them to restore calm in the region. Rather, he appeared to be attempting to neutralize his political foes. In November 2000, some 3,000 Islamist protestors clashed with PA police over the arrest of Mahmoud Tawalbi, a popular PIJ leader. In February 2002, Palestinian police clashed with more than 200 demonstrators outside a jail in Hebron, in the West Bank, where 60 PIJ and Hamas prisoners eventually escaped. Repeated clashes throughout the Gaza Strip prompted one prescient Israeli intelligence official to predict that PA rule there would "disintegrate" and that Arafat would be "replaced by Hamas and Islamic Jihad."[57]

The Palestinian territories experienced an acute financial crisis too. Although there was little to no fiscal transparency under Arafat's rule, according to some reports, the PA's annual revenue fell from more than $600 million (at the height of the peace process) to just $27 million by 2001.[58] Indeed, the PA's total worth was down by more than two-thirds after one year of the intifada, thanks to widespread corruption (Arafat alone reportedly had squirreled away many millions of dollars), a precipitous decline in productivity, and the drying up of foreign aid.[59]

To make matters worse, these financial woes forced the PA to cut administrative salaries. Without pay, PA functionaries could not be expected to work. Thus, as Palestinian daily newspaper *al-Hayat al-Jadida* reported in September 2001, senior figures in the PA were "leaving the area that is their responsibility without permission from above."[60]

The financial crisis caused other problems as well. Public infrastructure in the West Bank and Gaza Strip had disintegrated. As the editor of the *Jerusalem Post* noted, "public health standards, just seven years ago the highest in the Arab world, are among the lowest." More broadly, he observed that, just 16 months into the uprising, the al-Aqsa intifada had reduced the Palestinians "to the most desperate conditions they have seen since the creation of Israel in 1948."[61]

Conditions were particularly bleak among the minority Palestinian Christian population. Amid the lawlessness, Islamist youths raided stores and private homes that reportedly sold liquor. In one case, a nightclub was burned to the ground, although there were conflicting accounts about whether this was a case of arson.[62] As the Islamists' strength grew, many Christians perceived their place in the predominantly Muslim Palestinian society as significantly less secure. Although numbers are not readily available, many reportedly left or made plans to leave.

But Christians were not the only Palestinians seeking to depart. One year into the uprising, the Israeli *Haaretz* daily reported a dramatic rise in the number of Palestinians who sought to leave the territories. *Haaretz* reported that these Palestinians had "no way to keep going in the present situation, so they decide[d] to leave."[63] With unemployment estimated at a staggering 70 percent, the moderate voices who might have contributed to a future state fled.

The intifada impacted the Palestinians of the West Bank and Gaza in one other important way. After a string of Hamas and Islamic Jihad suicide bombings in December 2001 and again in spring 2002, Israel reached a breaking point. The Hamas suicide bombing on the first night of the Jewish holiday of Passover at the Park Hotel in Netanya, in particular, had the Israeli population calling for retaliation. Thirty people were killed in that attack, and 140 were injured during a ritual celebration.

Although Hamas took credit for the attack, Israel fingered the Palestinian Authority, specifically Arafat, for not doing enough to prevent terror. After all, it was Arafat who elected to launch the intifada. In April 2002, the IDF launched a large-scale counterterrorism campaign known as Operation Defensive Shield. It destroyed key PA security and government targets in Palestinian cities and refugee camps alike. The IDF hammered target after target in a contained but sustained effort to root out the groups responsible for the wave of attacks against Israel. The damage to the Palestinian government and civil infrastructure was catastrophic. With precious little holding together the Palestinian Authority, analysts began to predict a Palestinian collapse from within.

Some analysts claim that the Palestinian people may have benefited from their campaigns of violence against the Israelis. However, the deleterious cost of these uprisings to the very fabric of Palestinian society is beyond dispute. The first uprising crippled the Palestinian nationalist movement; after the Arab revolt, the movement was rendered leaderless, ineffectual, and paralyzed. When the surrounding Arab states declared war on the newly established State of Israel in 1948, the Palestinians could do little to control their own destiny.

The second uprising also led Palestinian society to the verge of collapse—until Israel and the Washington intervened with plans for a Palestinian state. Only through sheer will, and perhaps false hope, did Israel and the United States steer the Palestinian people toward an interim state. The Palestinian economy was decimated; Palestinians were increasingly engaging in internecine conflict; radicalism was on the rise; and while there was cooperation among the UNLU, there was no clear vision for a future Palestinian state. That lack of vision forced the United States and Israel to set goals and benchmarks for the Palestinian Authority during its formative years.

The 2000 intifada was also a blow to the Palestinian people. Violence once again decimated their economy, while radicalism, fratricide, and internal squabbles eroded society from within. The third uprising also undermined the confidence of the supporters of the "peace process" in the United States, Israel, and the Arab world. The result, particularly in Israel and the United States, was a swing to the right of the political spectrum and a lingering distrust of Palestinian institutions and their objectives. It took more than a half-decade for the international community to test the waters again for the possibility of rapprochement, when President George W. Bush convened a peace conference in Annapolis, Maryland, in late November 2007.

The fact that several Palestinian terrorist attacks caused American fatalities further damaged the Palestinian relationship with the United States. The July 31, 2002, Hamas attack on a cafeteria at the Hebrew University of Jerusalem was particularly galling to Americans; the Frank Sinatra cafeteria was a popular hangout for overseas students in a school known for hosting thousands of foreign students per year. That attack alone killed five Americans.

Finally, the third Palestinian uprising had a lasting impact on the Fatah-Hamas rivalry. The Fatah-backed Palestinian Authority emerged broken and bloodied from the al-Aqsa intifada. The Palestinian governing infrastructure, along with the society that relied on it, was all but destroyed.

Poor decision making on the part of Yasir Arafat also severely weakened the Fatah-backed PA. As the leader of the Palestinian people, Arafat provided no clear vision of what the future might look like or what his people could expect. At times, he embraced Islamism and violence. At other times, he embraced secularism and talked of peace. The result was a decline in confidence, which only helped Hamas gain support.

Hamas, for its part, was in far better shape than the PA. The organization's cell structure, which had enabled it to survive since 1989, remained intact. The intifada of 2000 also generated more support from oil-rich Gulf Arab states and the Palestinian diaspora, leading to an increase in both financial and political assistance. Moreover, the group had not changed its message. Yassin and the other Hamas leaders had not wavered as Arafat had.

As the West Bank and Gaza Strip smoldered, and with the Palestinian cause in retreat after yet another failed uprising, many frustrated Palestinians began to look toward Hamas for new answers. Hamas understood that it was closer to the possibility of overtaking Fatah. Now it had an important choice to make. Would its leadership divert from the traditional policy of eschewing internecine violence and issue a direct challenge to Fatah and the PLO?

CHAPTER SIX

FITNA

As violence engulfed the Palestinian-Israeli landscape, the international community largely wrote off the peace process. Upon taking office in January 2001, the George W. Bush administration signaled that it would not devote the president's resources to a struggle that the Palestinians did not want to solve. Indeed, the president refused to meet with Arafat, who had enjoyed numerous meetings with Bush's predecessor at the White House.

Meanwhile, Israel elected Ariel Sharon, a heavyset, white-haired veteran politician, as its new prime minister. It was hoped that Sharon, viewed as an extremely competent military man, could save the beleaguered country from this latest round of Palestinian violence. Palestinians vilified the former general for allowing Christian Lebanese forces to massacre Palestinians (reports vary from 700 to 3,500) at the Lebanese refugee camps of Sabra and Shatila in September 1982. Thus both the Palestinians and Israelis grew increasingly distrustful of the other, and the sputtering peace process ground to a halt.

While the mainstream American media over-reported the violence between the Palestinians and Israelis, the internal Palestinian struggle between Fatah and Hamas received little to no coverage in America. The Palestinian Authority increasingly exchanged sharp words and even gunfire with Hamas. Arafat claimed that the tension stemmed from the PA's efforts to halt Hamas violence, but this was only part of the equation. The PA was struggling with Hamas for control of parts of the government. Notably, Hamas had an iron grip on the charity committees in the Ministry of *Awqaf* (religious endowment), and Fatah could not wrest control of them.[1] Reports also indicated that Hamas had penetrated the PA's education ministry and even its security services. Hamas was able to gain critical intelligence about the PA's counterterrorism operations by bribing several officials, who sometimes tipped Hamas off to pending arrests of its operatives. According to one intelligence document, the PA recognized that Hamas had "begun to constitute a real threat to the PA's political vision, its interests, presence, and influence."[2]

More broadly, as noted in the previous chapter, Hamas was gaining control on the streets of the West Bank and Gaza. Economic turmoil and political instability, natural by-products of the intifada, had made it nearly impossible for the PA to govern. It had become one faction among many. In an attempt to regain control, Fatah was forced to battle Hamas.

For years, Hamas insisted that it sought to avoid *fitna,* a word commonly used to describe internal strife among Muslims, at all costs. But history clearly demonstrates that Hamas and Fatah have long engaged in hostilities. As described at length earlier, the ideological battle for the hearts and minds of the Palestinian people began soon after the eruption of the 1987 intifada. Within a few short years, the political rivalry developed a confrontational military component.

As early as May 1991, Israeli terrorism analysts began to note that the Hamas-Fatah rivalry was heating up. Violent clashes erupted, some of which were marked by the use of live weapons.[3] These were not merely isolated reports of internecine violence. In late 1991 as well as the summer and fall of 1992, Hamas-Fatah tensions again boiled over, leading to more violent clashes for control.[4] Observers noted that these clashes "marked the beginning of a dangerous stage in the relations between the two groups, and instilled fear among Palestinians that such violence was a prelude to a Palestinian civil war."[5]

In 1993, as the Islamist opposition repeatedly announced its steadfast rejection of the Palestinian-Israeli peace talks, several Fatah officials were murdered by unknown assailants. In mid-October 1993, for example, Assad Saftawi, a Fatah founder and senior PLO official, was killed in the Gaza Strip. The murder was brutal. Saftawi was shot at least twice in the head as he sat in a car waiting to pick up his nine-year-old son, who witnessed the killing. The boy told reporters how masked gunmen had smashed the windshield with their pistols and then killed his father.[6] Predictably, Hamas denied responsibility, but Fatah suspected its involvement.[7] Saftawi reportedly had heated arguments with Islamists linked to Hamas since the 1980s.[8]

In April 1994, Hamas launched its first successful suicide car bombing against Israeli civilians in the town of Afula. The attack killed eight people and wounded dozens of others. Seeking to calm his nation, Foreign Minister Shimon Peres stated on Israeli radio: "The primary lesson to be learned is that there are still many people who seek to kill the peace process, who seek to murder Jews because they are Jews, and we cannot remain silent." Peres promised that Israel would "spare no effort to root out the murderers, to stamp out the organization which seeks to kill, to murder and to destroy everything that is good in the Middle East."[9]

After the bombing, Washington and Jerusalem called on Arafat and the new PA to crack down on Hamas as a precondition for future negotiations. Arafat was almost certainly pleased at the prospect of dismantling the organization that challenged his authority. Thus PA crackdowns against Hamas began, with the PA picking up Hamas operatives off the street both to consolidate power and to appease its peace partners. As one veteran journalist noted, "A delicate balance between the two forces was upset, setting in motion a chain of events that verged on all-out civil war."[10]

In autumn 1994, in one particularly bloody conflict, at least 13 people died and 200 were wounded in a firefight between Hamas and PA supporters near a Gaza mosque. According to hospital officials, more than 20 of the wounded victims had been shot with Soviet-model automatic rifles—the kind carried by Palestinian police. Eight people had apparently been shot point blank in the head with other weapons. Fatah, however, was quick to place the blame on outside actors, implying that Israel was somehow involved. "We have reason to believe there have been instigations and attempts to blow this up into a major civil war," said Nabil Shaath, a polished PA spokesman. "We believe these parties used bullets and shot at both sides."[11]

In an effort to maintain damage control, the PA also distributed leaflets after the incident, slamming Hamas. "They want to create the impression that they are above the law," the leaflet stated. The PA charged that Hamas was attempting to establish "a government within a government."[12]

According to Amnesty International, PA security forces illegally detained a number of Palestinians in 1995. Detainees were tried in courts that did not meet international standards. Some detainees were reportedly tortured and even died while in custody.[13] Repressive PA measures against Hamas continued through 1996. The PA made a determined effort to shut down Hamas mosques and charity committees as a means to weaken the group's underlying support.[14] However, the more the PA attempted to undermine Hamas, the more the enmity grew, and the more alarmed the PA became about the Hamas challenge to its authority.

Interestingly, repression was only part of Arafat's larger strategy. For example, the PA used diplomacy in an attempt to co-opt Hamas. PA officials reportedly met with several Hamas representatives in Cairo in 1995 in an attempt to persuade Hamas to join the PA, halt attacks against Israel, and support negotiations—a call Hamas rejected.

PA documents also indicate that Yasir Arafat had a number of Hamas leaders on his payroll in an attempt to control the organization from within.[15] Arafat even sought to buy off Hamas leadership by providing Ahmed Yassin a Land Rover and a Palestinian diplomatic passport when he was released from Israeli prison in 1997.[16]

But Arafat could not control Hamas. The Islamist group grew increasingly bold in its efforts to discredit the PA. At one point, the Islamists dropped leaflets throughout the territories exposing alleged business ventures between PLO chief negotiator Nabil Shaath and Israel. This was a serious allegation, implying that Shaath's business interests might trump the interests of the Palestinian people.[17]

In March 1996, after four Hamas suicide bombings killed 57 Israelis and threatened to destroy the peace process, Fatah's top Gaza advisor, Mohammed Dahlan, reportedly asked Arafat for permission to "go after Hamas," and was granted that permission. Also known as Abu Fadi, Dahlan was part strongman and part politician. He understood that one could gain power politically only by controlling militias on the Palestinian street. His forces made "frequent raids on homes" of Izz al-Din al-Qassam Brigades members.[18] As one Hamas leader describes, it was a campaign that involved "pursuit, arrests, assassinations, dismantling of institutions, and so on."[19] The PA security services, with the aid of Israeli and U.S. intelligence, rounded up and jailed hundreds of Hamas operatives.[20]

One journalist reports that "hundreds, if not thousands, of families of Islamic sympathizers began living in constant fear—of being followed, of informers reporting on their conversations in the mosques." Some Palestinians "were held for two, three, four months or more, without seeing a lawyer, without being tried, without charges being brought against them."[21]

In 1998, a senior commander of the Izz al-Din al-Qassam Brigades was killed under mysterious circumstances. Muhi al-Din Sharif was found naked outside an explosives lab in Ramallah, in the West Bank, on March 29. The Palestinian Authority alleged that Sharif was shot and then blown up in an inside job.[22] Arafat's forces accused two of the commander's Hamas underlings of the assassination, arrested them, and forced them to confess. Hamas, in turn, accused the PA of helping Israel with the assassination. The PA responded by raiding three universities, seizing publicity materials, and arresting several Hamas-aligned students.

The following month, PA forces detained two senior Hamas leaders after a Hamas leaflet called for the resignation of senior PA officials and accused the PA of collaborating with Israel in Sharif's killing. With this, the Islamist group had crossed a red line. The PA sent a message by detaining senior Hamas leader Abdelaziz Rantisi, a stern-looking man with glasses who would eventually become the target of an Israeli assassination attempt. "Rantisi has been taken for questioning regarding statements made against our national interests and the Palestinian Authority," said one Palestinian police official.[23] By May, the president of Yemen, Ali Abdullah Saleh, publicly called for unity and an end to the factional fighting.[24]

Tensions appeared to worsen after Bill Clinton hosted a peace summit at the Wye River Plantation, in Maryland, in October 1998. As a result of the negotiations, Prime Minister Netanyahu and Chairman Arafat signed the Wye River Memorandum on October 23 in a ceremony also attended by a sickly looking King Hussein of Jordan, who was suffering from an aggressive form of cancer. Though emaciated and frail, the determined Hussein stood between Arafat and Netanyahu as the three men clasped hands in a photo that demonstrated to the world that the PA and Israel had again pledged to achieve regional peace. The Jordanian monarch succumbed to cancer four months later.

Hamas described the memorandum as an act of treason but surprisingly maintained a moratorium on its violent activity. Some analysts claimed at the time that Hamas's low profile was intended to facilitate the continuation of the rule of Benjamin Netanyahu, Israel's right-wing prime minister, and, implicitly, to undermine the PA's relations with Israel. It might also be argued, however, that Hamas tried to continue its campaign of violence but was stymied by the PA's successful security efforts.

When Ehud Barak replaced Netanyahu as prime minister in the summer of 1999, Hamas initiated a fresh round of West Bank shootings and ambushes against Israeli targets. Notably, it exploded three pipe bombs in the Israeli town of Netanya, wounding 27, in November. But it was almost certainly not the election of Prime Minister Yitzhak Rabin's protégé or the prospects for renewed peace talks that prompted the Hamas violence. In fact, Hamas had very little to lose. According to Amnesty International, the PA was still illegally holding hundreds of Palestinians who had challenged the PA, including members of Hamas, without charge or trial.[25] Violence was an obvious way for Hamas to challenge both Israel and the Palestinian Authority.

––––––––––

At the start of the Palestinian insurrection in late September 2000, after seven years of attempted peace making with Israel, Arafat elected to turn his back on the Oslo process. In defiance of Washington and Jerusalem, he released hundreds of Hamas operatives from PA jails. According to media reports, Arafat's men simply unlocked the cells, and the inmates let themselves out. During this time, the PA reassured the world community that some of the highest-ranking Hamas officials and terrorist masterminds were still behind bars.[26] But even the one Hamas terrorist to be tried and convicted in Palestinian court, Mahmoud Abu Hanud, was set free in October.[27]

Once the Hamas operatives were back out on the streets of the West Bank and Gaza, Arafat's Fatah militia and PA forces actually cooperated with Hamas fighters in terror attacks directed against Israel. The "National and Islamic Forces," a 13-member coalition that included Fatah, Hamas, and Islamic Jihad, was formed to coordinate violent acts of terror among the groups.[28] While the PLO's "Radio Palestine" called on West Bankers and Gazans to take to the streets, Hamas dropped leaflets with the same message in both territories, much as it had dropped leaflets in defiance of the PLO during the first intifada.[29]

Yasir Arafat had miscalculated, however. As was the case during the previous uprising, Hamas was not interested in following Fatah's lead. As Hamas viewed things, the al-Aqsa intifada had created ideal conditions for an even stronger resurgence of Islamism in the West Bank and the Gaza Strip. Hamas soon ratcheted up its own independent operations and once again served as a threatening opposition to Fatah. As one Palestinian journalist noted, "Hamas had no intention of recognizing the PLO, and what was really going on was that it was trying to blaze its own trail to power."[30]

At the start of the 2000 intifada, journalists at Israel's *Haaretz* newspaper observed that the "strength of the radical Islamic organization Hamas seems to be growing."[31] The newspaper soon reported "concerns among senior PA officials over the possibility that Hamas [was] trying to reap political capital among traditionally-minded Palestinians."[32] Arafat likely realized his grave error; in an attempt to reconsolidate his waning power, he offered Hamas an alliance in January 2001 but was again rebuffed.[33] Hamas also rejected Arafat's offer to become part of the Fatah-led Palestinian cabinet in June.[34]

In August 2001, a poll indicated that Fatah's popularity among Palestinians had declined sharply to 26 percent, while 27 percent supported Hamas.[35] With support for his government waning, Arafat almost certainly realized that he could not weaken Hamas's popularity. Thus he attempted to weaken Hamas financially by shutting down the al-Islah Society, a charitable group that helped to fund the organization.[36] Indeed, the entire Islamist welfare system of Hamas posed a constant challenge to the PA. Shutting down al-Islah, however, did little to quell the ongoing violence. Interfactional tensions ensued, with regular reports of street violence in both the West Bank and the Gaza Strip.

In September, Hamas leaders publicly challenged the patriotism of Marwan Barghouti, commander of Fatah's al-Aqsa Brigades, which led to an unusual exchange of public barbs between the two groups.[37] In October, when a Hamas operative killed Colonel Rajah Abu Lihyah of the PA's security forces, clashes between the two groups led to the deaths of five Palestinians. It was later reported that Lihyah's death was not the result of random gang violence; rather, Hamas leader Abdelaziz Rantisi reportedly had ordered the assassination.[38] The PA subsequently moved against Hamas in Gaza, again rounding up dozens of operatives, and declared an emergency. Arafat also ordered PA security personnel to put Yassin under house arrest, which prompted more gun battles on the streets.[39]

As Yasir Arafat grew older, and rumors of his failing health circulated, Hamas leader Mahmoud al-Zahar denied the possibility of the potential for civil war in a post-Arafat period. "Israel would like to see Palestinians killing one another," he said, "but we will not present it with this gift."[40]

Yet the fighting continued, which Hamas may not have viewed as a negative development. According to documents seized in the Gaza Strip by the Israel Defense Forces during the al-Aqsa intifada, Hamas recognized Fatah's weakness and saw itself as one of the "influential forces in the Arab-Zionist equation." Indeed, Hamas noted that the PA had "collapsed, its infrastructure has been destroyed, and it suffers rifts and divisions . . . in short, the PA has been dismantled and must be reassembled according to new conditions."[41] Those "new conditions" likely persuaded Hamas that it could legitimately claim a place of primacy and that it had nothing to gain by submitting to the PA.

Hamas also appeared to have realized something of equal significance. Every time it attacked an Israeli target inside Israel's Green Line or Jewish settlers in the disputed territories, a swift and often brutal Israeli military response followed. At times, Israel responded with targeted assassinations and manhunts of senior Hamas operatives. However, just as often, Israel retaliated against Arafat and the PA infrastructure (e.g., police stations, government buildings, and even Arafat's presidential compound in Ramallah). After all, the Israelis correctly recognized that Arafat and his Fatah faction had launched this uprising. In the aggregate, Israel's military responses appeared to weaken the Palestinian Authority (and Arafat's Fatah faction) more than it weakened Hamas.

To put it another way, Hamas realized that it could kill two birds with one stone. By attacking Israel, it boosted its popularity on the Palestinian street, and it elicited an Israeli military retaliation that, in most instances, damaged the infrastructure of the PA, paved the way for Fatah's disintegration, sparked more anti-Israeli anger among the Palestinians, and drove new recruits to the Hamas fold. Given these tangible rewards for terror, Hamas had absolutely no reason to desist.

As the PA crumbled, Arafat's Fatah faction was without direction. International support had clearly been Fatah's ticket to power in the late 1980s. But violence and rejectionism combined for a proven strategy for success at home. Hamas's surging popularity in both Palestinian territories, resulting from its continued attacks against Israeli targets, was a clear testament to that. Thus, Arafat called for "martyrdom"[42] and a "just peace" with Israel.[43]

Realizing that his simultaneous adoption of diametrically opposed approaches had left him devoid of power on the Palestinian street and that it had stripped his credibility as a statesman, Arafat jumped at a proposal by the Quartet (a Middle East peace-building coalition of the United States, United Nations, European Union, and Russia). This proposal, known as the Road Map for Peace, promised a de facto Palestinian state, with final borders to be set by 2005. For this road map to be implemented, however, the U.S.-led Quartet stipulated that an initial period of calm on the ground was necessary. This prompted Fatah to make yet another overture to Hamas, asking the group to halt suicide bombings for a period of three months. As Palestinian legislator Ziad Abu Amr noted, Hamas realized it could "play the role of the spoiler" and was a "factor for instability."[44]

In November 2002, at Washington's urging, Egypt attempted to broker a deal whereby Hamas would end attacks on Israeli civilians for the proscribed three months, provided Israel halted political assassinations (targeting Hamas members). Initially, the talks were to take place between Khaled Meshal, head of the Hamas politburo, and Mahmoud Abbas (also known as Abu Mazen), Fatah's second in command. However, Arafat lowered the profile of his delegation when he sent Zakaria al-Agha, a relatively unknown member of the PLO executive committee. Hamas, in turn, yanked Meshal and sent a lesser figure, Musa Abu Marzook.[45] Not surprisingly, the talks failed to produce results. On November 21, Hamas carried out a suicide bombing on a Jerusalem bus, killing 11 Israelis and wounding 50 others. It was clear that neither Egypt nor Fatah could rein in Hamas.

In Gaza, tensions between Fatah and Hamas escalated as clashes between the factions led to the deaths of a man and his five-year-old child.[46] Fatah responded by burning a Hamas press office and fired shots at the homes of two Hamas leaders.[47] Chaos overtook Gaza and the West Bank, and the PA steadily lost control.

Tensions continued as the two factions exchanged blistering public barbs. A Fatah leaflet released on December 10 warned Hamas: "Anyone who wants to challenge [Fatah], his end will be in our hands, never mind who he is." Days later, the PA minister of supplies, Abu 'Ali Shahin, accused Hamas of "concocting problems with Fatah in the Gaza Strip to weaken and marginalize the PA."[48]

A few days later, Hamas spokesman Usama Hamdan, while not mentioning Fatah by name, defiantly declared, "We are not ready to be ordered to stop the resistance."[49] The following week, Hamas founder Ahmed Yassin held a rally of some 30,000 Hamas supporters at a soccer stadium in the Sheikh Radwan neighborhood of Gaza City, a Hamas stronghold. There, the white-bearded sheikh assured the fervent crowd that "jihad will continue."[50]

Despite the continued tensions, Arab commentators insisted that the problems between the two factions could be worked out through dialogue. Jihad al-Khazen, an often-vitriolic columnist for the London-based *al-Hayat,* wrote that he had personally talked with Khaled Meshal, who had assured Arafat "that Hamas has no intention of taking the Authority's place and that reports to this effect are a plot with obvious aims and sources." He accused those of recognizing the potential for civil war (including this author) as being "enemies of the Palestinian cause."[51]

Al-Khazen's hopeful assessment notwithstanding, tensions continued. In January 2003, reconciliation talks between the two factions were again postponed, after Egypt failed to establish an agreed-on starting point: a halt on terror attacks against Israel.[52] Even the buoyant al-Khazen appeared deflated, admitting that his "recent contacts [with the two factions] were not encouraging."[53] In an interview with Yassin published on January 10, the Hamas leader explained that his organization's rejection of the proposed cease-fire stemmed from Fatah's inconsistency. He noted that "the PA itself supports the jihad activities and the suicide attacks, whilst at the same time it requests us to put a stop to them."[54]

Upon the urging of Washington, Egypt continued to try to bring the two sides together. Hamas, however, complained that Egypt's proposed meetings were not inclusive of other Palestinian factions. Hamas finally agreed to the talks after it was determined that they would include no less than ten other

Palestinian factions.[55] Meanwhile, Gaza-based Hamas cofounder Abd al-Aziz Rantisi, stated Hamas would "not agree to any project or document demanding an end to resistance."[56]

In the end, the talks collapsed primarily because of Hamas's refusal to compromise on the question of violence. Fatah criticized Hamas in the Palestinian media for not helping "the national interest of the Palestinian people."[57] Hamas repeatedly explained that the talks failed because it would never agree to end its attacks against Israel.[58]

Yassin's explanation for his rejection of Fatah's demands in January 2003 had some merit. Fatah's insistence that Hamas cease its attacks against Israel was unquestionably hypocritical. Shortly after the outbreak of violence in 2000, in an attempt to compete with the popularity of Hamas on the Palestinian street, Fatah had created the al-Aqsa Martyrs Brigades, which co-opted Islamic symbols and slogans, drawing heavily from the Quran and Islamic tradition.

Fatah also carried out violence against Israel through its other militias, which included Force 17, the Presidential Guard, and other small factions. The Brigades, however, were the only Fatah splinter to rival Hamas with spectacular and bloody terrorist attacks coupled with Islamist zeal. In fact, during the early months of the intifada, Fatah and Hamas actually sponsored joint attacks. However, as Hamas made it clear that it was challenging Fatah's primacy, the joint attacks became less common.

By 2002, the al-Aqsa Martyrs Brigades had claimed responsibility for dozens of attacks in which Israeli civilians were killed. The group rivaled Hamas in its headline-grabbing attacks against Israelis. In March 21, 2002, for example, a Martyrs Brigades suicide bomber detonated himself in the middle of the bustling King George Street in Jerusalem, killing 3 and injuring 86. Less than three weeks earlier, another Brigades suicide bomber killed 10 and injured 50 at a bar mitzvah celebration.[59]

The Martyrs Brigades was also the first of the jihadi organizations to use a female suicide bomber. On January 27, 2002, a 28-year-old nurse walked into a Jerusalem shopping area and detonated a bomb that killed herself and an Israeli, and injured 150 other Israelis. Initially Yassin denounced the use of women for attacks against Israel, asserting that their place was in the home, in order to raise children in the path of jihad. However, Hamas changed its stance on women suicide bombers in 2004 when Reem Rayashi blew herself up at the Erez crossing on the Gaza border, killing four Israeli soldiers. Yassin called this a "new strategy" in combating Israel.[60]

By 2003, al-Aqsa Martyrs Brigades members openly admitted their membership in Arafat's Fatah faction. Malik Jallad, a Brigades commander in Tulkarem acknowledged, "We belong to Fatah." One Brigades foot soldier told *USA Today,* "Our commander is Yasir Arafat himself."[61] Even Arafat's spokesman Mohammed Odwan confirmed that the Martyrs Brigades were "loyal to President Arafat."[62] Papers subsequently seized by the Israeli military from PA offices also demonstrated financial links. In one documented example, Arafat paid $20,000 to the group. From other captured files, it became clear that Fatah financed everything from explosives to guns and gas money.[63]

By challenging Israel through the Brigades, Fatah believed it could bolster its standing in a Palestinian culture that put a premium on radical rhetoric and deed. However, the ties between the al-Aqsa Martyrs Brigades and Fatah quickly became public knowledge, serving only to further estrange the Fatah faction and the PA from the United States and other international backers that could save them from what appeared to be an inevitable demise. Moreover, the Palestinian people, while perhaps supportive of the al-Aqsa Martyrs' attacks, still recognized Hamas as the primary Islamic "resistance" organization; it could not be rivaled by an Islamist faction of the secular Fatah party, which continued to lose Palestinian popular support.

Finally, it can be argued that Arafat's adoption of the al-Aqsa Martyrs Brigades was the last straw for Israel. A little more than one year into the 2000 intifada, the IDF surrounded Arafat's presidential compound and kept him under house arrest, essentially sapping Fatah of any strength it may have had to continue its war against Israel and, by default, its war against Hamas.

Beginning in 1991, Fatah sought a dual strategy of repression and diplomacy to weaken, destroy, or co-opt Hamas. After a dozen years of sporadic fighting, Hamas had survived and its leaders were defiant. Indeed, Hamas withstood PA efforts to dismantle the organization and eventually emerged as the stronger faction. In 2003, Khaled Meshal gloated in an interview that "the PLO met Hamas in the beginning with total disregard, then cast doubt on its authenticity, then it endeavored to belittle it and refuse to recognize it, then it went into a state of open confrontation followed by an attempt to contain it."[64]

By 2003, Hamas leaders may have determined that the era of subservience to Fatah was over. Hamas had created a parallel government and a parallel network of social services that served its own supporters while the PA served a separate constituency.[65] Accordingly, Mahmoud al-Zahar, who would serve as foreign minister of the Hamas government after the Gaza Strip coup, noted that his faction was "absolutely" prepared to take over leadership of the Palestinians, "politically, financially, [and] socially."[66]

CHAPTER SEVEN

HAMAS DIGS IN

As the al-Aqsa intifada lost its intensity, Israel took no comfort in the fact that the Palestinian Authority (PA) was working to dismantle Hamas for its own gain. After all, Hamas had carried out some 50 suicide bombing operations inside Israel, contributing to an atmosphere of public fear. Nightclubs, cafés, and buses were all possible targets. Going out to public places became an act of courage or even defiance for Israelis.

Nor did Israel take comfort in the fact that the United States Treasury had designated several Hamas charities Specially Designated Global Terrorist (SDGT) entities and frozen their assets, including those of the Holy Land Foundation for Relief and Development (December 2001) as well as Palestine Relief Committee, Interpal, and Sanabil Association for Relief and Development (all in August 2003). Over the decade before it was shut down, Holy Land alone was believed to have raised more than $50 million in charitable contributions from which Hamas funds were drawn.[1] True, these designations constituted a blow to the Hamas fundraising apparatus, but a few quick strikes could not decimate Hamas's deep foundations.

Jerusalem soon embarked on a systematic campaign designed to weaken Hamas and strengthen its own deterrence through a three-pronged strategy including:

1. A campaign of targeted assassinations against Hamas leaders;
2. The erection of barriers to separate Israel from the West Bank and Gaza Strip;
3. The controversial strategy of unilateral withdrawal from the Gaza Strip in the fall of 2005.

In retrospect, the first two strategies appeared to have hurt Hamas while the third appeared to have helped it.

––––––––––––––––––––––––

Sheikh Ahmed Yassin, the wheelchair-bound founder and spiritual guide for Hamas, was killed on March 22, 2004, when an Israeli helicopter launched a missile strike at him while he was leaving a Gaza City mosque. According to news reports, the Israeli prime minister, Ariel Sharon, personally ordered and monitored the three-missile attack. Eyewitnesses recounted that the first missile strike threw Yassin from his wheelchair, but it was unclear whether that strike killed him. As other member of Hamas ran for cover, the Israelis launched two more missiles, killing at least seven people. Two of Yassin's sons were among the 15 wounded.[2]

Although perhaps shocking, the missile attack came as no surprise. The 67-year-old cleric was an avowed enemy of Israel who justified suicide operations through his interpretation of Islamic law and ordered them to be carried out against Israeli citizens. Sharon called him the "mastermind of Palestinian terror" and a "mass murderer who is among Israel's greatest enemies."[3]

The Palestinian people, however, loved Yassin. Indeed, he was so well loved by Hamas and other Islamists that some 200,000 Palestinians mobbed the streets of Gaza City for his funeral procession, marking one of the largest demonstrations in recent memory. "Sharon, start preparing your body bags," the frenzied crowd chanted as Yassin's coffin, draped in a green shroud, made its way through the sea of angry people. Many of the mourners were armed, as if to imply that the crowd might march straight from the funeral into Israel; even some of the women bore automatic machine guns. Finally, when Yassin's coffin reached its burial place, it was carried between two rows of 200 masked Hamas fighters armed with antitank missiles and machine guns. After prayers and speeches by senior Hamas leaders, flags throughout the territories flew at half staff. It was the closest thing one could get to a Hamas state funeral.[4]

Israel believed that Yassin's assassination would strike a major blow to Hamas. However, many nations condemned Israel for an operation that the Jewish State considered self-defense. Even Hamas critics claimed that the missile strike against the paraplegic figure only strengthened the group's hand, while its apologists went on an anti-Israel offensive.[5]

Israel was undeterred, however. It was secure in the knowledge that if it did not attack Hamas leaders, those leaders would again plan and order the attacks of even more Israeli civilians. Thus the Israelis assassinated Yassin's successor, Abdelaziz al-Rantisi. A physician by training, Rantisi was a cofounder of Yassin's *dawa* network. In December 1992, Israel deported him to southern Lebanon, along with some 400 other Hamas members. After his return in 1993, he was often detained by PA security forces for his outspoken criticism of the ongoing peace process with Israel. Fearing his own assassination, Rantisi went into hiding after Yassin's death, but on April 17, 2003, about four weeks after he had been named the leader of Hamas, he paid a rare, full-day visit to his family in Gaza City. Soon after he left the house, the Israelis killed him with missiles shot at his car by helicopter, according to family members.[6]

Several months later, on August 21, 2003, Israeli choppers again launched missiles at a car carrying a Hamas leader. This time, the Israelis eliminated Ismail Abu Shanab, Hamas's third most senior leader.[7]

One missed opportunity for the Israelis was Mahmoud al-Zahar, a stern-looking, bearded man with a high forehead and a wart on his nose. He did not just look like an enemy to Israelis; he was the coordinator of the Hamas coup in Gaza in 2007. On September 10, 2003, Israeli warplanes dropped several large bombs on his home in Gaza, killing his son and one of his bodyguards. He, his wife, and his daughter survived.[8] Al-Zahar, incidentally, would lose another son in 2008 during yet another Israeli military operation in Gaza.

After the wave of targeted assassinations in 2003, the *New York Times* speculated that "each Israeli killing only seems to enhance the popularity of Hamas on the street."[9] But more worrisome for Israel was the notion that the assassinations actually may have helped Hamas become a leaner, more diffuse organization. As one Hamas spokesman stated on the Hamas Web site in 2007, "after the assassinations of Sheikh Yassin . . . Abu Shanab, and Dr. Rantisi, we have gained strength from these painful losses, and our organization became more powerful. We are not a figurehead organization; we are a resistance movement with deep roots."[10]

Nevertheless, the targeted assassinations appeared to have achieved their desired effect. The Hamas leadership was in disarray. Yassin had been a respected cleric, and he had legitimized the Hamas organization. Indeed, he had backed up its violent agenda with scholarly credentials. Moreover, he was a popular leader who had gained the trust of the community by providing a valuable welfare network when the PLO did not. To be sure, his shoes would be difficult to fill.

After Yassin's death, Hamas never found a religious leader to replace him. None of its other leaders had formal religious training. The closest thing Hamas had to a legitimate cleric was Sheikh Yousuf Qardawi, a white-bearded, Qatar-based televangelist on the al-Jazeera satellite television network, often photographed in a clerical white hat and robe. Qardawi was widely associated with the Union of Good (*al-I'tilaf al-Kheir*), an umbrella organization of some 50 charities identified by PA intelligence as one of the largest Hamas support organizations.[11] But while Qardawi had issued religious rulings in support of Hamas, and while the Union of Good was known to support Hamas, Qardawi had always sought recognition as a Muslim Brotherhood figure, not a Hamas cleric. Moreover, as the Egyptian political analyst Khairi Abaza notes, "Qaradawi could never be a Hamas cleric because he's Egyptian, not Palestinian. As an Egyptian he could probably only identify with the Muslim Brotherhood."[12]

Thus, Yassin's death made Hamas increasingly vulnerable to the widely held perception that it was a blunt and violent terrorist organization that sought only to inflict violence on Israel. Under Yassin, Hamas was traditionally viewed as fighting with a gun in one hand and a Quran in the other; now it was viewed as toting a gun in each hand.

The Israeli targeted assassinations of senior Hamas leaders also sparked what might be called a locality crisis. When Rantisi was named the new Hamas leader, he was seen as perhaps the only local leader known to Gazans who could carry Yassin's message into the future. His designation was also important in that it kept Hamas leadership in Gaza. However, after the deaths of Rantisi and Abu Shanab, Hamas appointed its new leader in secret so that Israel would not be able to assassinate him easily. Meanwhile, the new public face of Hamas became Khaled Meshal, an intense-looking figure with cropped salt-and-pepper hair, a round face, and a closely trimmed beard. Meshal, the leader of the Hamas political bureau, was expelled in 1999 to Damascus by Jordan's king, Abdullah II. After Rantisi's assassination in 2004, Meshal publicly coordinated much of Hamas's military, political, and financial activities from his base in Syria.[13]

Meshal quickly became a liability for Hamas. The longer the most recognizable Hamas leader was based in Syria, the more potential there was for Hamas to experience friction and fragmentation between local Gaza fighters and the decision makers abroad. Moreover, having a high-profile leader in Damascus gave Hamas the unmistakable appearance of being an international terrorist organization rather than a local and organic "resistance" group, as it always purported to be.

Reinforcing this negative perception was the fact that Meshal turned increasingly to the mullahs of Iran for both financing and training during this difficult period for Hamas.[14] This situation undoubtedly hurt the Hamas image at home among the predominantly Sunni Palestinian people who did not wish to be clients of a Shi'ite state. This also made it harder for Hamas's legions of academic and political apologists to defend the organization in the United States. Meshal would do additional public relations damage in 2005 when he rushed to the defense of the Iranian president, Mahmoud Ahmadinejad, for having the "courage" to dismiss the Holocaust, in which an estimated six million Jews died, as a myth, and for stating that Israel should be "wiped off the map."[15]

The Israeli assassinations put Hamas on the defensive. The surviving Hamas leadership recognized that Israel had almost complete freedom in its operations against them. International expressions of disapproval had little impact on Israel's actions. Following the bold targeted assassinations of Yassin and Rantisi, a number of Hamas leaders were forced underground, fearing for their lives.[16]

Another part of the Israeli counterterrorism strategy was to build security fences around both the West Bank and the Gaza Strip as a means to keep terrorists contained in the two territories. The idea for fencing off the Palestinians was tested seriously in the mid-1990s, when Israel had prevented untold numbers of terrorist attacks by erecting a fence around the Gaza Strip.

After the outbreak of the intifada of 2000, Palestinians tore down much of the Gaza fence, and many terrorists subsequently crossed into Israeli territory to carry out attacks inside the Green Line. Under Prime Minister Ehud Barak, Israel rebuilt the fence in late 2000 and early 2001. According to one senior IDF official, the "experience gained by the IDF's Southern Command in the Gaza Strip [was] the basis for [its] efforts to implement the new fence in the West Bank." Indeed, Israel stopped approximately "30 percent of hostile actions near the fence and 70 percent inside the territory through offensive actions."[17]

Israel was eager to prevent suicide bombings, particularly from Hamas strongholds in the northern West Bank but also by Arafat's Fatah-affiliated terror squads, including the al-Aqsa Martyrs Brigades, the Tanzim, and others throughout the West Bank. Indeed, Fatah was as much the cause as Hamas for the ultimate erection of the West Bank fence, for which construction began in 2002. As more installments of the fence were built under the direction of Prime Minister Sharon, Hamas became less effective in its ability to carry out its patented, attention-grabbing suicide bombings against Israeli citizens. Fatah was also stymied. As violence against Israelis dropped and violence among Palestinians rose, Sharon set about creating a more extensive, state-of-the-art West Bank security fence.

Interestingly, Sharon was initially hesitant to build the barrier, particularly because the idea of a separation fence originated with the Israeli left.[18] Indeed, building a fence was an indication that Israel was willing to accept a two-state solution at a time when the Palestinians had not yet renounced violence. Sharon agreed to build the barrier only after Israel could come up with no other alternatives to prevent Hamas and Fatah from shedding Israeli blood. He called it a "dam against brotherly hatred" and "murderous fanaticism."[19]

Once the IDF began to build the fence, the international criticism against Israel was overwhelming. Notably, former U.S. president Jimmy Carter charged that Israel was creating an apartheid situation in Israel, the West Bank, and Gaza.[20] Carter insisted that he sought to bring the Palestinians and Israelis closer together, but his allegations only served to alienate Israel. As countless officials explained, Israel was not interested in segregating the Palestinians or in exploiting them. Rather, the fence was a last resort taken to prevent further bloodshed caused by Palestinian terrorists.[21]

Moreover, the Israelis made a good faith effort to abide by international law in setting the course of the fence. They built their barrier roughly along the 1949 armistice line (the Green Line) that the United Nations had established following the 1948 Israeli War of Independence. It should be noted, however, that while the barrier hugged the Green Line, it also included some recently erected Jewish settlements to protect their large Jewish populations from Hamas violence.[22] The International Court of Justice demanded that the portions of the fence built on what was commonly recognized as Palestinian land should be torn down. The UN also ordered Israel to pay reparations for any damages caused by the building of the fence.[23]

Faced with intense international pressure, but recognizing that the fence was saving lives, Israel continued to pour its resources into the controversial and astronomically expensive barrier. Indeed, the fence cost about $1 million for every kilometer erected. After adding in bases, sophisticated transit points, and control systems, that figure swelled to $2 million per kilometer.[24] By 2007, the fence was estimated to be about 700 kilometers (435 miles) in length[25] but still did not seal off the entire West Bank border with Israel. Nevertheless, it had denied Hamas the ability to dispatch terrorists into Israeli cities. To the surprise even of Israeli security officials, in the areas where the barrier was fully operational, there was zero terrorism.[26] The Israeli government called the barrier "a vital, urgent, and critical imperative in order to save civilian lives."[27]

Not all Israeli analysts were thrilled with the fence, however. Some argued that it was a defensive measure that would not help Israel attain its long-term security goals. As analyst Hillel Frisch noted in 2007, no study compared the efficacy of Israel's fence to "offensive military measures such as targeted killing, penetration into 'enemy territory' on search and surprise missions, and most importantly, massive onslaughts and temporary conquest of areas in which terrorist infrastructure had taken root." But even without a comparative study, Frisch sought to prove the fence could be seen only "as a supplementary measure." He argued that the value of the barrier in the long run would "continuously depreciate in the face of Palestinian attempts to circumvent it by other means."[28]

The Palestinians, particularly in the Gaza Strip, had already found ways of circumventing their fence. While Hamas had been able to smuggle relatively small amounts of certain goods and weapons from Egypt's Sinai Peninsula into Gaza through tunnels beneath an area known as the Philadelphi Corridor (separating the Sinai from Gaza) during the Oslo period, by 2003 it became apparent to Israeli officials that Hamas was increasingly using its tunnel network to import weapons into Gaza that could prepare the group for the next round of fighting. Officials further noted that Egypt, despite its peace agreement with Israel, tacitly allowed for this illicit subterranean activity. Indeed, the Egyptian military border guards often allowed Hamas to smuggle weapons through the tunnels with utter impunity.[29]

According to one retired senior Israeli military official who did not want to be identified, the Israelis had found more than 70 tunnels originating in Egypt and leading to Gaza between 1993 and 2003, with the greatest number discovered during the al-Aqsa intifada and after. In retrospect, the Hamas leadership likely realized that, with the Israeli campaign of targeted assassinations and intermittent PA efforts to weaken the organization, it required more firepower in order to survive.[30]

To ensure a continued, steady stream of weapons, both Hamas and Palestinian Islamic Jihad, sometimes with the tacit approval of PA officials, facilitated the building and maintenance of the tunnels, which were often more than 100-yards long and cost up to $200,000 apiece to burrow.[31] But these groups were never responsible for the entire financial burden; Iranian funding undoubtedly helped bankroll these underground operations.

As the weapons poured in, the Israeli Engineer Corps destroyed a great many tunnels. However, military officials in Israel were frustrated by the fact that the Palestinians were able to dig them as fast as they were found. The Israelis redoubled their efforts when intelligence revealed that increasingly dangerous weaponry was arriving in Gaza. The smuggled weapons included everything from armor-piercing weapons and automatic rifles to mines and rocket-propelled grenades. The weaponry, according to a former Israeli military source, came from Egypt, Sudan, and Libya. Raw materials necessary to build homemade Qassam rockets as well as high explosives for suicide bombings also passed through the tunnels. On October 9, 2003, the IDF launched Operation Root Canal, its most ambitious operation yet in the Gaza Strip town of Rafah, where the tunnels typically emptied.[32]

To protect the subterranean supply lines, Hamas and the other terrorist groups burrowed more than 60 feet beneath the earth's surface to evade sophisticated Israeli sonar detection equipment. The mouths of the tunnels were equally hard to detect; some actually opened up into Palestinians homes in Gaza. According to Israeli sources, at least three or four tunnels were operational at any one time. They were reportedly extremely difficult to find without the help of good intelligence.[33]

Upon launching the operations that would destroy the tunnels, the Israelis took care to distribute brochures to the local population, explaining that their operations were designed only to uncover and destroy tunnels, as a means to minimize casualties. However, as the Israelis set about dismantling the tunnels, Hamas often hit the Israelis with heavy weaponry, including grenades, antitank missiles, and other ordnance.[34]

The Israeli operations certainly destroyed a number of tunnels and yielded caches of weapons and explosives, but they were unable to stem the flow of weapons to Gaza. During raids on Hamas strongholds, the Israelis found that the group was hiding smuggled arms and explosives under kindergarten playgrounds.[35] This prompted Israeli authorities to wonder what else Hamas had and where it was hidden. A September 2003 arrest and subsequent interrogation of one tunnel digger revealed that eight antiaircraft missiles had been smuggled through the tunnels. According to the Palestinian suspect, the missiles were designed to counter Israeli attack helicopters. However, they also could be used to target commercial airliners.[36]

In retrospect, debriefings with tunnel diggers and other intelligence may have yielded misinformation. The Israelis came to view this feverish tunneling activity as a threat to Israel—which it was—but not as a threat to the ruling Palestinian Authority, which it also was. To be sure, Hamas utilized the weapons and explosives in firefights with Israeli forces and terrorist operations. It also used the materiel to make its increasingly deadly Qassam missiles, which the group fired indiscriminately into Israeli population centers. But Hamas stashed the bulk of its weapons. While the Israelis were justifiably concerned that Hamas would one day use them in an offensive against the Jewish state, they gave little thought to the notion that the Islamist group may have also been anticipating a full-scale confrontation with its better-armed and better-trained rival, Fatah.

———————

In December 2003, as Hamas busily stockpiled weapons, Israeli Prime Minister Sharon announced his surprising plan to begin a unilateral "disengagement" process that would extricate Israel from the hostile Gaza Strip. He sought to disengage from Gaza for several reasons. For one, the former IDF general believed that Israel stood to gain little by protecting some 9,000 Jews living in a sea of angry Palestinian refugees. He was also certain that Israel would face a demographic threat, particularly if the Jewish state one day included Gaza. As Sharon reasoned, annexing Gaza would one day guarantee that the rapidly reproducing Palestinians would force Israel to choose between its Jewish character and its vibrant democracy. Moreover, he believed that withdrawal from Gaza would engender goodwill with the United States, which had laid out its road map for peace through the Quartet. Among the road map demands for Israel was the uprooting of settlements.[37]

In a speech at a conference in December 2003, Sharon announced:

> Israel will initiate the unilateral security step of disengagement from the Palestinians. The purpose of the Disengagement Plan is to reduce terror as much as possible, and grant Israeli citizens the maximum level of security. The process of disengagement will lead to an improvement in the quality of life, and will help strengthen the Israeli economy. [Such disengagement would also] relieve the pressure on the IDF and security forces in fulfilling the difficult tasks they are faced with. The Disengagement Plan is meant to grant maximum security and minimize friction between Israelis and Palestinians.

Sharon stressed that he still sought

> direct negotiations, but do not intend to hold Israeli society hostage in the hands of the Palestinians. I have already said—we will not wait for them indefinitely. [Disengagement is] a security measure and not a political one. The steps which will be taken will not change the political reality between Israel and the Palestinians, and will not prevent the possibility of returning to the implementation of the Roadmap and reaching an agreed settlement.[38]

Nearly two years after Sharon first announced his intentions, in August and September 2005, Israeli troops facilitated the evacuation of the Gaza Strip. As expected, Israelis engaged in heated debate over the ramifications of Sharon's bold step. Some argued that by making the Palestinians responsible for a quasi-state in Gaza, Israel could respond to aggression with traditional military might. Others asserted that the Gaza Strip would become a hotbed for terrorism—and one in which Israel's defense forces would not be able to regain control easily.

In retrospect, unilateral separation was a mistake from the Israeli perspective. For one thing, the withdrawal allowed Hamas and other terrorist groups to more easily manufacture explosives and other weapons, without needing to worry about possible raids by Israeli troops. Moreover, illicit tunneling became easier without Israel monitoring the border. Finally, as Israeli Likud party figure Benjamin Netanyahu noted, the withdrawal amounted to a defeat for Israel and an overall victory for Hamas since "it could claim that terror works."[39]

Hamas found new ways to inflict pain on Israel. Without the threat of unpredictable and debilitating Israel counterterrorism operations, Hamas leaders realized that the organization could continue to kill civilians and damage property by launching rockets and mortars into Israeli territory. Palestinians terrorists in Gaza thus indiscriminately launched some 1,500 Qassam rockets into Israel between 2005 and 2007. Many hit the Israeli town of Sderot, killing only a few people but wounding many, creating a climate for fear and causing millions of dollars in damage.[40]

Finally, disengagement impacted the ongoing Hamas-Fatah mini-war. Although largely overlooked at the time, the separation and isolation of Gaza actually exacerbated a geographical and sociological separation that already existed between the two Palestinian territories. Indeed, unilateral separation drove a wedge between the already disparate Palestinian territories (their differences are described at length in chapter 10), perhaps sparking the notion among Hamas leaders that their group had the potential to govern Gaza, particularly since the Hamas social infrastructure had already helped it establish dominance there. Indeed, when Israel withdrew from the fenced-in Gaza Strip, Hamas and Fatah were left to finish a fight that began during the first intifada. Hamas began to prepare for that inevitable confrontation.

In November 2004, after the death of Yasir Arafat, Abbas stepped in as the interim leader of the PA. In January 2005, the Palestinian people officially elected Fatah's second in command to represent the PA. Abbas, however, was largely powerless to quell the intra-Palestinian violence. One Palestinian official noted his concern for Abbas's safety "because of the campaign of incitement waged against him by Hamas and several other groups." In response to these threats, the PA official threatened a "Fallujah-style" operation against Hamas and its supporters, making a blunt reference to powerful U.S. military operations against al-Qaeda strongholds in Iraq.[41]

In an interview with al-Jazeera, however, Abbas assured the Arab world that the two Palestinian factions "have not clashed and nothing happened between us." He further noted that "shedding Palestinian blood with Palestinian hands is completely banned." He even claimed that after talking with Hamas leaders, "there was no disagreement on the substantial issues."[42]

In February 2005, attempting to regain control of the territories still beset by seemingly uncontrollable factional fighting, Abbas reached out to Hamas. The new PA leader offered Hamas a period of calm, or *tahdiyya*, which is neither a peace treaty nor a truce. In this context, it was a cooling-off period; the PA would not arrest members of Hamas. Abbas also assured the Islamists that he would work with Israel to reduce operations against the Islamist group, in exchange for assurances from Hamas that it would allow the Palestinian elections scheduled to proceed as planned.[43]

The very need for a cease-fire between the two factions marked a low point in Palestinian history. After some deliberation, Hamas agreed to Abbas's offer. The period of calm began in March 2005. "Those who violate it," Abbas warned Hamas, "will be outside the national consensus and must be struck with an iron fist because we cannot allow any individuals . . . to take the law into their own hands."[44] Only one attack against Israel was attributed to Hamas during the *tahdiyya*. It came in August 2005, but Israeli authorities did not believe that Hamas's military leadership sanctioned it.[45] Thus, it appeared to outsiders that Abbas was slowly regaining control of the West Bank and the Gaza Strip.

Abbas, however, was struggling in his new role. Filling the void left by Yasir Arafat was a Herculean task. As one former PA cabinet member noted, after the death of Arafat, the Fatah-backed PA would face "the threat of disintegration and the prospect of losing pre-eminence within the Palestinian society."[46] This was not hard to imagine. Arafat had almost absolute control over every aspect of the Palestinian Authority. One might even argue that Arafat *was* the Palestinian Authority.[47]

As one senior Israeli journalist explained, Fatah, the PLO, and the PA were all designed to make Arafat "the exclusive arbiter in every matter." Arafat was able to do this by creating short chains of command that all reported to him directly. He also ensured loyalty through a patronage system, which ensured that his subordinates were paid well for their allegiances. Moreover, he created an intricate network of rival security and intelligence operations that competed for power and budgets that only he could bestow.[48] As one frustrated Palestinian parliamentarian quipped, the legislature should have declared Arafat "god of Palestine."[49]

Arafat even looked like the Palestinian cause. In dramatic fashion, he wore military fatigues to government business meetings, along with his signature *keffiyeh* that when, draped over his shoulder, took on the shape of pre-1948 Palestine. Arafat was almost never clean-shaven; he reportedly sought to demonstrate that he was working tirelessly to "liberate Palestine" and did not have time to worry about his personal appearance.

By contrast, Abbas was a mild-mannered man with a mustache who wore a suit and tie. He parted his white hair carefully to one side and had the air of a western politician. Indeed, he appeared to be anything but a revolutionary. When Arafat died from a mysterious illness in November 2004, Abbas, who had long been the heir designate, was officially installed as the new figurehead of the Palestinian Authority. However, he was never seen as a natural leader by his people. This would remain a challenge for him, and likely contributed to the Hamas attack against his authority in 2007.

The fact that Abbas was not a cult of personality was not his only problem. He also had to struggle with several difficult realities. Economic devastation from the al-Aqsa intifada was just beginning to register on the

Palestinian street. The Erez industrial zone in Gaza, for instance, had been a place for work for thousands of Gazans seeking to benefit from the economic cooperation between Israel and the Palestinians, but was abandoned by the Israeli government and businesses in 2005 as punishment for the violence and concern over the lawlessness. The World Bank estimated that the economic damage done between 2000 and 2005 in the West Bank and Gaza Strip exceeded that of the Great Depression in the United States, with the Palestinian gross domestic product falling by almost 40 percent.[50] Meanwhile, many of the Fatah leaders from the Oslo era owned businesses and property outside of the territories. The perception was building that Fatah had gone corrupt during the period in which it negotiated with Israel. This common belief ultimately helped Hamas in the elections and the battles that followed.

Abbas also struggled with his efforts to bring all of Fatah's violent factions, spawned during Arafat's long reign, back under his control. In December 2003, Palestinian political scientist Abd as-Sattar Qasim had predicted that "Fatah will definitely disintegrate and polarize into many groups and factions."[51] This was not far from what happened. Gangs and factions challenged the law and the president's authority. In some cases, they threatened the population and forced Palestinians to pay for protection. They also disrupted the electoral process. The chaos was exacerbated by Abbas's struggle to gain control of the younger generation of Fatah fighters who had, for more than a decade, been seeking to share the power and patronage systems that were jealously guarded by the older guard. As if that were not enough, Abbas was also forced to contend with disgruntled old guard members of the PA security forces as he went about addressing the wider issue of security reform.[52] This disarray would also benefit Hamas during the June 2007 war.

While Hamas was hit hard by Israel's campaign of targeted assassinations and the construction of barriers that prevented them from the attacks that gained them popularity, the PA was in even worse shape. It is important to note that the PA's woes directly impacted the lives of Palestinians. As the PA struggled to rebuild itself, Hamas took the opportunity to rebound from its losses, stock up on weapons, and train its ranks for future battles. This dynamic undoubtedly benefited Hamas for the challenges ahead.

Hamas appeared to have recognized its own strength and popularity. Thanks to its social welfare network, which remained in place despite PA and Israeli attempts to dismantle it, the Islamists were in an advantageous position to enter the Palestinian elections planned for early 2006. Thus, the *tahdiyya* likely marked a change in Hamas strategy from concentrating most of its efforts on attacking Israel to seeking nothing less than control of the PA.[53]

Specifically, plans for a Hamas political victory were in the making. According to one Palestinian journalist with good access to the Hamas leadership, Hamas plotted for a surprise electoral victory in early 2006; after it announced its intention to compete in the election, the group instructed voters to trick pollsters by not revealing their electoral choices.[54] According to this strategy, if Hamas was not forecast to win the elections, Fatah would not campaign as hard, believing that another electoral victory was at hand.

Meanwhile, Hamas had maintained a strong constituency in Gaza as well as the West Bank through its welfare system of mosques, charitable associations, sports clubs, and other services. The group also sought to influence the Palestinian people through its media network. In addition to its print and Internet publications, Hamas broadcast its message via a terrestrial channel in the Gaza Strip called al-Aqsa Television. Programming on this channel included messages from Hamas leaders calling for jihad, songs of incitement to murder, glorification of "martyrdom," videos of Hamas gunmen, and even promises of Israel's destruction.[55]

Although Hamas clearly announced that it would take part in the January elections, and analysts mused the potential impact of its gains at the polls, other dramatic events took place in the weeks before the vote that overshadowed the Islamist organization's participation in PA elections. On January 4, 2006, Ariel Sharon suffered a massive stroke, leaving him in a permanent vegetative state. The former general was rushed to hospital in Jerusalem after complaining that he did not feel well. The stroke reportedly took place during the hour-long ambulance journey from his home to the hospital.[56] Ehud Olmert, Sharon's deputy, became acting prime minister when it was determined that Sharon was incapacitated. The contrast between Olmert and Sharon was stark. Olmert was bald, thin, and serious looking. His predecessor was obese with an easy smile; some called him "larger than life." Critics of Olmert also noted that the new prime minister lacked Sharon's strong military background.

The uncertainty surrounding the loss of Israel's leader weighed heavily on the region. As Hussein Agha and Robert Malley wrote in the pages of the *Boston Globe*, "With Sharon's stroke, the Israeli political scene has lost a central actor. With Hamas's electoral participation, the Palestinian political scene is gaining a new one. An already impossibly complex situation is about to become more complicated still."[57]

CHAPTER EIGHT

PRELUDE TO WAR

"We have lost the elections; Hamas has won," said Saeb Erakat, a Palestinian official aligned with the Fatah faction. Erakat was visibly shaken. A heavyset, bald man with glasses who often appeared on television during the Palestinian uprising of 2000 to defiantly lambaste Israel's counterterrorism measures in the West Bank and Gaza, Erakat appeared anything but defiant here. His surprising announcement came even before the final election tally had been made.[1]

Fatah members had fired celebratory gunshots into the air in Ramallah the night before. But these celebrations were premature. The Palestinian Central Elections Committee shocked the world on January 26, 2006, when it announced that the Islamist party had won a majority of seats in the Palestinian parliament. There was no refuting the fact that Hamas had earned a legitimate landslide victory; the election was considered by observers to be as free and fair as elections can be in the Arab world. More than one million Palestinians went to the polls to cast their votes. Hamas claimed 76 of the 132 seats (74 under the Hamas banner, plus independents), granting it the right, by Palestinian law, to form a coalition.[2]

Some sympathetic analysts argued that, despite the results, the Palestinians did not truly seek an Islamist government. Rather, their votes for Hamas were an expression of a need for "change and reform," which was the name of the Hamas electoral platform. Others, however, argued that it was "condescending to argue that the Palestinians were somehow unaware that they were casting ballots for the party that advocates violent jihad."[3] Indeed, it was impossible that they were unaware of Hamas's history of brutal violence against Israel dating back to the outbreak of the first intifada in 1987. Moreover, the

Palestinian people knew from the Hamas election manifesto dated January 25, 2006, that Hamas sought a shari'a state and all the trappings that came with it.[4] Further, had they merely wished to protest Fatah, they could have voted for other parties. Thus, the Palestinians were fully responsible for the electoral choices they made.

On the day the election results were announced, Hamas leader Ismael Haniyeh flashed a broad smile and held up his forefinger in front of photographers and journalists in Gaza. With cropped salt-and-pepper hair and a neatly trimmed beard, Haniyeh projected a calm confidence, unlike many of his cohorts, whose nerves had been visibly frayed by years of Israeli counterterrorism operations. Haniyeh came of age during the 1987 intifada (he was 24 when it erupted) but had already been active in Islamist politics at the University of Gaza in the early 1980s. His credentials as a Hamas leader were further bolstered by several Israeli arrests and the fact that he was among those deported to South Lebanon in 1992 for his involvement in Hamas. After the wave of assassinations of Hamas leaders that followed the al-Aqsa intifada, Haniyeh emerged as one of the group's top leaders.[5]

Haniyeh's jubilation over the elections results was short-lived, however. After he formed a new coalition on March 29 (he was named "prime minister"), the territories fell into turmoil. Fatah, which took only 45 seats in the election, was unprepared to let go of the power it had enjoyed since the creation of the Palestinian Authority in 1994. Clashes between various Palestinian factions and clans soon erupted in the streets of Gaza.

How did Hamas win? As described in previous chapters, the group's popularity grew steadily over two decades of confrontations with Israel. Palestinians of the territories and the diaspora alike came to view Hamas as a source of hope for Palestinian renewal, particularly since the Islamist group had always refused to take part in what was widely viewed as a corrupt Palestinian political system (although it should be noted that Hamas had participated in previous municipal elections). Indeed, the prevailing perception was that Hamas was a pious and ascetic organization that could not be corrupted. Hamas exploited this belief by casting the PLO returnees (*a'idoun*)—the wealthy Fatah officials who returned from the diaspora to the Gaza Strip and West Bank after the Olso Accords—as corrupt and spoiled by the money they had amassed while in exile.[6] The prevailing Palestinian perception was that Hamas was tenacious and unwavering in its rejection of the Palestinian-Israeli peace process, despite immense international pressure, not to mention coercion by Fatah from within. Hamas also gained popular support from its expansive social networks that provided much-needed services to appreciative Palestinians in ways that the PA never did. Hamas enjoyed a baseline of popularity simply by buying off a sector of the Palestinian people; the group provided monetary support to the families of suicide bombers and handed out meat to needy families on holidays.

For the Israelis, options were few after the election. The 2006 Hamas legislative victory severely dampened any hopes that Prime Minister Olmert may have harbored for peace. The unilateral withdrawal had backfired. Hamas was now the representative of the Palestinian people through a free and fair election. Above all else, Hamas rejected the very existence of the State of Israel and refused to negotiate that point. If there had been any doubt about Hamas's intentions, its leaders stated immediately after the elections that they had no plans to pursue peace talks or disarm the party's armed wing, the Izz al-Din al-Qassam Brigades.[7]

Washington's options were similarly limited. "I have made it very clear," George W. Bush stated solemnly, "that a political party that articulates the destruction of Israel as part of its platform is a party with which we will not deal." He added, "I don't see how you can be a partner in peace if you advocate the destruction of a country as part of your platform."[8]

America's stance was not a surprise. The Hamas election was an embarrassing black eye to the U.S. democratization efforts in the region. The Palestinian elections that brought Hamas to power had been spawned by the Bush doctrine, which was designed to promote democracy throughout the Arab world. The U.S. president viewed free elections and transparent governance as a means to combat the ideology of radical Islam, which continued to spread unabated and inspire violence against the United States and the West. Obviously, this was not the outcome the administration had been hoping for.

America's decision to back the Palestinian elections was a calculated one. It was due, in no small part, to polling data that all but guaranteed a Fatah victory over Hamas, falsely affirming the popularity of the U.S.-backed government in the West Bank and Gaza Strip. The polls were produced primarily by Khalil Shiqaqi's Palestinian Center for Policy and Research, which conducted three critical studies of Palestinian opinion in June, September, and December 2005. The data indicated that Fatah's support among Palestinians ranged from 44 percent to 50 percent, while Hamas support was said to range from 32 to 33 percent.[9] "With each new Shiqaqi poll," scholar Martin Kramer notes, "U.S. policymakers grew more lax when it came to setting conditions for Hamas participation."[10]

In retrospect, U.S. reliance on these polls was a grave error. Kramer suggests that the polls may have been part of Fatah's election propaganda, in an attempt to project its strength.[11] Alternatively, some analysts quietly wondered whether Shiqaqi, whose brother was the late Fathi Shiqaqi, a founding member of the Palestinian Islamic Jihad, sought to deceive the United States, Fatah, or both. Others, however, defended Shiqaqi, contending that he was a "scapegoat" for America's unexpected and crushing defeat in the Palestinian-Israeli arena.[12]

The elections also constituted a severe blow to Fatah, which captured just 45 seats out of a possible 132. These dismal results were a sign that without Yasir Arafat, the party had little appeal to the Palestinians of the West Bank and Gaza Strip. "This is the choice of the people," admitted 70-year-old Ahmed Qureia, a member of Fatah's old guard. "It should be respected."[13]

While the people had spoken, Qureia's younger colleagues in Fatah wanted the last word. Immediately after the elections, Fatah and Hamas members clashed in front of the Palestinian parliament building in Ramallah.[14] Tensions between the two factions soon spread, continuing regularly in the weeks and months that followed. According to a 104-page report issued by the Palestine Center for Human Rights (PCHR) immediately after the elections, there were reports of "attacks on public institutions; armed personal and clan disputes; attacks on international organizations; abductions of internationals . . . armed conflicts between security services and armed groups; and attacks on officials."[15] Over 15 months, according to PCHR, 350 Palestinians were killed in the clashes, including 20 children and

18 women, while 1,900 were wounded. The center also estimates that 248 Palestinians were killed "by an escalation in the state of lawlessness."[16] How the center differentiated between casualties from clashes and casualties from lawlessness is unclear.

The first serious clashes, which foretold the real possibility of a civil war, were reported in mid-April, when hundreds of Fatah activists marched to Gaza's parliament compound, throwing stones and shattering windows in a government building. Elsewhere in the territories, tens of thousands of Fatah members marched through the streets, denouncing Hamas, setting tires ablaze, and waving the Fatah party's flag. In Nablus, Fatah-affiliated gunmen stormed a courthouse, ejected dozens of employees, and shut it down.[17]

Tensions worsened on April 22, 2006, when hundreds of students representing the Hamas and Fatah factions at Gaza's al-Azhar University and the Islamic University threw stones and homemade grenades at one another. Fifteen people were wounded, two seriously.[18] Two weeks later, in early May, at least nine Palestinians were wounded in two days of Gaza Strip fighting between the two rival factions. At least four schoolchildren were wounded in the crossfire of predawn gun battles.[19] In another incident, Hamas activists responded to the assassination of one of their members by launching a shoulder-fired missile at a Fatah security services truck, killing two passengers inside.[20]

The violence grew worse after the creation of the "Executive Force" (EF), a new military unit deployed on April 20 by Hamas Interior Minister Said Sayyam, a teacher for 20 years in the Gaza Strip with a long history of Hamas involvement. For weeks, Sayyam had complained that forces loyal to Fatah and the PA were not following Hamas directives. Palestinian President Mahmoud Abbas, as it turned out, had actually ordered Gaza's police officers to stay home in exchange for receiving their salaries as a means to deny Hamas the power that it had earned at the ballot box.[21] It soon became apparent, however, that the EF was not a legitimate police force. Rather than filling the void left by the PA forces and restoring law to the streets of Gaza, the EF became an authoritarian tool that Hamas used to intimidate and exterminate its political foes. The EF adopted many of the extremist views associated with Hamas's military wing, the al-Qassam Brigades. As one new recruit noted, "I'm not Qassam, but I'm in the police force. It's considered jihad."[22]

When Hamas elected to deploy the EF, Fatah correctly viewed the move as a direct challenge to Abbas's PA forces. This again raised the specter of an all-out civil war. Fierce clashes erupted for nearly an hour between the two sides on May 22, as the two factions exchanged fire in front of the Palestinian Legislative Council (PLC) building near the police headquarters in Gaza.[23]

In early June, more brutal fighting was reported between Hamas fighters (including the al-Qassam Brigades) and Fatah fighters (including the al-Aqsa Martyrs Brigade), which led to the death of a pregnant woman and a deaf man, among others. Assaults launched by the two opposing factions against each other continued throughout the month, with reports of abductions, grenades, and rocket fire.[24]

Amid the chaos, Hamas and other terrorist factions did not forget to attack Israel. On June 25, Hamas carried out a daring raid near the Kerem Shalom crossing on the Gaza border. Eight Hamas fighters reportedly utilized an underground tunnel to approach and ambush an Israeli tank, resulting in the deaths of two Israeli soldiers as well as the capture of Corporal Gilad Shalit. Hamas had knowingly crossed an Israeli red line. It was common for the Israelis to endure shelling or other attacks. But when its soldiers were kidnapped, the IDF responded with stronger force. Thus, two days after Shalit's abduction, the IDF launched Operation Summer Rains against several key Hamas targets, adding to the pandemonium that plagued the Gaza Strip.[25]

According to Prime Minister Olmert, the aim of the invasion was "not to mete out punishment, but rather to apply pressure so that the abducted soldier will be freed." Prior to the dawn raid, Israeli fighter planes attacked three bridges and the main power station in Gaza, in order to limit the mobility of Shalit's captors. If they had not taken out those targets, the Israelis feared that the captured soldier could be removed from Gaza or transferred to another location.[26] In the end, however, Shalit was not recovered. Seeking retribution, Israel continued to target Hamas in the Gaza Strip, even as the Islamist group tangled with Fatah forces.

Surprisingly, the Israeli rage over the Hamas kidnapping of one of its soldiers was almost a side plot during the summer of 2006. While recovering the kidnapped soldier was a high priority for the IDF, the war with Hizbullah on Israel's northern border quickly overshadowed Israel's Gaza operations. That war was provoked when Hizbullah fighters, on July 12, infiltrated Israeli territory from Lebanon and attacked two IDF armored jeeps patrolling the border, killing three soldiers and kidnapping two: Eldad Regev and Ehud Goldwasser. Hizbullah, like Hamas, had knowingly violated an Israeli red line. The result was a 33-day war, marked by thousands of Hizbullah rockets fired on Israel's north and an even greater number of Israeli reprisal strikes against Hizbullah targets mostly in southern Lebanon and Beirut. The conflict raged until the United Nations brokered a cease-fire that took effect on August 14, 2006.

The Lebanon war did not deter the Palestinian factions from warring with one another, however. Armed clashes continued between Hamas and Fatah throughout the summer and fall. By October, the violence had spread throughout the West Bank towns of Ramallah, Nablus, Jericho, and Hebron.[27]

In December 2006, Hamas accused Fatah of attempting to assassinate Palestinian Prime Minister Haniyeh in an attack at the Rafah crossing in Gaza that killed one of his bodyguards. In the war of words that followed, Hamas claimed that Mohammed Dahlan, a senior Fatah strongman in Gaza, was behind the attack. Violence again erupted between the two factions, leading to 20 injuries.[28]

Seeking to regain control, Abbas called for an early election to bring down the Hamas government. Fatah activists in Gaza and the West Bank celebrated this political maneuver, taking to the streets and firing celebratory machine-gun bursts into the air. In response, Hamas accused Abbas of launching a coup against its democratically elected government.[29]

Even before Abbas made this call for early elections, Hamas complained that the Fatah-backed PA had refused to engage with it on issues of governance.[30] There had also been reports of tensions between the Hamas appointees and Fatah functionaries in various ministries as well as fragmentation within the security services. Indeed, each faction retained and developed its own militias.[31] In retrospect, Abbas's call for a new government was probably justifiable. The political tensions that characterized the Hamas-Fatah power struggle had paralyzed the Palestinian legislature.

Meanwhile, violence worsened between the two groups in January and February 2007, leading to a sense that the West Bank and Gaza were more lawless than ever. Specifically, Hamas carried out a string of abductions of Fatah and PA figures. Those who were kidnapped were often beaten; in some cases, "their limbs were fired at to cause permanent physical disabilities." According to PCHR, the Hamas EF stormed private homes and executed their Fatah enemies by shooting them, point blank, in the head. Reportedly Hamas also hijacked a convoy of PA trucks, marking a turning point in the conflict. The EF was not simply trying to kill Fatah members; it was attempting to cut off their supply lines as well.[32]

In an effort to halt the fighting, King Abdullah of Saudi Arabia intervened and invited the leaders of Fatah and Hamas to Mecca to engage in a dialogue designed to end the conflict. Abdullah, a heavyset man often photographed in a headscarf, sunglasses, and a dyed-black goatee and mustache, likely gloated over his high profile diplomatic endeavor with the Palestinians, particularly since it did not include Egypt, his country's political rival. Abdullah was also likely happy to do something positive for the United States; Washington often complained to the Saudis about their role in financing terror and the propagation of radical Wahhabi propaganda.[33]

The top leaders of Hamas and Fatah represented their factions at the Saudi talks, demonstrating a seriousness of purpose and perhaps concerns about the future. Fatah's representatives included Abbas and Dahlan, while Ismael Haniyeh and Khaled Meshal represented Hamas. After three days, the two high-level delegations reportedly reached an understanding, leading to the February 8, 2007, Mecca Agreement. The agreement was based on the so-called Prisoners Document of May 2006. The Prisoners Document was penned by Marwan Barghouti of the Fatah faction and Abdul Khaleq al-Natshe of Hamas, as well as several other prominent Palestinian prisoners in Israeli jails.[34]

According to the text of the Mecca Agreement, both Hamas and Fatah agreed:

> First: To ban the shedding of Palestinian blood and to take all measures and arrangements to prevent the shedding of Palestinian blood and to stress the importance of national unity as the basis for national steadfastness and confronting the occupation and to achieve the legitimate national goals of the Palestinian people and adopt the language of dialogue as the sole basis for solving political disagreements in the Palestinian arena.
>
> Second: Final agreement to form a Palestinian national unity government according to a detailed agreement ratified by both sides and to start on an urgent basis to take the constitutional measures to form this government.
>
> Third: To move ahead in measures to activate and reform the Palestine Liberation Organisation and accelerate the work of the preparatory committee based on the Cairo and Damascus Understandings.
>
> Fourth: To stress on the principle of political partnership on the basis of the effective laws in the PNA [Palestinian National Authority] and on the basis of political pluralism according to an agreement ratified between both parties.[35]

A little more than one month later, on March 17, 2007, the two sides agreed to form a national unity government. But, predictably, the brokered calm did not last long. There was virtually no way to sweep aside the pain and animosity that lingered; the bloodshed between Fatah and Hamas had resulted in hundreds of deaths and injuries in 2006 and 2007. In March 2007 alone, the same month that the agreement was signed, there were 46 reported kidnappings of civilians in the Gaza Strip as well as more than 25 killings. The intra-Palestinian violence got to the point that one human rights activist announced that Gaza had "become worse than Somalia." Yasir Abed Rabbo, an executive committee member of the PLO, simply described the situation as "anarchy."[36]

The Palestinian violence had other negative consequences, particularly in the Gaza Strip, where Hamas enjoyed the most control. Foreign aid workers and armed military advisors, who initially sought to provide various forms

of aid to the Palestinians, began to flee for their lives. According to one report, several Egyptian military officers stationed in the Gaza Strip were re-
called to Cairo due to the raging hostilities. Fearful of violence, the two
Egyptian generals who stayed on spent most of their time in Israel, a country for which most Egyptians have little love.[37] The United Nations even
considered declaring the Gaza Strip a "dangerous zone," a move that would
prompt the evacuation of nearly all foreigners, including the United Nations
Relief and Works Agency and other international aid organizations that have
provided handouts to the Palestinians for decades.[38]

The violence in Gaza was also directly correlated to a rise in crime.
While Hamas and Fatah forces were killing one another, no one was policing
the streets.[39] Indeed, the Palestinian media, not known for its candor about
negative developments within Palestinian society, reported that crimes, including car theft and abductions, had skyrocketed.[40]

Gaza's decrepit infrastructure also paid the price. While the fighting
raged, in March 2007, a sewage-treatment pool collapsed in Umm al-Nasser,
a North Gaza village. The disaster was ultimately blamed on local residents
who were stealing sand from an embankment and selling it to local building
contractors. It was later learned that the sewage basins from which they stole
were already stretched well beyond their maximum capacity. The ensuing
"sewage tsunami" killed 3 women and 2 toddlers and injured 25. The raw
sewage submerged at least 25 homes, flooded the streets, and caused untold
damages to the 3,000-person village. Fadel Kawash, head of the Palestinian
Water Authority, told the Associated Press that a number of sewage projects,
including the one in Umm al-Nasser, had been halted after the Hamas electoral victory in January 2006. In fact, a Japanese project to repair the sewage
system had been cancelled.[41] According to one UN official, it was "a tragedy
that was predicted and documented."[42]

As Hamas-Fatah violence continued, there were also numerous reports of
Islamist groups attacking secular and Christian targets throughout the Gaza
Strip. A group calling itself the Islamic Swords of Truth, a self-appointed vice
squad, claimed responsibility for bombing the Gaza Bible Society's Christian
bookstore and two Internet cafés.[43] In response to these and other attacks, one
of Gaza's largest clans gathered to blockade a main road in northern Gaza to
protest the targeting of one of their shops by a vice squad. The family demanded that the government bring law and order back to the streets.[44]

Even journalists who covered the Palestinian conflict paid a price. Access to both Hamas and Fatah became more difficult as the fighting raged. Indeed, covering the violence endangered the journalists. In April 2007, Hamas security guards broke up a peaceful protest of journalists who were angered over the Hamas government's inability to secure the release of Alan Johnston, a BBC journalist who had been kidnapped by Gaza's Hamas-linked Dughmush clan in March. The confrontation resulted in three injured journalists.[45]

Thanks to little mainstream media coverage of the turmoil, most of the western world was unaware of the factional violence that continued between Fatah and Hamas through the spring of 2007. Multiple kidnappings took place, as well as machine-gun clashes, peppered with explosions caused by homemade bombs and other projectiles. Both sides suffered many casualties, but Hamas was particularly devastated by the killing of Ibrahim Suleiman Maniya, the 45-year-old leader of the al-Qassam Brigades, who was shot in the chest during a fierce clash between Hamas and Fatah on May 15. Fighting between the two factions during that week resulted in the deaths of 47 Palestinians and wounding of hundreds of others, mostly noncombatants.[46]

Sensing that the violence could get even worse and perhaps threaten regional security, the government of Egypt stepped in to attempt to broker a cease-fire on May 19. As was the case with previous Hamas-Fatah cease-fires, this one lasted only for a few weeks. Soon another round of fighting erupted, which quickly came to be known as the six-day Palestinian civil war.

CHAPTER NINE

HAMAS CONQUERS GAZA

On June 7, 2007, Hamas launched a military offensive to conquer the Gaza Strip. By June 13, its forces controlled the streets and Palestinian Authority (PA) buildings, including the presidential compound of Mahmoud Abbas and the massive security compound known as al-Suraya. By June 14, it was clear that all of Gaza was under Hamas control. Abbas had no choice but to dismiss the Hamas-led unity government that the Saudis had helped create in March. He soon appointed outgoing Finance Minister Salaam Fayyad to lead an emergency government in the West Bank. In so doing, Abbas all but conceded that he had lost the Gaza Strip.

The sight of Hamas and Fatah engaging in open battle on the streets of Gaza was certainly not a surprise, given the long history of animosity between the two groups. What was striking, however, was the dismal performance of the Fatah-aligned PA security forces. The battle for Gaza lasted a mere six days, resurrecting memories of another painful six-day war that drastically altered the future of the Palestinian people: the lightning victory of Israel over Egypt, Jordan, and Syria in 1967.

Fatah's forces, trained and armed by the United States and other western nations, had failed miserably in war. According to numerous reports, PA fighters either left the field of battle or even joined the Hamas fighters. Those PA fighters who stood their ground were likely not prepared for their brutal and zealous enemy. According to the Palestinian Center for Human Rights (PCHR), while both factions engaged in countless acts of violence, much of the Hamas violence was indiscriminate, demonstrating a willful disregard for the conventions of war.

According to PCHR, the mid-June violence in Gaza was characterized by "extra-judicial and willful killing," including incidents where Hamas fighters pushed two Fatah faction members from the roofs of tall buildings. Hamas also abducted and executed some political enemies. Reportedly Hamas even killed PA supporters who were already injured,[1] or shot Fatah fighters at point-blank range to ensure permanent wounds.[2] PCHR further reported attacks against private homes and apartment buildings, hospitals, ambulances, and medical crews associated with the Palestinian Authority. All told, the June civil war claimed the lives of at least 161 Palestinians, including 7 children and 11 women. At least 700 Palestinians were wounded.[3]

Although history will almost certainly cast Hamas as the aggressor in the battle for Gaza, reports of two authoritative human rights organizations on the June civil war (Amnesty International and PCHR) were careful to blame both Fatah and Hamas. Both reports issued pleas to both sides to end the violence, protect the civilian population, and return to negotiations.[4] The United Nations also sought to be evenhanded. Some states worked to include a clause in a proposed resolution citing "concern about an illegal takeover." The verbiage, however, fell short of assigning blame.[5]

When the guns fell silent, Sami Abu Zuhri, the dark-skinned, bearded Hamas senior spokesman who appeared regularly on Arab television networks, announced that the war had been a defensive one. In what many Fatah leaders viewed as an utterly audacious statement, Zuhri claimed that Hamas had entered into battle to defend itself from a Fatah cadre that was collaborating with the United States and Israel. "There is no political goal behind this but to defend our movement and force these security groups to behave," Zuhri said. He also stated that his organization sought to unify the various armed Palestinian factions under its command, insisting that it still sat atop a unity government. He even stated that the United States should "sit with [Hamas] at the dialogue table on the basis of mutual respect, respecting the elections." [6]

Zuhri did not need to do much to get a rise out of the White House. According to the *Wall Street Journal*, U.S. security services were already furious over the loss of the Fatah security complex, which housed the PA's intelligence and military infrastructure—infrastructure the United States had helped to create. After the compound was captured, Hamas claimed to have "acquired thousands of paper files, computer records, videos, photographs, and audio recordings containing valuable and potentially embarrassing intelligence information gathered by Fatah." Washington's fear, reportedly, was that Hamas had gained "access to important spying technology as well as intelligence information that could be helpful to Hamas in countering Israeli and U.S. efforts against the group."[7] Both Washington and Jerusalem also feared that Hamas had stolen the advanced weaponry that had been given to the PA, which Hamas could use on the battlefield, making its fighters harder to defeat.

As Hamas assumed control of the Gaza Strip, it began to govern through a combination of violence, authoritarianism, and Islamism. Ismael Haniyeh, the ascendant ruler of Gaza, officially denied accusations that Hamas intended to establish an Islamic emirate.[8] However, as noted previously, Islamists had launched a string of attacks on Internet cafés and Christian institutions. By November, the British press reported that "only believers feel safe" in Gaza and that "un-Islamic" dress sometimes resulted in beatings.[9]

According to Asma Jahangir, the United Nations Special Rapporteur on Freedom of Religion or Belief: "Women seem to be in a particularly vulnerable situation and bear the brunt of religious zeal. I was informed about cases of honor killings carried out with impunity in the occupied Palestinian territory in the name of religion. Reportedly some women in Gaza have recently felt coerced to cover their heads not out of religious conviction but out of fear."[10]

Hamas proved once again that terrorist groups, much like their Fatah predecessors, were unfit to govern. The Islamist group exhibited an almost criminal indifference to the suffering of Gaza citizens impacted by the violence, lack of services, deepening poverty, collateral damage from the battles, and the predictable Israeli reprisals that resulted from Hamas attacks. Moreover, as PCHR noted in its report, the de facto Hamas government attacked the media and peaceful demonstrations and engaged in the "destruction, seizure, and robbery of governmental and non-governmental institutions."[11] The few, reluctant steps toward liberalization that the PA had taken during its 13-year rule in Gaza—small advances in press and political freedoms, for example—had been wiped out in a matter of days.

Hamas, of course, attempted to highlight the positives. Within a week of the takeover, the Islamists boasted that crime, tribal clashes, and kidnapping had all dropped precipitously in the Gaza Strip.[12] But as former U.S. Envoy to the Middle East Dennis Ross noted, this drop in crime was more than likely the result of fear on the part of Gaza residents rather than a sign of increased or improved law enforcement.[13]

Some reports indicated that Ahmad al-Ja'abari, a senior member of the Izz al-Din al-Qassam Brigades, was behind the dangerous new conditions. Al-Ja'abari, an angry-looking man with an unkempt beard and crooked teeth, spent 13 years in Israeli jails and 2 years in the PA jails.[14] He also survived at least one Israeli assassination attempt.[15] According to the Israeli *Haaretz* newspaper, he was ignoring the moderating advice of Haniyeh and Syria-based Khaled Meshal.[16] Regardless of who was making the decisions, Gaza was suffering.

The first sign of religious violence in the Gaza Strip against non-Muslims— or "Talibanization" as some analysts called it, in reference to the Taliban regime that mistreated non-Muslims and harbored the al-Qaeda terrorist network in the 1990s—was the way in which Hamas mistreated the minority Christian community, mostly Greek Orthodox, which had lived in relative peace for centuries amid Gaza's predominantly Sunni Muslim population. When the June violence first subsided, Hamas announced on Palestinian television that the coup marked the "end of secularism and heresy in the Gaza Strip." On June 14, masked gunmen attacked the Rosary Sisters School and the Latin Church in Gaza City. According to Father Manuel Musalam, the leader of the small Latin community in the Gaza Strip, the Hamas gunmen used rocket-propelled grenades to storm the main entrances of the school and church. Then they destroyed almost everything inside, including the cross, bible, computers, and other equipment. The attack appeared to be entirely religiously motivated, since there were no reports of Fatah fighters in the church or the school. "This is more than vandalism," Musalam said. "They forced open the door and entered and destroyed everything. They even put the sisters' beds on fire." [17]

Later that month, according to the *Jerusalem Post,* Hamas kidnapped Professor Sana al-Sayegh, a teacher at Palestine University in Gaza City, and forced her to convert to Islam against her will. Her family's attempts to meet with Hamas leaders to find her repeatedly failed. Requests by community leaders representing Gaza's 3,000 Christians to meet with Haniyeh were also turned down. Finally, the Haniyeh government asked Ala Aklouk, a senior Muslim cleric in Gaza City, to look into the case. Aklouk soon told Sayegh's family that the professor had made a personal decision to convert to Islam. "She was too afraid to inform her family that she had converted to Islam," he said. [18]

In September, an attack against an elderly Christian woman triggered fresh fears among Gaza's Christians. A masked man in black clothes knocked on her door late at night, forced his way into her home, beat her on her hands, called her an "infidel," and stole her money and jewelry. [19]

In October, a Palestinian news agency reported that the body of 30-year-old Rami Ayyad, the owner of the Holy Bible Association, was found in an eastern suburb of Gaza City. Ayyad had been missing for a day, and had been receiving death threats from Islamists after they torched his organization's building in late summer. [20] The Holy Bible Association had also been the target of a grenade attack during protests stemming from the cartoons of the Prophet Mohammed that appeared in the Danish newspaper *Jyllands-Posten* in 2005. [21]

According to a Christian news service, Hamas attempted to force all Christians under its rule to become Muslims, submit to Islamic law, or leave the Gaza Strip. [22] By one count, more than 50 attacks had taken place in the first few months following the June coup. Targets included barbershops, music stores, and even a UN school where boys and girls played sports together. [23]

In December 2007, four masked gunmen in the Gaza Strip tried to kidnap a Christian. The man escaped unharmed, but as one Christian leader stated, the incident was "aimed at sending a message to all the Christians here that we must leave. Radical Islamic groups are waging a campaign to get rid of us and no one seems to care." [24]

In February 2008, unidentified gunmen believed to be aligned with Hamas blew up the YMCA library in the Gaza Strip. Two guards were temporarily kidnapped, offices were looted, a vehicle was stolen, and more than 8,000 books were destroyed.[25] That attack came only days after a Hamas "modesty patrol" attacked a Christian youth's car after he was seen driving a female classmate to her home. Both were injured in that attack.[26]

Hamas issued a statement on the Muslim Brotherhood's Web site condemning the YMCA attack, claiming that it sought to preserve the "historic patriotic Islamic-Christian relationship in Palestine," and that the attack served Israel's "agenda."[27] This did little to placate the fears of local Christians, living mainly in the Sheikh Radwan, Zeitun, and al-Daraj neighborhoods of Gaza City.

In May of the same year, unidentified gunmen bombed another Christian institution in Gaza, the Rosary Sister's school. [28] No one was hurt and only minor damagers were reported, but the message was clear. As one Gaza Christian lamented, "the Islamic revival has brought intolerance in its wake."[29]

It was not necessarily easy being a Muslim in the Gaza Strip after the June coup, either. Some 1,000 people, almost all members of Fatah and the PA, were illegally arrested in the first months of Hamas rule by the Executive Force (EF) and the al-Qassam Brigades. They were detained in 23 different locations, according to Amnesty International.[30]

One Palestinian news agency reported that the leader of the EF, Jamal Jarrah, admitted to the use of torture and violence against Hamas's political enemies. Jarrah stated in August that torture occurred in Hamas prisons but that the EF was trying "to minimize violations and avoid them through the training of our members." In response to reports alleging that more than 100 Fatah members were languishing in Hamas jails, Jarrah stated that "if there are, they are there for criminal reasons and not on a political background [sic]."[31]

The allegations of torture continued, however. In September, the EF reportedly abducted five Fatah men who were then transferred for treatment in a Gaza hospital, where evidence of torture was reported.[32] PCHR began to document Hamas torture on its Web site, citing Fatah members who "sustained fractures to the feet" as a result of beatings with sticks. In other instances, Fatah men were "handcuffed and blindfolded" and had pieces of cloth stuffed in their mouths to stifle their screams.[33]

The new rulers of Gaza also abducted and held a number of PA officials without stated cause. In some cases, those victims had held high-profile political positions. In July, for example, Hamas arrested the director of Gaza's electricity company, who was held without charges until December.[34] In August, Hamas also arrested the manager of a bank for no stated reason.[35] In some cases, Fatah leaders were abducted and intimidated in an attempt to persuade the group to cease its challenge to Hamas rule. For example, in January 2008, Hamas abducted one Fatah leader who was later returned to his home without the hair on his head or his mustache.[36] In May, human rights groups noted that Hamas gunmen had illegally detained the governor of Khan Younis in southern Gaza, along with three Fatah activists.[37]

In many cases, the de facto Hamas Interior Ministry in the Gaza Strip justified these arrests as part of its efforts to dismantle networks of "collaborators." As Hamas explained, these were people allegedly hired by Israel to snoop around or even carry out anti-Hamas activities.[38] However, labeling its enemies as "collaborators" was the easiest way for Hamas to detain its Fatah foes, since no proof of their activities was required.

Hamas also took over former government buildings and "nationalized" them. In February 2008, gunmen claiming to be from the Hamas interior ministry forcibly took over the Financial and Administrative Control Bureau offices in Gaza.[39] Two months later, unidentified gunmen set a Fatah building ablaze.[40]

For Gazans who had their rights trampled, there was no redress. According to Amnesty International, Abbas's decision to freeze the salaries of the judiciary in Gaza as punishment for the Hamas coup opened up this legal vacuum. Haniyeh responded by filling the legal void with his own personnel. But by January 2008, only four judges had been appointed.[41]

Shari'a courts became the primary arbiters of disputes in Gaza. These courts, presided over by Hamas-appointed judges, did not adjudicate cases on their legal merit but rather through the prism of Islamic jurisprudence. As Amnesty International noted, the judicial replacements lacked "adequate independence, impartiality, training, oversight, and public accountability."[42] Rights groups were further alarmed when Hamas also created "Palestine Islamic Scholars Association" branches in every district across Gaza. These quasi-legal entities employed up to eight religious scholars per branch but lacked trained legal professionals.[43]

The rulings from these Islamic courts caused further alarm. In one example, two university students reportedly were taken to court in November for "having a romance." The court tried to force them to marry, but the families, which were feuding, refused. In the end, the court "ordered the woman's family to keep her at home and her boyfriend to leave the city for a year."[44]

Those Palestinians who challenged the ad hoc judiciary also paid the price. The al-Qassam Brigades reportedly seized legal papers from a lawyer that attempted to document the confiscation of a car by Hamas. The militiamen ripped the lawyer's affidavit from his hands at gunpoint. According to the *Jerusalem Post,* the Fatah-allied Palestinian chief prosecutor, Ahmed Mughami, was assaulted by Hamas, which alleged that he had "smuggled very important and dangerous information" and had broken the law.[45] Human and legal rights groups documented these and other incidents, but they had no way to resolve them.

Those who held demonstrations against the lack of law in Gaza also suffered. According to the al-Jazeera Web site, two months after the coup the EF beat peaceful Fatah demonstrators who chanted "What is happening in Gaza is not acceptable" and "What has happened to security and human rights?" According to one journalist in Gaza, "Cameramen recording the protest were not allowed to film, or [to] get out of their cars."[46]

In August, Hamas banned unlicensed demonstrations by the Fatah party, citing Islamic law as its basis. According to a Hamas spokesman, the demonstrations were "being used to create chaos and terrorism."[47] In response, Fatah leaders found their own Islamic scholars to issue a ruling against the religious edict so that Fatah could hold open-air prayers on Friday, the Muslim sabbath.[48]

Hamas's apprehension over the prayers was understandable; these gatherings often turned into angry demonstrations against Hamas rule. It was suggested that Fatah even recruited for these gatherings by tempting each attendee with a prepaid phone card worth approximately $50.[49] Once under way, demonstrations often turned violent, particularly when Hamas security forces began forcefully dispersing the crowd, firing in the air, or beating demonstrators and reporters.[50] Associated Press television documented other abuses when it broadcast images of Hamas men beating an unarmed protester with long sticks.[51] In some cases, according to Amnesty International, Hamas forces deliberately shot unarmed demonstrators. In two specific cases, Palestinians were shot and killed while trying to help other demonstrators who were injured.[52]

It is also interesting to note that when Hamas threw rocks at Israelis during the 1987 and 2000 uprisings, the group called this "resistance"; when Palestinian protestors threw stones at Hamas, the new rulers of Gaza called them "outlaws" and arrested them.[53] Once when Fatah supporters threw stones at police, the Hamas forces opened fire with live rounds rather than rubber bullets or tear gas, as the Israelis usually did. Seven people were killed in those clashes, including a young boy, and dozens were wounded.[54]

In one anti-Hamas rally in November 2007, a group of female Fatah protestors gathered in front of a Gaza police station controlled by Hamas, chanting "Shi'a, Shi'a, Shi'a!" This was a bold and audacious reference to the fact that Hamas was receiving funds from Iran. Unwilling to be insulted, Hamas police attacked the girls and beat some with batons, according to *The Times* of London.[55]

In early January 2008, Hamas violence against Fatah demonstrations reached its zenith. Seven Palestinians were killed and 40 were wounded after a firefight erupted just outside of a mosque in the southern Gaza town of Khan Younis. Hamas alleged that Fatah supporters instigated the clash by firing on worshippers leaving their prayers. The fighting soon spread to other areas around the Gaza Strip. Pro-Fatah rallies were held across Gaza the next day to mark the group's 43rd anniversary. Tensions ran high, marked by blistering verbal attacks, but no violence was reported.[56]

Sadly, there were indications that the Hamas-Fatah rivalry even had made its way to the schoolyard. The *Observer* newspaper in Britain reported that Hamas EF members were intimidating children who wore a Fatah *keffiyeh* and, in some cases, beating them.[57]

According to one Fatah intelligence operative, Fatah welcomed Hamas brutality to some extent. Indeed, it began to view its role in the Gaza Strip as one of provocateur in order to "weaken the Islamists in the eyes of the public." Demonstrations that ultimately ended in violence, the operative explained, helped Fatah in the battle for popular support on the Palestinian street.[58]

Most of the violence, however, went largely unnoticed in the West. One rare but shocking report in the *New York Times* in April 2008 documented Hamas brutality against Fatah activists at al-Azhar University, in which one woman was struck in the leg with an ax.[59]

Hamas understood that attacking its own citizens would not engender goodwill in Gaza or around the world. Therefore, it worked assiduously to cover its own tracks. As journalist Khaled Abu Toameh reported, the EF soon prevented, for a short period, the distribution of three Fatah newspapers, including the *al-Ayyam* and *al-Hayat al-Jadida* dailies, in the Gaza Strip. This is the first time that West Bank newspapers were barred from the Gaza Strip.[60] Hamas even took some of the circulation officials of the papers into custody for a short time. The EF closed a pro-Fatah television station and radio station. In fact, by late summer, Hamas controlled all electronic media in Gaza, except one radio station linked to the Palestinian Islamic Jihad, another Iran-backed terrorist organization.[61]

The Palestinian media were not the only ones subject to Hamas restrictions. According to the al-Jazeera Web site, Hamas attacked two cameramen from the Abu Dhabi satellite television channel in August and stormed the Gaza bureau of the al-Arabiya satellite channel.[62] The EF also detained a German television crew in November after they shot footage in the Gaza town of Khan Younis.[63] In February 2008, Hamas halted the publication of *al-Ayyam* again after it published a cartoon that lampooned Haniyeh.[64]

To control the reporting out of Gaza, Hamas began to issue government press cards to journalists. Predictably, journalists whom Hamas did not like did not receive credentials. The Palestinian Journalists Syndicate protested that the tactic threatened journalists and prevented them from doing their jobs. The syndicate alleged that under the Hamas government's draconian rules, phrases such as "Hamas militias" and "ousted government" were banned.[65] Hamas also announced it would ban stories that did not support "national responsibilities" or those that would "cause harm to national unity."[66]

The more journalists complained, the more difficult Hamas made it for them. The Union of Palestinian Journalists reported that after a series of threats, Hamas forces raided the home of one journalist, Hisham Saqalla. The union further noted that its ranks had been threatened and blackmailed by Hamas on a daily basis.[67] The Foreign Press Association confirmed these reports, claiming Hamas had engaged in "harassment of Palestinian journalists in Gaza."[68] In one example, Hamas prevented journalists from attending a sit-in to protest the fact that the EF was holding two reporters. Hamas warned that anyone who attended the sit-in would be arrested.[69]

Within just months of the June coup, international nongovernmental organizations documented more than 9 assaults on journalists by Hamas and 21 illegal arrests.[70] Reporters Without Borders, an international media watchdog group, noted that Hamas "failed to investigate" these incidents.[71] In May 2008, press reports indicated that Hamas would begin to block Web-sites deemed "unfit according to Islamic rules," raising new concerns over the lack of media freedom under Hamas rule.[72]

By the end of summer 2007, Gaza residents were growing restless. One article in *ash-Sharq al-Awsat*, a London-based newspaper, entitled "Hamas: A Lawless Authority," noted that Gazans openly expressed the fact that they felt "miserable and suffocated" under Hamas rule. The article stated that "law is absent as a result of a paralysis in the legislative tools—all of which have been replaced by Hamas's Executive Force." Gaza was suffering from an "unprecedented paralysis" in nearly every sector of society.[73]

Due to Israel's sanctions against the Hamas government, stores in Gaza were out of many products, and hospitals ran low on crucial supplies, including anesthetics and antibiotics. Seeking to avert a humanitarian crisis, the Israelis eventually allowed certain medical supplies into Gaza but vowed to withhold other nonessentials. Israel's plans for sanctions against Gaza, approved in October 2007, also included the disruption of fuel supplies. Predictably, Hamas dubbed these sanctions a "crime" against the Palestinians. Ban Ki-Moon, the UN's secretary general, also weighed in, saying that cutting off energy from Gaza was unfair punishment. The rationale behind Israel's sanctions, however, stemmed from the realization among Israeli decision makers that if Israel allowed goods to flow through Gaza, it would be providing assistance to its enemy.

Several leftist Israeli organizations attempted to thwart the Israeli measures and appealed to the Israeli Supreme Court to allow fuel, in particular, to flow back into Gaza. The Court denied the motion in January 2008, but the activists vowed to appeal. Israel soon made public its plans for punitive disruptions of electricity in response to Qassam missile attacks out of Gaza, with plans for longer cutoffs, or even permanent cessations, in the future.[74] In an attempt to stave off these punitive measures, Hamas admitted on its Web site that "not every Palestinian who lives in [the Gaza Strip] fires Qassam rockets or even support[s] firing the Qassam rockets."[75]

But Hamas could not blame Israel for all that Gaza was forced to endure. After the coup, numerous newspaper stories documented a repeat of the "sewage tsunami." As a result of Hamas mismanagement, several Gaza sewer pipes burst, which flooded homes and businesses with a foul river of waste that was several yards high.[76] Gazans were infuriated when it was learned that the Israeli-made pipes that were intended to repair Gaza's decrepit sewage system had been sold to Hamas but used to assemble Qassam missiles and bunkers.[77]

The most anger, however, likely stemmed from the Hamas government's decision to raise taxes on cigarettes. A very large percentage of Palestinians in Gaza smoke (exact numbers are unavailable), and many were said to be "fuming." Lucky Strikes used to cost 10 shekels ($2.50) per pack. After Hamas came to power, the same pack of cigarettes cost 16 or 17 ($4.00 or $4.25) shekels. Reports just a few months later indicated that other American cigarettes could cost Gazans upward of 40 shekels per pack ($10.00).[78] With a faltering economy that was squeezed tighter by sanctions, and most Gazans living below the poverty line, residents could scarcely afford to smoke.

The nicotine withdrawal that many Gazans were experiencing did not help Hamas popularity. Some residents turned to locally grown tobacco and rolling papers but were clearly unhappy about it. As one smoker said, "I roll my cigarettes, and seal them with my mouth, and before I close my lips, I spit on Hamas and Fatah that are squabbling between them for their own interests."[79]

In fact, by December 2007, Gazans were complaining that even the simplest pleasures were hard to find. The goods that Israel barred from entering Gaza included batteries, tobacco, coffee, gasoline, diesel, and even chocolate.[80] Even some locally grown goods were hard to come by. For example, the price of chicken had doubled. Concurrently, there was a surplus in goods such as strawberries, which helped feed the Gaza population. However, whatever was not eaten was left to rot, due to the Israeli blockade on goods coming out of Gaza.[81]

One *Haaretz* story noted that a 15-year-old became an instant celebrity at her Gaza school because her father gave her a can of Coca-Cola that he had purchased abroad. The children in the class all wanted to be photographed with the girl and her can, since carbonated drinks were nearly impossible to purchase inside Gaza.[82]

By January 2008, according to journalist reports and Hamas spokesmen, some 50 to 80 percent of the Gaza population was unemployed, thousands of factories were shut down, and as many as 85 percent of Gazans were living below the poverty line.[83] In less than a year, Hamas had effectively destroyed the small steps the PA had taken in the Gaza Strip, largely with U.S. aid, to make the territory bearable for its people.

CHAPTER TEN

FATAH'S WEST BANK

As the Gaza Strip fell into turmoil, Mahmoud Abbas had problems of his own in the West Bank. After the Hamas takeover, the Fatah-backed Palestinian Authority was an emergency government that ruled over the West Bank only, and it had not even been elected. Indeed, the new cabinet, headed by Salaam Fayyad, was a stopgap measure. Moreover, the June Hamas coup in Gaza had thoroughly demoralized the once-dominant Palestinian faction.

Abbas and Fayyad clung to power in Ramallah even as some of their longtime colleagues appeared to have abandoned hope. Senior Fatah leaders such as Nabil Shaath, Mohammed Dahlan, and Hassan Asfour, all formerly powerful ministers in the PA, retreated to Cairo with their families and their wealth. There was even talk that several Fatah leaders had absconded with some $2 billion of Yasir Arafat's hoarded funds after the guerrilla leader's death in November 2004.[1] Analysts questioned whether Fatah would hold a congress in 2008, due to questions about the faction's viability.[2] As one observer quipped, Abbas was "no more than the president of the Muqata compound in Ramallah."[3]

The series of blows that Fatah had endured in 2006 and 2007 prompted Abbas's supporters in Israel and the West to question whether Fatah and the PA could survive in the West Bank. Indeed, as the Hamas Executive Force and the Qassam Brigades built fortified military positions throughout the Gaza Strip in preparation for the next military encounter, questions arose over whether the PA could control West Bank security. Some of the elite PA forces had capitulated immediately to Hamas's more zealous and motivated troops; some, as noted earlier, did not even put up a fight. It stood to reason, then, that this weakness and lack of will was pervasive throughout the once-formidable PA security apparatus.

Hamas also sensed this vulnerability and sought to exploit it. The Gaza-based Islamists taunted Abbas in late October 2007, saying that "in the autumn, the leaves fall and Abbas will fall."[4] The following month, Mahmoud al-Zahar, the architect of the Hamas military coup, threatened that "what happened in Gaza will also come to the West Bank." He further taunted his Palestinian rivals by saying that his organization "took over Gaza because Fatah is weak and the corrupted ones. They are not trusted. We won twice, once with elections and once again through our Gaza takeover in June."[5]

The West, particularly U.S. president George W. Bush, realized that in order to halt the spread of Hamas rule to the West Bank, Fatah would need an infusion of both funds and weapons. Thus, when it became apparent that Abbas still maintained a modicum of control over the West Bank after the guns in Gaza fell silent, Washington lifted its embargo on direct aid to the Palestinian Authority government (imposed after the Hamas electoral victory). Both Israel and the European Union also joined the United States in an expression of support for a moderate West Bank.

By supporting the decimated Fatah organization when it needed it the most, Israel and America likely realized that they might be able to exact concessions for an Israeli-Palestinian peace deal once Abbas returned to a position of strength. Thus began the flood of aid to the PA in the West Bank.

The West certainly did not believe that Fatah was a party of reformers and democrats. Rather, most world leaders viewed Fatah as the less aggressive of the two warring factions. Since there were no other dominant factions, the West had to back one of them.

On June 18, the U.S. secretary of state, Condoleezza Rice, appeared before a crew of cameras at the State Department and read carefully from a script. Rice announced that up to $86 million in U.S. aid that been previously slated to aid the PA's security forces against Hamas would be redirected to ensure the continued viability of a Fatah-controlled Palestinian government in the West Bank.[6] President Bush followed up in October by announcing a six-fold increase in aid promised to the Palestinians. He allotted $435 million in aid to the PA in addition to the funds earmarked earlier in 2007. The funds were slated for stronger security capabilities but also to avert a possible financial crisis that would send the West Bank into a meltdown.[7]

Abbas appealed to the international community for even more funds. Indeed, international donors promised a total of $7.4 billion through 2010, which amounted to nearly double the traditional combined PA budget for both Gaza and the West Bank.[8] As one analyst noted, the West Bank had not necessarily become stronger. Rather, it had become an "international ward," which did little for its legitimacy.[9]

After a Paris donors' conference in December, the international community continued to promise cash infusions to the PA. Predictably, Hamas spokesman Fawzi Barhum condemned the conference as a "dangerous conspiracy" to divide the Palestinians. He charged that Abbas was "cozying up to the Zionist enemy and the American project in exchange for millions of dollars to strengthen his security forces for his own personal interests."[10]

The most surprising pledges came from Israeli Prime Minister Ehud Olmert, who announced that he would allow Palestinian security forces in the West Bank town of Nablus to receive 25 armored vehicles from the Israeli defense industry along with 1,000 rifles and 2 million rounds of ammunition. The move was shocking in that it was a reversal of Israel Defense Forces policy. Indeed, the Israelis had withheld military materiel from the PA for seven years, after Israel discovered that the copious amounts of rifles and bullets it had provided the PA during the Oslo years for internal Palestinian security purposes were used against it during the al-Aqsa intifada beginning in September 2000.

Olmert's decision was also shocking given Israel's lack of confidence in the long-term viability of Abbas's government. Notably, Likud party politician Benjamin Netanyahu predicted that the new vehicles and weapons Olmert had pledged would also "eventually fall into the hands of Hamas."[11] After all, Hamas inherited a windfall of weaponry after it sacked PA strongholds the Gaza Strip, creating a security crisis for Israel.

The Israelis soon began to question the logic of providing the PA with weapons. In March 2008, Israeli Defense Minister Ehud Barak openly challenged General James Jones, the U.S. Special Envoy, over the need to provide the PA with armored vehicles and weaponry. The fear, he stated, was that Hamas could conquer the West Bank, as it did Gaza, and reap another weapons windfall.[12]

With numerous financial promises in place, Fatah set out to get even with its Hamas rivals in the West Bank. The Fatah-controlled Palestinian security services had rounded up hundreds of known Hamas activists throughout the West Bank as the June fighting raged in Gaza. In one naked act of retribution, masked Fatah gunmen kidnapped Ahmed al-Khaldi, the justice minister of the former Hamas government, as he left a mosque in Nablus.[13] It was not known whether Abbas or any of the PA leadership was involved in that kidnapping or the scores of other reported around the West Bank.

Abbas was, however, directly responsible for dismantling a number of Hamas-controlled city councils (including the one in Nablus) via decree, and he ordered a full review of all charities and businesses tied to Hamas in the West Bank. Some Hamas-run charities, businesses, and political offices were set ablaze before the review even was launched. More than 100 charities were initially closed.[14] In less than one year, some 200 were shut down.[15] Others reportedly have sought to deemphasize their ties to Hamas for fear of being dismantled by PA forces.[16]

In the weeks and months after the coup, numerous media reports confirmed that the Fatah-affiliated Palestinian security forces were working with Israeli security services to arrest or assassinate Hamas members throughout the West Bank.[17] One human rights organization reported that approximately 600 suspected Hamas members had been arrested in the West Bank between June and October 2007.[18] Amnesty International estimated that the figure was closer to 1,000.[19]

Roundups continued into the fall as PA security forces confiscated weapons, set up roadblocks throughout the West Bank, and even fired radical imams (mosque prayer leaders) who supported Hamas.[20] The Saudi *Arab News* also reported in October that Fatah had raided several mosques in the West Bank, confiscating print material produced by Hamas.[21] PA security forces also monitored imams' sermons in West Bank mosques.[22] One rights group alleged that PA security was using "the same practices on

Hamas detainees that Hamas is using on Fatah detainees in Gaza." In one example, a Hamas activist was reportedly yanked out of bed in the middle of the night and dragged to a Hebron prison, where he was beaten while hooded and handcuffed.[23] Arrests continued in to the summer of 2008.[24] Palestinians began to wonder whether the Fatah-backed PA was any less brutal than Hamas in Gaza.

Fatah also engaged in heavy-handed press restrictions. PA officials lobbied Egypt to stop airing the Hamas-sponsored al-Aqsa television channel on the state-owned Nilesat satellite system.[25] After Egypt refused, the PA's security services arrested numerous nonviolent members of Hamas, including journalists from the Hamas-sponsored al-Aqsa television channel.[26] PA police also arrested the director of the Amal television channel, which is not affiliated with Hamas but had aired a speech by Hamas's political leader in Gaza, Ismael Haniyeh, which the police said was "illegal."[27] PA police also briefly detained two Hamas officials in November for attempting to hold a press conference in Ramallah.[28]

In December, after the PA shuttered additional West Bank charities in an effort to constrict Hamas's finances, Abbas contemplated a law that would require all political parties to reveal their funding sources and to disclose personal information about their activists. While Hamas was not named specifically, it was clear that this was yet another measure taken to weaken the organization's West Bank apparatus and to cut off funds coming in from Iran and other foreign donors.[29]

By the end of 2007, according to Hamas sources, Abbas's forces had arrested more than 1,000 Hamas members in the West Bank.[30] These roundups and other repressive measures almost certainly helped the Palestinian Authority gain increased control over the West Bank and protect the territory from an attack from within.[31]

For the Israelis, Abbas's successes were bittersweet. For years, the PA had claimed that the very presence of Israeli forces in the West Bank made it impossible to detain Palestinians linked to terrorist attacks. Thus, Hamas, Palestinian Islamic Jihad, and the al-Aqsa Martyrs Brigades continued to carry out suicide bombings and other attacks against Israeli civilians. Finally, with a clear interest in neutralizing Hamas, the PA accomplished what it always insisted it could not: an effective clampdown on terrorist operatives within its jurisdiction.

The PA's moderate successes against Hamas notwithstanding, in October 2007, the United States voiced misgivings over the ability of PA security forces to assume the responsibility for securing the West Bank.[32] The PA took crucial steps to improve its military capabilities.

For example, the PA established an officer school to ensure that its senior security personnel learned vital skills. Additionally, the new Palestinian prime minister, Salaam Fayyad, shrank the PA's armed forces by one-third (from 83,000 to 50,000) as a means to save money and produce a better-armed yet more controllable force. Fayyad, a serious and clean-shaven man with glasses, was more of an accountant than a soldier. He made few friends in the security forces when he announced that personnel over the age of 45 were slated for removal, along with thousands of other men and women who were on the payroll but who never served on the force. Some old guard Fatah fighters accused Fayyad, a former official from the International Monetary Fund, of "starving our children." Fayyad responded by promising to remunerate the Fatah security personnel who were cut, but a risk remained that these former Arafat loyalists might switch sides and support Hamas in a bid to take down the Palestinian Authority in the West Bank.[33]

There were additional concerns as well. Fatah and the PA faced an uphill challenge in bringing all of the West Bank under control. The territory is about the size of Delaware, with its estimated 2.5 million residents dispersed among almost a dozen major population centers. For some time, it was believed that the remaining Israeli military presence in the West Bank might help the PA maintain control. Questions remained, however, about security there if the Israelis turned over full control to the PA.[34]

By late October 2007, as 3,500 PA security forces were deployed to the Hamas stronghold of Nablus, the West Bank's second largest town with a population of about 170,000, concern arose that these forces could be out-gunned. Specifically, Abdullah Kmeil, the head of PA intelligence in Nablus, admitted that there was only one rifle for every ten officers.[35] U.S. and Israeli military and financial assistance probably fixed this problem, but the crisis of confidence in the PA's military capabilities remained.

With U.S. and Israeli support, Fatah set about addressing other security concerns in the West Bank. In December, Abbas deployed an estimated 500 military personnel to the town of Tulkarem. The men set up checkpoints, searching for weapons and other contraband.[36] In an attempt to restore authority, the PA also began to rebuild its military compounds, which had been destroyed by Israel after the outbreak of the 2000 intifada. The PA also began to pay its soldiers more money as a means to maintain loyalty.[37] Fatah continued to shut down Hamas charities. However, due to international fears that dismantling Hamas services could spark a financial crisis among the Palestinian poor, Prime Minister Fayyad vowed to create 11 new government-approved charities to ensure continuity.[38] In March 2008, the PA announced the creation of a new socioeconomic network—financed by the United States, Israel, the United Nations, the European Union, and Russia—to counter the Hamas *dawa* system by providing aid to some 60,000 persons in the West Bank.[39]

The success of this program, along with continued military assistance, was seen as critical to the survival of the PA's West Bank regime. According to a senior Israeli defense official, the IDF assessed that without a significant Israeli military presence in the West Bank, "Hamas would take over the institutions and apparatuses of the Palestinian Authority within days."[40] The Israeli newspaper *Maariv* also cited concerns that thousands of weapons and millions of bullets—many from Iran—were being smuggled into Hamas hands in the West Bank.[41] Ironically, while Israel was fending off Hamas advances into the West Bank, the PA occasionally tried—and even sentenced to death—West Bank Palestinians for collaborating with Israel.[42] This only contributed to the sense among Israeli and American policymakers that the PA lacked an understanding of its own security predicament.

Washington and Jerusalem, in their bid to save the PA, shared fears about possible Hamas infrastructure lying dormant in the West Bank. Specifically, questions arose over the possibility that Hamas's broad social welfare infrastructure could be used for military advantage.[43] The PA continued to break up Hamas cells; it reportedly arrested some 250 operatives in the West Bank in the first days of January 2008.[44] But finding every fighter was virtually impossible. In early February, one West Bank–based Hamas member made his way into Israel and detonated a suicide belt, killing himself and an Israeli woman while wounding 11 other Israelis. Hamas's cell structure had eluded Israeli forces during both intifadas; it was not hard to imagine that Hamas could continue to survive underground in the West Bank until it could attempt another coup.

Abbas repeatedly expressed public concerns that Hamas already had plans to overtake the Palestinian Authority in the West Bank. He stated that Hamas would try to overthrow him with the help of outside parties, including Iran, Syria, and even Qatar.[45] He continued to order the arrest of Hamas members throughout the West Bank.[46] One arrest led to the controversial death in February 2008 of Hamas member Majed Bargouthi, a West Bank mosque preacher and father of eight, who died in a PA prison. Hamas alleged that Bargouthi had been tortured, sparking an outcry among Hamas members who claimed the PA was engaged in "factional cleansing."[47]

In March, after the February 13 assassination of Hizbullah operations chief Imad Mughniyeh in Damascus, Syria, a senior Palestinian official stated that he believed that Hizbullah was becoming more active in the West Bank, making PA security increasingly complicated.[48] The PA continued to push for more weapons and faster progress with Israel on a final status peace agreement, as a means to solidify power. In April, Palestinian spokesman Saeb Erekat warned that Abbas's government would disappear if peace was not reached.[49]

In early May, the first class of Palestinian security officers trained under a multi-million dollar U.S. program designed to bolster the PA hit the streets of the West Bank. The training had been characterized by numerous difficulties. In fact, one official called the training "a fiasco."[50] With memories of the al-Aqsa intifada lingering, the very sight of trained Fatah men elicited anxiety among Israel's military brass. In mid-May, the IDF rejected U.S. requests to arm the PA forces with personal armor, night vision goggles, and electronic communications.[51]

The PA's need for better equipment became increasingly apparent. Even amid the continued security crackdowns, Hamas occasionally demonstrated its strength. For example, Hamas created chaos in a West Bank refugee camp in May 2008. Fatah claimed that Hamas attacked a Fatah rally, and ransacked the home of a Fatah official.[52]

Fatah's manifold security weaknesses were only part of the problem. Palestinians had simply lost confidence in the long-time leading Palestinian organization. Allegations of corruption continued to haunt Fatah. It was widely believed that Ahmed Qureia, a former PA prime minister, had deposited $3 million in PA funds into his own account. He also battled allegations that his family-owned cement factory was supplying concrete for the construction of the Israeli security barrier, as well as for new homes in Jewish settlements in the West Bank.[53] The PA was further forced to fend off Hamas accusations that it was selling Palestinian land to foreigners.[54]

Given Fatah's struggles, its ability to control the West Bank was far from clear by the summer of 2008. Still, a few factors indicated that the PA might survive, including:

1. Abbas was prepared for a possible coup attempt, and his forces were on guard for a Hamas attack. This had not been the case in June 2007.
2. Abbas enlisted the help of the United States and Israel to protect the PA from a Hamas takeover.
3. It would be considerably more difficult for Hamas to operate in the West Bank if the people there truly did not want Hamas to remain. In light of the turmoil in Gaza, it appeared that West Bankers preferred the status quo.

CHAPTER ELEVEN

THE THREAT OF AL-QAEDA IN GAZA

"Through Hamas, al-Qaeda is entering Gaza," Palestinian Authority President Mahmoud Abbas said in the summer of 2007, just after the Hamas offensive. "It is Hamas that is shielding al-Qaeda, and through its bloody conduct, Hamas has become very close to al-Qaeda. This is why Gaza is in danger and needs help."[1]

Whether Abbas's claims could be verified or not, there is no denying that Gaza was a perfect breeding ground for al-Qaeda, the terrorist network that had carried out the suicide attacks against the World Trade Center in New York City and the Pentagon in Virginia on September 11, 2001. Usama bin Laden, the tall and soft-spoken Saudi millionaire who became the most wanted man in the world, had designed his terror network to exploit areas of weak central authority and weak states like the Gaza Strip. Indeed, bin Laden's fighters typically found it easier to establish footholds in areas characterized by deteriorating living standards, corruption, and a marked lack of civil society and social services.

Although the al-Qaeda leader was believed to be hiding in a remote cave in hinterlands of Pakistan, analysts believed that he had designs on the Palestinian territories and even Israel. In December 2007, bin Laden announced his intention to "expand our jihad" to conquer all of Israel "from the Jordan River to the sea." This announcement reportedly coincided with an intelligence report citing militants receiving al-Qaeda training in the Gaza Strip.[2]

With Hamas firmly in control of Gaza, but with little direct evidence of joint attacks by Hamas and al-Qaeda on record, western intelligence faced the challenge of deciphering the prospects of a partnership between the two Islamist terror groups. Fatah, for its part, needed to consider what an al-Qaeda presence in Gaza might mean for the long-term prospects of uniting the West Bank and Gaza Strip under the flag of the Palestinian Authority.

———

There are many differences between Hamas and al-Qaeda. Most notably, Hamas has a relatively recent territorial grievance while al-Qaeda seeks to reclaim Muslim lands from centuries past. There have also been occasional differences over strategy and tactics. For example, Hamas condemned al-Qaeda's terrorist attacks in Saudi Arabia (2003), London (2004), and Amman (2005).[3] Still, there is no denying the fact that Hamas and al-Qaeda share a common worldview. From justifying violence against civilians to lionizing "martyrdom," the ideologies may not be exactly the same, but they certainly overlap.

In 2004, Israeli intelligence discovered that Hamas was distributing computer disks throughout the West Bank and Gaza Strip lauding jihadist fighters in Afghanistan, Kashmir, and Chechnya. The disk featured a montage of the late Sheikh Ahmed Yassin, bin Laden, and the Chechen jihadist leader Shamil Basayev who threatened "kamikaze" attacks inside Russia. In this way, Hamas projected its identification with al-Qaeda, its lesser-known network of violent affiliate groups, and the broader jihadist movement.[4]

While bin Laden has always sought to target Jews (al-Qaeda was known in the 1990s as the World Islamic Front for Jihad Against Jews and Crusaders), after the attacks on the World Trade Center and the Pentagon in 2001, al-Qaeda demonstrated support for the Hamas cause by attacking Israeli and Jewish targets. Indeed, the global terror network attacked an Israeli hotel in Kenya (2002), synagogues in Tunisia (2002) and Turkey (2003), and a Jewish center in Morocco (2003).

More important, the jihadist ideologies of the two groups, founded within a year of one another, have the same roots. As discussed in chapter 1, Hamas was founded in 1988 during the eruption of the first intifada as a breakaway faction of the Palestinian Muslim Brotherhood. The following year, prominent Palestinian Muslim Brotherhood figure Abdullah Azzam founded al-Qaeda with a young Saudi named Usama bin Laden. Al-Qaeda became an important umbrella organization for mujahideen from all over the Muslim world who played an important role (thanks to arms and funding from the U.S. Central Intelligence Agency) in the defeat of the Soviet army and its 1989 withdrawal from Afghanistan. As one Israeli official noted, "Azzam could have just as easily returned to the West Bank and joined Hamas. . . . He could have become one its early leaders."[5] Subsequent al-Qaeda figureheads, including Ayman al-Zawahiri, bin Laden's second in command, and Khaled Sheikh Mohammed, the mastermind behind the September 11, 2001, terrorist attacks, were also Muslim Brothers.

Unquestionably, al-Qaeda and Hamas were both founded on the Islamist principles of the Muslim Brotherhood. They both embrace the xenophobic and chauvinistic worldview that Hassan al-Banna, the Brotherhood's founder, preached in the 1930s. Both organizations believe that this political interpretation of Islam should dominate the globe and subsequently concluded that violence to achieve that end is not only justifiable but an imperative. Finally, both groups believe that compromise, particularly with the West, is not an option.

The ideologies of the two groups are so intertwined that al-Qaeda publicly chastised Hamas for betraying its Islamic principles when it entered into a secular, democratic political contest with Fatah in the 2006 PA elections. Zawahiri blasted Hamas, saying it "joined the surrender train" and that it "sold out so it can keep a hold of a third of government."[6] Similarly, the leader of al-Qaeda in Iraq, Abu Musab al-Zarqawi (killed in June 2006 by U.S. forces), denounced Hamas for taking part in the elections, saying that Palestinians had "other choices"—perhaps a reference to joining forces with al-Qaeda.[7]

After Hamas assaulted and overthrew Fatah's forces in the Gaza Strip in 2007, however, Zawahiri issued an audio message assuring "our brothers, the Hamas *mujahideen,* that we and the entire Muslim nation stand along side you." When Hamas rejected power-sharing in the Gaza Strip in favor of brute force, bin Laden's deputy changed his rhetoric, pledging to help facilitate the "passage of weapons and supplies from neighboring countries" into the Gaza Strip.[8]

The transfer of weapons from al-Qaeda to Hamas would not be the first time that the two Islamist groups worked together. In the early and mid-1990s,

Hamas members received paramilitary training and even attended Islamist conferences in Sudan that bin Laden and members of his budding network reportedly attended. The government of Sudan, under the influence of radical ideologue Hassan al-Turabi, was aligned with the worldwide Muslim Brotherhood, further underscoring the ideological connection between the nascent Hamas and al-Qaeda network.[9]

When the al-Aqsa intifada erupted in the Palestinian territories, bin Laden reportedly sent emissaries to Hamas on two separate occasions (September 2000 and January 2001).[10] Most analysts believe that Hamas rejected al-Qaeda's overtures to assist in the coordinated violence against Israel, but apparently Hamas never closed the door. The *Washington Post* quoted official U.S. government sources as confirming a loose alliance "between al-Qaeda, Hamas, and Hizbullah" in 2002. Specifics were not disclosed.[11]

Reports from the Indian press suggest that communication between the two groups continued through 2006, when senior Hamas figure Muhammad Sayyam reportedly met with members of the terrorist organization Hizbul Mujahidin, an al-Qaeda affiliate group, in Kashmir.[12] Although the two groups have little to nothing in common, given the geographic distance that separates them, they reportedly found business to discuss.

The Arab media also reported in 2006 that Hamas chief Khaled Meshal met in Yemen with Abd al-Majid al-Zindani, whom the U.S. Treasury officially designated as a terrorist in 2004 for his ties to al-Qaeda. Zindani, an elderly and visibly feeble man, had a bright red beard colored with the herbal dye henna—a common look among elderly Yemenis who still wish to be seen as fighters. He reportedly fought with bin Laden in Afghanistan in the 1980s and was believed to have recruited new fighters for al-Qaeda's training camps.[13] Zindani was quoted as stating that "the support we can provide [to Hamas] at present is money."[14]

Zindani is not the only known financier to back both groups. Fellow Yemeni national Mohammed al-Moayad, a prominent Islamist businessman, also claims to have provided funds and materiel to both al-Qaeda and Hamas. Moayad, a flat-nosed Yemeni with thick, dark glasses and a bushy white beard, reportedly provided $3.5 million to Hamas and $20 million to al-Qaeda, including $70,000 to the London-based Hamas charity Interpal.[15]

Further, the U.S. Treasury designated Saudi businessman Yasin al-Qadi as a terrorist financier in 2001.[16] He was believed to have provided funds to al-Qaeda and Hamas.[17]

The U.S. government has identified several U.S. charities as supporting both groups. The Holy Land Foundation (HLF) and Benevolence International Foundation (BIF), shut down by the U.S. Treasury in 2001 and 2002 respectively, may have had financial ties to both Hamas and al-Qaeda. Bank al-Taqwa, another known source of terrorism financing, has funded al-Qaeda and facilitated the transfer of some $60 million to Hamas in 1997.[18]

Analysts also noted an overlap of financial networks between the al-Qaeda affiliated International Islamic Relief Organization (IIRO) and Hamas.[19] Documents uncovered by Israeli security services further detailed "an IIRO program devised to financially compensate the families of Hamas suicide bombers." Until the early 1990s, IIRO was led by bin Laden's brother-in-law, Mohammed Jamal Khalifa. According to an Israeli diplomat, the Israel army uncovered PA documents demonstrating that the IIRO donated some $280,000 to known Hamas charities.[20]

The cases of HLF, Taqwa, BIF, and IIRO prompt questions as to whether Hamas and al-Qaeda knowingly cooperate on fundraising. Future Treasury designations, in which sensitive information is sometimes declassified for public consumption, may provide a clearer picture.

In 2000, Israeli security services uncovered an al-Qaeda network in the Gaza Strip led by Hamas operative Nabil Okal, who had trained with al-Qaeda in Afghanistan in the late 1990s.[21] Thus began a long string of alarming discoveries.

In 2003, Israel arrested three Hamas fighters returning from al-Qaeda training camps in Afghanistan. That same year, Jordanian security officials confirmed to *Time* magazine that two Hamas members went on a recruiting mission in Afghanistan for al-Qaeda fighters.[22] Israel also learned that British citizens-turned-suicide bombers Mohammed Hanif and Omar Sharif might have been recruited by al-Qaeda to carry out Hamas attacks.[23] These men of Pakistani origin were responsible for the April 30,

2003, suicide carnage at Mike's Place, a popular Tel Aviv bar near the American embassy, which killed 3 and wounded 50.

In 2005, Hamas leader Mahmoud al-Zahar told the Italian media that al-Qaeda was in the territories. "Yes, it's true," he said, "a pair of men from al-Qaeda has infiltrated into Gaza and other contacts happen by telephone with the centers of the organization in a foreign country."[24] There were also reports in October of that year that an organization named Al-Qaeda Jihad in Palestine dropped leaflets in a Gaza mosque,[25] while stories circulated regarding the alleged formation of Jundallah (Army of God), an al-Qaeda affiliate comprised of disgruntled Hamas and PIJ members.[26] Months later, Israel announced that it arrested two al-Qaeda operatives, Azzam Abu al-Ads and Bilal Hafnawy, in Nablus in the West Bank in March 2006. The two reportedly had planned to carry out suicide attacks inside Israel.[27] In early 2008, news services reported that a previously unknown organization called Army of Believers/Al-Qaeda in Palestine Organization carried out an attack on the American International School in Gaza, just as U.S. president George W. Bush was visiting the region.[28]

In 2006, Hamas Interior Minister Said Sayyam, the man ultimately responsible for deploying the Hamas EF, announced that he would not order the arrests of any operatives who carried out attacks against Israel.[29] This declaration was tantamount to an invitation for al-Qaeda and other terrorist groups to join Hamas in its violent campaign against Israel.

After the 2007 coup, embattled PA President Abbas stated that al-Qaeda maintained a presence in the West Bank and the Gaza Strip. While Abbas may have been trying to frighten the West into supporting his Fatah faction over Hamas, dangers seemed more apparent after Hamas breached the wall separating Gaza and Egypt in early 2008. According to the Egyptian daily *al-Masry al-Youm*, during the 12 days in which the Egyptians allowed Palestinians and Gazans to cross the border freely and without documentation, some 2,000 Egyptian jihadists entered the Gaza Strip.[30] Unknown numbers of Egyptians rushed to Gaza to join Hamas.[31] Among them, according to Major General Amos Yadlin of the IDF, were al-Qaeda operatives, including individuals that received "training in Syria and Iran, including snipers, explosives experts, and engineers." Yadlin also stated that large amounts of money and ammunition were smuggled in during the 12-day breach.[32]

One additional concern among terrorism analysts was that members of the al-Qaeda network had significant interaction with the tens of thousands of Palestinians living in Lebanon's refugee camps. For example, a known al-Qaeda affiliate group called Asbat al-Ansar operates freely in Lebanon's cramped and poverty-stricken Ein al-Hilweh refugee camp about 30 miles south of the capital, Beirut. According to a 2004 State Department terrorism report, Asbat "receives money through international Sunni extremist networks and bin Laden's al-Qaeda network."[33] Hamas is also active in Ein al-Hilweh. There is no question that the two groups have overlapped over the years.[34] However, the extent to which they may cooperate is a subject of speculation.

Nahr al-Bared is another refugee camp in Lebanon where Palestinians have been exposed to both Hamas and the broader al-Qaeda network. The refugee camp made headlines in May 2007, when Fatah al-Islam, a new al-Qaeda affiliate group, clashed with Lebanese forces there, leaving dozens dead. Fatah al-Islam was led by Shaker Abssi, a Palestinian whose photos only depict a man with dark skin, dark eyes, dark eyebrows and glasses; the rest of his face is obscured by a black-and-white checkered keffiyeh. Abssi's jihadi pedigree stemmed from his ties to the late Abu Musab al-Zarqawi, the famous al-Qaeda third-in-command whose life was cut short by the U.S. military in June 2006. Both men had been sentenced to death in absentia in Jordan for killing U.S. diplomat Laurence Foley in 2002.[35] On the morning of October 28, 2002, Foley was riddled with bullets as he walked to his car outside his home in Amman, the capital. Months later, Jordanian security services arrested two men who allegedly confessed that Zarqawi and Abssi had been involved in planning the attack.

Asbat al-Ansar and Fatah al-Islam undoubtedly exposed the already-radicalized Palestinian refugee populations of Lebanon to the broader al-Qaeda network. In late December 2007, however, Palestinian officials reported that Fatah al-Islam was operating inside the Hamas-controlled Gaza Strip, firing homemade rockets into Israel. One aide to Mahmoud Abbas stated, "Hamas is responsible for the presence of Fatah al-Islam in the Gaza Strip. . . . The presence of this dangerous gang of mercenaries in the

Gaza Strip will bring more tragedies and disasters to the Palestinians."[36] The extent to which Hamas welcomed Fatah al-Islam into the Gaza Strip was not known.

There are those who would argue that Hamas's cooperation with Iran, a Shi'ite country, would preclude its cooperation with al-Qaeda because al-Qaeda is a Sunni terrorist network. Of course, Sunnis and Shi'ites have been at odds, to varying degrees, since the death of the prophet Mohammed in 632 C.E., when a succession disagreement erupted between those who sought a leader with the prophet's bloodline (Shi'ites) and those who sought a leader who adhered to Islamic orthodoxy (Sunnis). Although the two sects have lived harmoniously in many places over the years, there has also been recent bloodshed between them during, for instance, the Lebanese civil war (1975–1990) and the recent Iraq insurgency (2004–present).

It must first be noted that Iran has always financed Palestinian groups that attacked Israel, including Fatah and the PLO. However, Fatah made a series of errors that strained the relationship in the early 1990s. For one, Arafat supported Iraq during the Iran-Iraq war (1980–1988). The mullahs were also unhappy over the prospect of Arafat's participation in the Oslo peace process with both the United States and Israel—the "Great Satan" and "Little Satan," as Iran sometimes describes the two. As punishment, Iran gradually threw its support behind Hamas. By 1994, Iranian demonstrators broke into the PLO embassy in Tehran, calling the secular organization "agents of Israel and the Americans." Osama Hamdan, a Hamas representative to Iran in 1994, openly gloated that the growing ties between Hamas and Iran came at the expense of the PLO.[37]

Throughout the 1990s, Hamas enjoyed financial support from both Iran and Sunni Arab states, notably Saudi Arabia. Notably, according to David Aufhauser, a former senior U.S. Treasury official, "it is not a crime to give to Hamas in Saudi Arabia."[38] Indeed, Hamas is seen as a legitimate "resistance" organization. Thus, the Saudis reportedly raised millions of dollars for Hamas in the first two years of the al-Aqsa intifada. In the past, U.S. petitions to persuade the Saudis to cease their support to Hamas were largely ignored. Even PA officials registered official complaints with the Saudis over their support to Hamas, to no avail.[39]

The Saudi spigot began to dry up beginning in 2004.[40] However, that change was almost certainly not connected to a change of heart regarding the use of violence against Israel. More than likely, elements within the Saud family may have realized that supporting terrorism abroad, as they have done for decades, had led to the creation of a terrorist infrastructure at home. Indeed, during this time, the Saudis were struggling with an al-Qaeda affiliate group called Al-Qaeda of the Arabian Peninsula that wrought havoc throughout the kingdom.

Without the same stream of Saudi money, Hamas soon turned to Iran to fill the void. Iran became even more vital to the group's finances after Hamas's January 2006 electoral victory and the western embargo that followed. Indeed, a Hamas spokesman confirmed that Iran "was prepared to cover the entire deficit in the Palestinian budget, and [to do so] continuously." The *Bonyad-e Mostazafan za Janbaza* (Foundation of the Oppressed and War Veterans), a splinter of the Iranian Revolutionary Guards Corps, is believed to provide Hamas with critical financial support.[41] During a visit by Hamas leader Ismael Haniyeh to Tehran in December 2006, Iran pledged $250 million in aid to compensate for the western boycott.[42] In October 2007, the U.S. secretary of state, Condoleezza Rice, openly stated her concerns about Iranian support to Hamas during testimony to the United States Congress.[43]

Just as Saudi Arabia was not deterred from contributing to a cause that Iran supported, al-Qaeda most likely would not be deterred either. Indeed, Sunni-Shi'ite enmity has not stopped Iran from cooperating with al-Qaeda in certain circumstances. For example, Ansar al-Islam, an al-Qaeda affiliate group that had been based before the Iraq war of 2003 in northeast Iraqi Kurdistan on the Iranian border, enjoyed support from Iran.[44] The 9/11 Commission, the National Commission on Terrorist Attacks Upon the United States, even noted that as many as ten of the September 11 hijackers may have passed through Iran in late 2000 and early 2001; Iranian border guards reportedly were instructed to allow al-Qaeda associates to travel freely.[45]

Based on this history, it seems unlikely that Hamas ties with Iran would deter al-Qaeda from seeking a foothold in the Gaza Strip. Should Hamas allow al-Qaeda to nestle in Gaza, it would be a worrisome development for western intelligence agencies seeking to promote peace in the Middle East and to control terrorism worldwide.

———

In May 2008, as Israel celebrated its 60th anniversary, Usama bin Laden issued an online audio message insisting that the Islamist war against Israel would continue, and that Muslims would not cede "one inch of Palestine." The al-Qaeda leader sounded as if he had taken a line straight from the Hamas charter.[46] The following month, Zawahiri released an audio tape that called upon all Muslims to "break the siege of Gaza."[47]

Hamas and al-Qaeda will always share core ideological tenets. This common worldview, based on the Islamist foundation of the Muslim Brotherhood, will likely produce individuals and cells sympathetic to both groups well into the future. Accordingly, as long as the two organizations exist, al-Qaeda and Hamas can be expected to share financial networks, such as those dismantled by the U.S. Treasury Department in recent years.

Similarly, as long as the two terrorist groups exist, Israeli and American intelligence organizations can be expected to uncover operational and logistical connections. The most obvious overlaps probably will be observed in Lebanon. But since Israel's destruction is Hamas's ultimate goal, and al-Qaeda can help plan and mount attacks against the Jewish state, cooperation cannot be ruled out in the Gaza Strip. Indeed, the chances of al-Qaeda infiltrating Gaza appeared increasingly likely after January 2008, when Egyptian border security allowed Gazans to enter Egypt and Egyptians to enter Gaza without documentation.

Still, a significant al-Qaeda presence in the Gaza Strip is not likely, at least for the foreseeable future. Hamas, as described throughout this book, is a fiercely independent organization. The July 2007 coup handed the terrorist group its own territory, which it will jealously guard. Hamas would never knowingly allow any entity, including al-Qaeda, to challenge its authority. For this reason, as long as the Gaza Strip remains under Hamas control, Usama bin Laden's transnational network likely will be restricted to cooperation with Hamas in attacks against Israel. There is also a remote possibility that the two groups could target Egypt, which has been a perennial target for al-Qaeda since the network's inception, thanks to a cadre of disgruntled Egyptians who seek to overthrow the predominantly secular autocratic regime of Husni Mubarak.

Limited cooperation between Hamas and al-Qaeda, however, does not mean limited risk. Israeli security services began to understand that they faced new dangers. Al-Qaeda thinks big. Its attacks, real and imagined, tend to be spectacular. Bin Laden and his associates typically seek to destroy western nations' symbols of strength and deploy numerous attackers simultaneously, causing confusion and creating the sense that the terror network is omnipresent.

Hamas, for its part, had a history of launching relatively small yet painful attacks against Israel's public transportation system, public markets and eateries, and military targets. There was probably little in the way of technology, training, and even know-how that al-Qaeda could bring to a relatively sophisticated terrorist group like Hamas. Still, the ingenuity of al-Qaeda, marked by its penchant for spectacular attacks against critical infrastructure, remained a concern for Western security services. Moreover, as long as Hamas maintained control of the Gaza Strip, there remained a remote yet worrisome possibility of al-Qaeda and Hamas teaming up to attack PA interests in either of the Palestinian territories.

CHAPTER TWELVE

THE GAZA–WEST BANK SPLIT

As the internal strife between Hamas and Fatah became more pronounced, and as Hamas and Fatah became more entrenched in their new territories, it became increasingly evident that, if conditions continued to deteriorate, the West Bank and Gaza Strip could evolve into two geographically and politically distinct entities.

Such talk, of course, was considered heresy among Palestinians, who insisted that the entirety of Palestine would be one day redeemed under one flag. Supporting this notion was a recent flood of books and articles by academics (who were accused by some as being politically driven) attesting to long-standing Palestinian unity, patriotism, and a strong sense of nationalism. Also contributing to this belief in unity was the fact that American diplomats, in their continued attempt to be honest brokers in the Palestinian-Israeli conflict, have always sought to preserve the "territorial continuity" of the two Palestinian territories, despite the fact that the West Bank and Gaza Strip are separated by a large Israeli landmass known as the Negev desert. Even Israel, which sought to divide and conquer the Palestinian factions that carried out violence against its citizens, did not openly discuss breaking up the territories.

While the Palestinians nearly unanimously reject the notion of a Gaza–West Bank split, it is not so outrageous a concept. After all, Palestinian society always had been strongly characterized by tribalism and strong regional differences that set West Bankers apart from Gazans. In other words, while the West Bank is about 30 miles from the Gaza Strip, there has always been more separating the two territories than a patch of Israeli desert.

Competing patriarchal clans have long dominated local politics in the Arab world. The same holds in the West Bank and Gaza Strip. Although the Palestinians have talked of nationalism for nearly a century, nationalism is a recent concept in the Middle East; it was introduced by Western powers in the World War I era. Thus, despite arguments to the contrary, regionalism often trumps nationalism in the Arab world. And regionalism, in turn, often is trumped by family (*a'ila*) and clan (*hamula*) allegiances.

Regional, clan, and family allegiances have always guided the politics of the indigenous West Bank and Gaza Palestinians. According to the International Crisis Group, a nongovernmental organization, Gaza is home to six federations, consisting of a dozen or more tribes.[1] Gaza's stronger local families include, but certainly are not limited to, the Dughmush, Shawwa, Shafei, and Middein families. In the West Bank, the Nashishibi, Huseini, Shaka'a, Ja'abari, and Masri families historically have ranked among the dominant political elite. By nature, these clans are regional, and are often at odds. The patriarchs can act as representatives for their loyalists and have competed for economic, political, and social stature over the years.

It can be argued that Palestinian regionalism, along with clan or family rivalry, has been reinforced over the years by the Palestinian spoken Arabic dialects, which differ very subtly or even significantly throughout the territories. West Bank dialects have long been similar to the Jordanian dialect (reinforced by Jordanian occupation from 1948 to 1967) while the Arabic spoken throughout the Gaza Strip shows influences of the Egyptian dialect (reinforced by Egyptian occupation from 1948 to 1967).

Speakers of Gaza's dialect, to use just one small example, tend to pronounce the Arabic word for "fish" as *samag*, while West Bankers typically pronounce the word as it is written in standard Arabic: *samak*. According to one study conducted at Birzeit University in Ramallah, other differences can be found in intonation and lexicon.[2] As is the case throughout the Muslim world, dialect often is a clear indication of an Arab's precise origin. The same is true among indigenous Palestinians.

The absence of intermarriage between clans or families in the West Bank and Gaza Strip is another traditional dividing line. Although traditional marriages arranged between tribal chiefs are no longer common among Palestinians, one study notes that "kinship-based marriage arrangements now exist as a way to preserve the continued identity of dispersed communities."[3] These communities derive from specific, smaller areas of the former Palestinian mandate and rarely cross the West Bank–Gaza Strip divide.

Geopolitics have also reinforced Palestinian tribalism and limited the ties between the West Bank and the Gaza Strip. After the first Arab-Israeli war in 1948, Egypt controlled the Gaza Strip and Jordan controlled the West Bank. With the Gaza Strip under the control of Gamal Abd al-Nasser, the powerful and gripping speaker who championed a brand of socialism known as Arab nationalism, and the West Bank under the command of King Hussein, a royalist who was often wary of Nasser's socialist influence, ties between the two territories were often lukewarm, or even cold. Until the Jordanians and Egyptians lost their territorial spoils during the Six-Day War of 1967, two distinctly different political cultures took root in the territories.

The influence that Jordan and Egypt had on the two Palestinian territories during the early years of the Arab-Israeli conflict cannot be stressed enough. The West Bank cities under Jordanian rule, for example, enjoyed an economic infrastructure that the Gaza Strip did not. The Gaza Strip was largely neglected under Egyptian occupation; Jordan invested heavily in West Bank civil society through 1967. With an eye toward recovering the West Bank as Jordanian territory even after losing it in the Six-Day War, King Hussein continued to invest there until 1988, when he finally renounced Jordanian claims, fearing violence among his own Palestinian population. Thus, over time, the West Bank emerged as a more developed mini-state, with a modicum of upside economic potential, while the Gaza Strip wallowed in neglect.

When Israel assumed control of the West Bank and the Gaza Strip following the June 1967 war, the gap between the two territories widened in several ways. Israel placed tight travel restrictions on the territories for security reasons, as postwar tensions ran high. The Israelis also allowed tribal structures to remain in place and in some cases reinforced them. In the 1970s, for example, the Israelis employed Gaza's patriarchal leaders to preside over disputes as a means of maintaining order.[4] It can be argued that the influence of these leaders kept the Gaza Strip isolated and set in its provincial ways.

The West Bank, thanks to its shared border with Jordan, broadened its political and economic possibilities with Amman and other Arab capitals. However, Gaza, which borders the mostly barren Sinai Peninsula, had significantly less access to the rest of the Arab world. Thus, the two territories developed at different paces with different influences, which ultimately resulted in two distinct cultures. To demonstrate this point, as scholar Meir Litvak notes, the Muslim Brotherhood branches in West Bank and Gaza operated "as separate entities" until the intifada of 1987.[5] Thereafter, analysts observed that the character of Hamas was very different in the West Bank as compared to Gaza.[6] Most notably, the Gaza Strip became a hotbed of Hamas activity compared to the West Bank, particularly in the early years of the uprising.

When Israel and the Palestinians launched the peace process in the early 1990s, as analysts Justus Reid Weiner and Diane Morrison note, international expectations were that the Gaza Strip and the West Bank would be unified in one way or another. Terms such as "territorial contiguity," "territorial continuity," and "territorial connectivity" often were used to describe the foreseen outcome of the Oslo peace process. The 1995 Interim Agreement on the West Bank and the Gaza Strip, more commonly known as Oslo II, stipulated safe passage and transportation between the territories. Four years later, the two sides signed a document known as the Protocol Concerning Safe Passage Between the West Bank and Gaza Strip.[7] However, after the violence of the 2000 intifada by Hamas, Palestinian Islamic Jihad, and the al-Aqsa Martyrs Brigades, Israel rejected the notion of connecting the territories; transportation of goods or people between the two territories would expose Israeli sovereign territory to further attacks.

As the Palestinian violence worsened, Israeli security measures grew even tighter. It was not uncommon to hear Gazans complain of how they had to first travel to Egypt and then fly to Jordan in order to reach the West

Bank. After the June 2007 coup in Gaza, Israel sought to maintain this separation to isolate and protect the West Bank from Hamas infiltration.

As of summer 2008, Jordan and Egypt were working with the West Bank and Gaza, respectively, to provide electricity to the two areas. Jordan insisted that it was acting out of humanitarian concern for the West Bank, but as one Jordanian analyst noted, the move carried with it "political overtones."[8]

———

The post–World War II era was marked by several refugee problems. With the exception of the Palestinians, who refused to be repatriated, all have been settled. Six decades later, the Palestinian refugee problem continues and contributes to the growing divide between the West Bank and the Gaza Strip.

More than 34 percent of the Palestinians who declared refugee status after the Arab defeats in 1948 and 1967 are registered in Gaza's eight teeming refugee camps. By contrast, in the West Bank, less than 19 percent of the population is registered as a refugee. Indeed, even though refugee camps exist throughout the West Bank, many residents have invested in homes or businesses rather than choosing a life of suffering, living in hovels, and surviving on food and provisions provided by the United Nations or international nongovernmental organizations.[9]

The poverty associated with the problem of the Palestinian refugees has contributed directly to two distinct economies and, consequently, two different cultures. In 1997, more than 40 percent of Gazans were living below the poverty line ($650 year). That was four times the West Bank's 11 percent poverty rate, which was still high by most standards. Before the al-Aqsa intifada of 2000, 22 percent of all Gazans were unemployed, while only 9 percent of West Bankers were not working. Although the uprising and subsequent Israeli response to the Palestinian violence certainly took its toll on both territories in recent years, Gaza was unquestionably harder hit; unemployment topped out above 50 percent.[10]

In light of the sanctions imposed on Gaza after the Hamas coup in June 2007 and the monetary infusions enjoyed by the West Bank to support the PA, the gap between the two separate economies widened further. Given the devastating effects of the international sanctions against Hamas in 2006 and 2007, it may take years for the economy of Gaza to recover.

As economic and cultural differences emerged in the West Bank and Gaza, residents of the two areas have reportedly developed a quiet animosity toward each other. After conducting hundreds of interviews in the early 1990s, Khalil Shiqaqi, the aforementioned Palestinian sociologist and pollster embroiled in the 2006 elections controversy, noted "a psychological barrier between the inhabitants of the two territories and . . . mutual suspicion" that cannot be "disregarded or ignored."[11]

Shiqaqi's 1994 study, *The West Bank and Gaza Strip: Future Political and Administrative Relations* (published in Arabic), uncovered a prevailing West Bank belief that the Gaza Strip is "nothing but a big refugee camp." West Bankers also saw the Gaza Strip as a backward society with "increased crime . . . inclined to roughness, extremism, grimness, fanaticism, and instability."[12]

Gazans, in turn, resented the patronizing and discriminating West Bankers, who show them little respect. Gazans were frustrated that while they were often willing to accept the consequences of insurrection against Israel, "workers from the West Bank fill the work spots left vacant from when [Israel] prevents Gaza workers from coming to their jobs in Israel."[13]

Of particular note is the period between 1967 and 1971, when some 20,000 Gaza Strip residents moved to the West Bank towns of Tulkarem and Qalqilya. Shiqaqi's interviews revealed that tensions ran high during this first attempt at integration between the territories. West Bankers viewed Gazans as messy, dishonest, less cultured, less educated, and predisposed to poverty. Gazans saw West Bankers as "racists" who treated them as "third class" citizens.[14] Regrettably, Middle East studies professors and other regional specialists have largely avoided this issue, so there exists a gaping hole in our understanding of the way Palestinians from the two territories view one another.

On the eve of the 2000 intifada, the animosity between the two territories appeared to have changed little. One Israeli internal security report, released just before the violence erupted, noted "mounting hostility and a growing rift between the West Bank and Gaza Strip," to the point that "senior officials in the West Bank are against opening the 'safe passage' route [with the Gaza Strip], as the result could be to flood [the West Bank] with Gazans."[15]

After the launch of the intifada, Yasir Arafat sought to keep the two territories separate as a means to control them, particularly as the George W. Bush administration pressured the guerrilla leader to relinquish control of the territories. Arafat, suffering from the effects of Parkinson's disease, appointed two strongmen to control the two Palestinian areas. In the West Bank, Jibril Rajoub reigned, wielding strong influence in Palestinian paramilitary circles. The stocky, bald, and mustached figure appeared to be the diametric opposite of Gaza's strongman, Mohammad Dahlan, who was tall, dark-haired, and clean shaven. As head of Gaza's Preventive Security Force, Dahlan was reported to have strong ties with the PA's ruling elite, the Israeli government, and U.S. intelligence agencies (which did little to improve his standing on the Palestinian street). As one Israeli analyst noted in 2001, the PA resembled a "federation of geographical emirates," such that the "balance of forces in the Palestinian territories" would not allow any one strongman "to dominate the Gaza Strip and the West Bank."[16]

Over time, Dahlan and Rajoub came to compete with one another. Washington even played a small role in the competition. Inside the Beltway, both men were viewed as potential successors to Arafat, whom the Bush administration sought to remove. For a time, it appeared that Washington preferred Rajoub.[17] Arafat soon sacked him, perhaps fearing his political strength.

In November 2002, Rajoub accused Dahlan of taking part "in a battle against the preventative security forces."[18] In 2003, Arafat pitted the two men against one another when he rehired Rajoub in an attempt to prevent Dahlan from gaining increased influence over Palestinian forces as a power struggle played out between Mahmoud Abbas and Arafat.[19] This struggle between Rajoub and Dahlan may have only helped to widen the gap between the two territories.

With the death of Arafat in November 2004 and the rise of Abbas as the new leader of the PA, the gap between the two territories remained. Especially after the surprise Hamas electoral victory in 2006, the Fatah-Hamas conflict exacerbated the differences between the two territories. One Gaza official noted, after the Mecca Agreement, "instead of fighting each other directly, Fatah and Hamas have both incited the relatives of those killed and wounded either in fighting or in the crossfire to take revenge." Another official noted that the factions were "arming the families as surrogates with heavy weapons."[20] The collapse of the PA contributed to the growing strength of clans and families, which exacerbated the regionalism that divided the West Bank and Gaza.

Finally, the Hamas takeover of Gaza in June 2007 destroyed the vestiges of political ties that bound the two territories. Indeed, a different Palestinian leader assumed power in each territory. In Gaza, Hamas began to govern its people with a blend of authoritarianism and Islamism. According to the International Crisis Group, clan and family allegiances actually "helped prevent a total collapse." In the West Bank, Abbas kept his hold on the Palestinian Authority by mobilizing its military but stressing a more secular, nationalist approach. Family and clan also played a significant role in the West Bank, but Abbas's canton suffered less from the feuding and fighting between clans and families than in Gaza. In fact, Fatah actually sought to reignite family and tribal vendettas where there were none, particularly if they could be used against Hamas.[21]

Journalist Amira Hass noted another important dividing line between the two territories. The Hamas leaders in Gaza created new government institutions, separate from those of the Fatah-ruled West Bank. She notes that Hamas "tightened its grip on three important civilian institutions: the court system, the municipality, and the Central Palestinian Bureau of Statistics."[22] Hamas members also held sessions of the Palestinian parliament in Gaza, which were not attended by Fatah.[23]

While Hamas sought to establish a separate system of governance from the PA in Gaza, Abbas also considered holding presidential and legislative elections in the West Bank by the end of 2008. If Hamas remained in control of Gaza, analysts speculated that there was little chance the Islamists would be invited to take part.[24]

It is also important to note that sanctions exacerbated the disparate preexisting economic conditions in the West Bank and Gaza, pulling the two territories farther apart than ever before. The West Bank enjoyed the infusion of millions of dollars and euros, as the international community strove to ensure that Abbas would maintain control over a stable territory that would fend off Hamas advances. In the Gaza Strip, by contrast, the Israeli embargo on everything but ten basic items—cooking oil, salt, rice, sugar, wheat, dairy, frozen vegetables, frozen meat, medical equipment, and medicine—ground the economy to a halt.

By the end of the year 2007, roughly 75 percent of all Gazans lived in poverty, up 10 percent from the summer, when Hamas took over. Corner markets were running short of everything, from cleaning supplies and diapers to candles and sugar substitutes for diabetics. A sharp rise in prices ensued, as demand sharply outpaced supply. Businessmen closed up shop. Others were forced to work with less staff. Construction companies, for example, were forced to lay off some 35,000 workers due to a lack of cement and other raw materials.[25]

Finally, in late January 2008, ties between the two Palestinian territories were further strained when the Gaza-Egypt border was breached. Over a period of 12 days, Egypt allowed up to 750,000 Gaza residents to stream into the Sinai Peninsula to buy goods and products. As they swarmed several Sinai towns, several Israeli analysts correctly noted that "the Ramallah-based state is now further and more disconnected from Hamas than ever."[26]

Cut off from the West Bank, both physically and economically, the Hamas-ruled Gaza Strip turned to Egypt to break Israel's economic siege. Haniyeh stated in the Hamas newspaper *Falasteen* that "Gaza must maintain stronger economic links with Egypt as a way of economic disconnection from Israel." He hoped that Egypt would begin to provide the territory with the fuel and electricity Israel did not.[27] Ahmed Yousef, an advisor to Haniyeh, stated that Hamas had already generated plans to unite economically with Egypt.[28] Even Amnesty International called for Egypt to officially open its border to Gaza as a means to ease Palestinian suffering.[29]

One unnamed Israeli official, recognizing the possibility that Gaza could become Egypt's problem, called the breach a "blessing in disguise."[30] Indeed, Jerusalem appeared to welcome the development, but only as a means to rid Israel of the economic and political burdens associated with Hamas.[31]

Some Israeli analysts feared that Egypt could allow Hamas to arm itself with more sophisticated weaponry. But such concerns were negated by the fact that President Husni Mubarak had already allowed the smuggling tunnels to remain open, thus permitting Hamas to arm itself and prepare for its confrontations with Fatah and Israel alike.

Egypt, however, rejected the Hamas call for economic union outright and even reprimanded Hamas officials for suggesting a union. Mubarak recognized that reengaging in the Palestinian-Israeli arena as anything other than a diplomatic intermediary would upset the delicate balance Egypt and Israel had achieved in their nearly three decades of cold peace.

Additionally, he learned that sharing an open border with Gaza was not easy. Just before the border was breached, Egypt suffered the indignity of a Hamas-led protest of 400 Palestinian women who called Mubarak a coward for keeping his agreement with the United States and Israel.[32] When the Egyptians sealed their border again, after nearly two weeks, angry Palestinians began to throw rocks at the border guards, eliciting gunfire and tear gas.[33] As one Egyptian newspaper editor lamented, "The 'children of the stones' have changed since becoming Hamas fighters. They have forgotten their heroic past . . . now they aim their stones at Egyptian security forces deployed along the borders of a sovereign state."[34]

The Egyptian Sinai Bedouin also grew tired of the Gazans, who triggered food shortages and drove up prices, thanks to lack of supply and overwhelming demand.[35] According to one economic analyst, Gazans spent $130 million in Egypt in less than two days.[36]

Mubarak feared that Palestinian terrorism would spill over into Egypt. Some 9,000 Palestinians from the Gaza Strip went missing after the border breach, even after Cairo rounded up 3,000 and sent them back.[37] According to several reports, Egyptian security forces had captured Palestinians with suicide bombing belts in the Sinai; they allegedly planned to attack Israeli tourists at popular seaside tourist destinations.[38] According to other reports, some Gazans had made their way to Cairo, where tourism was even heavier.[39] This was an alarming prospect for Mubarak, who lamented that Egypt was essentially sharing a "border with Iran."[40] He understood that attacks against tourists in the Sinai, or perhaps even at the pyramids or other antiquities, would be catastrophic for Egypt's tourism industry.

According to Palestinian media reports in mid-February, Egypt was holding some 500 Gazans prisoner in a sports complex in the border city of al-Arish.[41] Days later, it was reported that Egypt released 21 Palestinians from custody; 12 were members of Hamas and had been captured with explosives.[42] After resealing the border, the typically mild-mannered, gray-haired Egyptian foreign minister, Ahmed Aboul Gheit, warned, "Whoever breaks the border line will have his foot broken."[43]

———

The drastic economic and political divisions that developed between the two Palestinian territories, made worse by the June 2007 coup and the January 2008 breach of the Gaza-Egyptian border, called into question whether the two territories would ever be rejoined, even in the event of political reconciliation between Hamas and Fatah. As the International Crisis Group observed, "[the] geographic split of Palestinian territories risks enduring."[44]

What an enduring split might look like is unclear. However, the notion is not unprecedented. In 1948, after the withdrawal of the British, Bangladesh and Pakistan became two separate, culturally distinct territories under a single rule. For more than two decades, Bangladeshis grumbled about their role as junior partner in this unlikely marriage. Then, in 1971, with a deepened sense of nationalism that could no longer be denied, Bangladesh seceded from Pakistan.

Of course, Palestinians would vociferously reject any similarities to the case of Pakistan and Bangladesh. The majority of Palestinians have been deeply distressed by the division, and they hold out hope that Palestinian nationalism will, in the end, reunite both territories under one flag. Even amid the fighting, Hamas and Fatah continue to discuss the importance of establishing a governing body that both groups would recognize in both the West Bank and Gaza. Hamas spokesman Ahmed Yousef even wrote an opinion piece in late February 2008 insisting, "Hamas Doesn't Want a Separate Gaza."[45] However, the repeated failure of talks geared toward rapprochement made the possibility of a Gaza-West Bank split increasingly difficult to ignore.

CHAPTER THIRTEEN

ANNAPOLIS AND THE HOPE FOR PEACE

On July 16, 2007, standing on the plush red carpet of Cross Hall in the White House, President George W. Bush announced to a live television audience that he would

> call together an international meeting this fall of representatives from nations that support a two-state solution, reject violence, recognize Israel's right to exist, and commit to all previous agreements between the parties. The key participants in this meeting will be the Israelis, the Palestinians, and their neighbors in the region.

The president announced that Secretary of State Condoleezza Rice and her counterparts would

> review the progress that has been made toward building Palestinian institutions. They will look for innovative and effective ways to support further reform. And they will provide diplomatic support for the parties in their bilateral discussions and negotiations, so that we can move forward on a successful path to a Palestinian state.[1]

Bush's announcement came as a surprise to many. For nearly seven years, he had kept his distance from the Middle East peace process. Bush was wary of putting his presidency on the line the same way that former President Clinton had. Despite hundreds of hours of personal effort to bring the two sides together, Clinton left office in January 2001 without a peace deal. When Bush stepped in, he refused to meet with Arafat and the Palestinian leadership so long as the violence against Israel continued. After the attacks of September 11, 2001, Bush was even more determined to steer clear of any party that engaged in the tactic of terror.

Seven years later, however, Bush appeared determined to bring the Israelis and Palestinians together. As autumn approached, the White House announced that the peace conference was to convene in Annapolis, at the venerated naval academy on Maryland's eastern seaboard in late November 2007. In the months before the conference, countless newspaper editorials weighed the prospects of success, rehashing the depressing details of the peace process that had imploded in September 2000. Few of these analyses even briefly raised the question of the impact that the two warring Palestinian factions might have on negotiations.

As the conference drew near, Bush announced that he would deliver a speech and personally conduct three rounds of diplomacy with the Israeli and Palestinian Authority (PA) representatives present. The president also applied the full pressure of the White House to ensure that several Arab states, including the Kingdom of Saudi Arabia, would attend. Surprisingly, Syria agreed to join the diplomatic roster at the last minute, in what was seen in State Department circles as a boost of credibility for the conference. Critics, however, openly wondered why a designated state sponsor of terrorism had been invited to discuss Palestinian-Israeli peace in the presence of the president of the United States when it continued to provide support to Hizbullah and Hamas.

In the days before the conference, Rice announced that the goal would be nothing short of a comprehensive peace deal by the end of the Bush administration in January 2009.[2] Predictably, both Palestinians and Israelis, including the Palestinian and Jewish diaspora, responded with little to no enthusiasm. Few organizations representing either Palestinian or Israeli interests wanted to appear antipeace; however, few could forget the failures of the recent past. This fact made it difficult for even the president's most ardent supporters to react with anything but pessimism.

On the eve of Annapolis, the Palestinian-Israeli conflict fell into a familiar pattern: The PA and Israel began to jockey in the media for previously promised concessions, leading occasionally to angry responses and lines drawn in the sand. Notably absent were any substantive adjustments to a new reality in Gaza. Neither side seemed to want to recognize that some 1.4 million Palestinians were under Hamas rule in the Gaza Strip. With two Palestinian mini-states warring over already disputed territory, how could any agreement reached at Annapolis possibly take hold?

November 27, 2007, was a clear autumn day, with orange and red leaves still on the trees. Representatives from nearly 50 countries and organizations descended on the naval academy in Annapolis, as did protestors representing the Palestinian and Israeli points of view.

With hundreds of reporters listening at tables set up behind a dark blue curtain on the main stage, and millions of people across the Middle East watching on television, Ehud Olmert, Mahmoud Abbas, and Bush pledged to revive the peace process that had failed seven years earlier. Then the three men stepped outside for photos; all three appeared relaxed and flashed easy smiles.

Concurrently, across the Atlantic Ocean, a sea of angry Hamas supporters wearing green hats, waving green flags, and chanting Hamas slogans gathered in Gaza City to protest the U.S.-sponsored meeting. Gunmen wielding AK–47 automatic rifles took up positions along the street as Hamas leaders on stage bluntly rejected the notion of negotiating with Israel. Mahmoud al-Zahar stated, "Anyone who stands in the face of resistance or fights it or cooperates with the occupation . . . is a traitor."[3] Ismael Haniyeh urged Arab states to boycott the conference, saying "let the whole world hear us: We will not relinquish one centimeter of Palestine, and we will not recognize Israel."[4] After the conference, Hamas leader Khaled Meshal declared that Hamas was prepared to launch "a third and fourth intifada until the dawn of victory." Mushir al-Masri, another Hamas official, stated, "Jews, go back, because we have already dug graves for you."[5]

Hamas also vilified Fatah. Just days before the Annapolis conference convened, Fatah announced that Hamas gunmen had kidnapped a Palestinian intelligence officer along with four other Fatah members in the Gaza Strip.[6] Haniyeh then taunted Fatah by stating that the secular faction's normalization with Israel was tantamount to "treason."[7] The Hamas Web site also excoriated Abbas and Fatah for cooperating with Israel. The Izz al-Din al-Qassam Brigades Web site likened Fatah to "guards of the Zionist entity." They claimed that Fatah members in the West Bank were part of the Shabak, the Israeli security services (also known as the Shin Bet). The Web site called on the Hamas organization to "escalate its actions against the occupation to dispel enemy dreams of security and stability under the protection of his [*sic*] loyal friends in Ramallah."[8]

Elements within Hamas also launched a publicity campaign via al-Aqsa television and other outlets, claiming that the future of the al-Aqsa Mosque was in danger. The campaign was reminiscent of the one launched by Haj Amin al-Husseini in the late 1920s, which incited the Palestinians to launch their first ill-fated uprising against the local Jewish population and the British authorities.

This time around, Hamas alleged that Israel was digging tunnels beneath the third most holy site in Islam as "part of Israeli designs against the Mosque" which were described as "terrorist."[9] According to unconfirmed reports, Hamas further provoked Israel when it broadcast a three-hour radio program live from the Temple Mount. On the morning of December 19, 2007, Hamas reportedly broadcast an announcement boasting that its program was a "victory for the al-Aqsa mosque, which is suffering from Judaization efforts imposed by the Zionist government."[10] No mention of this broadcast appeared on the official *Sawt al-Aqsa* Web site.[11]

Curiously, while some elements within Hamas continued to provoke Israel or to warn Abbas that he was "not authorized to make decisions on behalf of the Palestinian people,"[12] other factions within the group made a surprising effort to "renew its call for dialogue and restoring the unity of the Palestinian people."[13]

Sensing an opening, the Saudis and the Egyptians attempted to bring representatives of the two opposing Palestinian factions together for formal talks, following several rounds of talks with lower-level representatives from both sides.[14] In mid-December 2007, after the close of the Annapolis summit, a Fatah-sponsored news service reported that Hamas had, after a meeting between Meshal and the Saudis, announced its willingness to engage in negotiations to form a central government with Fatah.[15] Reaching out to

Hamas, Palestinian Prime Minister Salaam Fayyad publicly called on Israel to lift the economic restrictions it had placed on Gaza.[16] Meshal stated in early January that Hamas was ready for "unconditional dialogue."[17]

In late March 2008, it appeared that the two sides had reached an agreement. Under the auspices of the president of Yemen, Ali Abdullah Saleh, Hamas leader Musa Abu Marzook and Azzam al-Ahmed from Fatah signed the Sanaa Declaration, named after the Yemeni capital. The two delegations issued a statement following the agreement: "Fatah and Hamas have agreed to accept the Yemeni initiative as a framework for dialogue . . . and a return the Palestinian situation to what it was before the events in Gaza."[18] Hours later, however, the two factions began to wrangle over the meaning of the accord. Fatah believed it called for the implementation of certain demands, namely ceding Gaza, while Hamas believed it was simply a pledge to begin dialogue.[19]

"Hamas is trying to lead us to endless talks without backing away from its military coup," said Fatah spokesman Yasir Abed Rabbo.[20] Days after the agreement crumbled, Abbas rejected a Hamas invitation to visit the Gaza Strip and attempt to jumpstart talks.[21] As such, the Palestinian hope for an end to the civil strife between Hamas and Fatah was short-lived. Still, according to a poll taken in 2008, a full 88.2 percent of the Palestinians living both in the West Bank and Gaza supported continued dialogue between the two factions.[22]

Before the Sanaa talks, several Arab newspapers reported that some members of Hamas were trying to persuade its military wing to stop firing Qassam missiles into Israel, in an attempt to prevent a large-scale military Israeli incursion.[23] Haniyeh reportedly offered the temporary cease-fire to Israel, using Egypt as its intermediary. The terms included a cessation of violence, including rocket fire, by all sides in exchange for a halt of Israeli incursions into Gaza.[24]

Israel had little to gain from a cease-fire at the time, however. As one analyst observed, all of Hamas's nine cease-fires during the Oslo peace process era were offered "at a time when Hamas needed a 'breather'—an opportunity to step back and regroup after an organizationally exhausting confrontation with a more powerful foe (Israel or the PA)." Moreover, the offering of a *temporary* cease-fire in no way changed Hamas's ultimate goal of destroying Israel and Fatah.[25]

Even dovish Israeli President Shimon Peres, the silver-haired 1994 Nobel Peace Prize winner, called the cease-fire proposal a "pathetic and misleading attempt to divert international attention away from the crimes of Hamas and Islamic Jihad." The Tunisian-born, right-wing Israeli parliamentarian Silvan Shalom added, "When the entire world is boycotting Hamas, should [Israel] be the ones to talk to it?"[26] Indeed, the last time Hamas had claimed it would honor a cease-fire had been with Fatah via the 2007 Mecca Agreement, which effectively ended when Hamas took the Gaza Strip by force.

Eventually, when Hamas realized that offers of a cease-fire would be rejected, it changed tactics. After launching dozens of Qassam rockets into southern Israel in January 2008, Hamas said that it believed escalation might force Israel to accept a cease-fire.[27] This, too, backfired. The barrage of homemade missiles, landing mostly in the town of Sderot and its environs, prompted Israel to review its military options. By February, an angry Israeli public was openly discussing the notion of a full-blown invasion of the Gaza Strip and remaining there until Hamas was ousted.[28]

For a short time, it even appeared that Hamas was interested in rapprochement with the United States. Following the Annapolis summit, Hamas sent a letter, written by Ahmed Yousef, the prolific advisor to Haniyeh, to Secretary of State Rice. In it, Yousef described Hamas's interest in starting a dialogue with Washington:

> Many people make the mistake of presuming that we have some ideological aversion to making peace. Quite the opposite; we have consistently offered dialogue with the U.S. and the E.U. to try and resolve the very issues that you are trying to deal with in Annapolis. . . . We are not anti-American, anti-European, or anti-anyone. The root of the problem which neither Israel nor the U.S. is willing to acknowledge, let alone address, is the dispossession of the Palestinian people upon the creation in their homeland of Israel in 1948.[29]

Yousef's insistence that Hamas was "not anti-American" appeared disingenuous. In a December speech, Haniyeh reportedly cited "resistance" in Afghanistan and Iraq against U.S. forces as two of Hamas's achievements in the Middle East, implying that Hamas was involved in the global jihad against America and the West.[30] In early January 2008, with President Bush en route to the region, Hamas stated flatly that the American leader was "unwelcome" and that he was "providing political and material aid to the enemy and working to deepen the internal divisions to help one Palestinian faction confront another."[31] As Bush worked to establish common ground between Abbas and Olmert, Hamas sponsored a mass protest in Gaza, in which protestors held up placards depicting the U.S. president as a vampire drinking Muslim blood.[32]

Upon Bush's departure, Haniyeh announced that Hamas rejected the president's vision of a "dwarfed Palestinian state"[33] and indicated that the group remained intent on conquering all of what it considered to be Palestine. He also stated that Bush's attempts to bring Olmert and Abbas together were "sowing the seeds of sedition" and an "attempt to create an atmosphere for internal Palestinian wars."[34]

Haniyeh's statements likely confirmed two things for Bush as he flew back to the White House on Air Force One:

1. Hamas would be anti-American as long as Washington either supported Israel or promoted peace between the Fatah-backed Palestinian Authority and Israel.
2. The Palestinian-Israeli conflict would likely not be solved unless the Hamas-Fatah conflict was solved first.

Indeed, a senior U.S. official openly acknowledged after the president's departure that the fate of the Palestinian-Israeli conflict would depend on the fate of Gaza. "I don't think in the long term that an agreement is going to work if Hamas continues to control Gaza," he said. "That's why we repeatedly said that the Palestinian Authority should resume its responsibility for the government in Gaza. . . . How that is going to work I don't know."[35] Neither Jerusalem nor Ramallah knew either.

CHAPTER FOURTEEN

THE EFFECT OF SANCTIONS

On February 18, 2006, one month after Hamas's surprising electoral victory, Mahmoud Abbas swore in the new legislators of the Palestinian Authority (PA) in Ramallah. Hamas members of parliament in the Gaza Strip were forced to participate in the ceremony via video link-up because Israel had barred them from traveling to the West Bank. According to al-Jazeera, some 2,000 diplomats and VIPs gathered in a government complex to view the historic moment, along with about 100 women from the Hamas Women's Union whose faces were covered by veils.

Standing at a wood-paneled dais with a dark blue curtain behind him, Abbas read from prepared remarks. Despite the knowledge that his words would almost certainly be ignored, he told the new Hamas-dominated parliament that it would have little choice but to work with Israel to find a negotiated solution to the conflict, calling negotiations with Israel the "sole . . . strategic choice" of the Palestinians. Not surprisingly, Hamas leader Ismael Haniyeh, who would soon become known in Gaza as the Hamas prime minister, stated that he differed with Abbas over the utility of negotiating with Israel. Still, he was careful to add that he sought to ensure that the differences he had with Fatah would be "resolved by dialogue."[1]

Israel was alarmed at the prospect of a government ruled by the same figures who had ordered suicide bombings against its civilians over the years.

Questions arose over what Hamas might be capable of doing with a territory of its own. In an attempt to minimize the dangers posed by the Hamas government, Israel quickly adopted a cocktail of sanctions aimed at restricting Palestinian travel, goods, and finances. After a long cabinet meeting, Israel also announced tougher security measures at checkpoints between Israel and Gaza, although this was largely symbolic, since it had imposed strict travel bans on the Palestinians since the 2000 uprising.

Israel issued an urgent appeal to international donors not to transfer funds to the Hamas-led PA. The Olmert government was quick to note, however, that Israel would continue to allow money into Gaza for humanitarian purposes. Israel also elected to freeze the customs duties it collected on Palestinians' behalf, which amounted to about $50 million a month, or about one-third of the PA's annual budget. Nayef Rajoub, a prominent Hamas leader, described the decision as "theft in broad daylight."[2]

Israel was not the only state to impose sanctions, however. In March 2006, the major aid donors to the Palestinian Authority—the United States, the European Union, and Canada—cut off aid as well. Their decision stemmed from the fact that Hamas refused to renounce violence, recognize Israel, or even acknowledge the previous agreements signed between Israel and the Palestinians. The legal basis for U.S. sanctions stemmed from the fact that the U.S. Treasury and State Department had officially labeled Hamas a terrorist organization. It was, therefore, illegal for the United States to provide financial assistance to the new Hamas government in either the Gaza Strip or the West Bank.

Seemingly unfazed, Hamas defiantly demanded that the United States remove it from Washington's list of designated terrorist groups. Notably, Musa Abu Marzook of the Islamist organization's political bureau insisted that keeping Hamas on the list was not justified, "because Hamas is a national liberation movement that confines its struggle to the occupied territories and had never targeted its weapons outside Palestine."[3] However, Syria-based Hamas leader Khaled Meshal did not help the Hamas cause when he traveled to Iran, another state on the U.S. terrorism list, asking for financial assistance. Within the first year of Israeli sanctions, Iran was believed to have provided Hamas with some $120 million in aid.[4]

For more than a year, Israeli and international sanctions pushed both the West Bank and the Gaza Strip to a desperate point. They also spotlighted the Hamas-Fatah conflict. Indeed, the sanctions sent a clear message to the Palestinian people that they would be held accountable for the Hamas government they had brought to power. The prevailing logic was that unbearable pressure might push the Palestinians to force Hamas to leave power and restore the Fatah faction to its former place atop the PA.

In keeping with this policy, after the Hamas takeover of Gaza in June 2007, the international community adjusted its sanctions. While the embargo against Gaza remained firmly in place, the international community allowed funds to flow freely to the new West Bank emergency government under PA president Abbas. The message to the Palestinians was clear: Life under Hamas rule would be hard; life under Fatah would be significantly less so.

"There won't be any obstacles, economically and politically, in terms of reengaging with this [Abbas-led] government," said the U.S. consul-general, Jacob Walles. He told reporters that Washington sought to provide "significant" financial assistance for West Bank economic development and Abbas's security forces. The Israelis estimated that $300 to $400 million in frozen Palestinian tax revenues could be transferred to Abbas. The economic and diplomatic embargo of Gaza, however, would remain.[5]

As the West Bank began to enjoy the flood of international aid and easing Israeli restrictions, the Gaza Strip suffered under continued sanctions. According to one Israeli human rights group, 59 percent of Gaza's electrical power came from Israel,[6] and an estimated 95 percent of local production depended on imports of raw materials from there.[7] Gaza Strip residents also historically relied on Israel for high-level medical care that they could not get in their own dilapidated and neglected hospitals. Moreover, Hamas would need to work with Israel, much as the PA did, if foreign diplomats, aid organizations, and journalists were to enter the Gaza Strip.

But working with Israel was dangerous for Hamas. It would be tantamount to recognizing the state and would constitute a clear violation of its own covenant. Thus, Hamas continued to hammer Abbas and the PA for engaging with Israel and launched hundreds of Qassam rockets into Israel from its new territory.

For six months, due largely to international pressure, Israel adopted what might be described as a wait-and-see approach, marked by occasional operations against Hamas targets inside Gaza. In November 2007, however, the Israeli government began to debate more serious sanctions. Specifically, it discussed the idea of shutting off Gaza's power as punishment for Qassam rocket and mortar fire. Jerusalem soon delineated Gaza as a "hostile territory."

As the Olmert government observed, as long as Israel continued to provide fuel to Gaza, Israel was effectively contributing to attacks on its own soil. Thus, even as an Israeli court debated whether cutting off electricity to Gaza would violate the country's responsibility to provide humanitarian services there, Israel began to cut fuel shipments.[8] By early December, 100 of the Gaza Strip's 150 gas stations had been shut down because of the fuel cuts. Owners of the remaining gas stations went on strike.[9] Hamas fighters were repeatedly accused by fellow Palestinians of stealing or diverting fuel from Gaza Strip hospitals to fill up their own vehicles.[10] By January 2008, Israel halved the normal amount of fuel shipped to Gaza's only electric plant.[11]

The resulting blackouts sparked international criticism. One UN official asserted that the punitive measures "cannot be justified, even by those rocket attacks."[12] However, as numerous analysts have noted, Israel was well within its rights to withhold both fuel and electricity, according to the Fourth Geneva Convention, so long as Israel continued to allow for the passage of food, clothing, and medicines for non-combatants.[13]

International law notwithstanding, demonstrations took place throughout the Arab world. In Amman, Jordan, where the Palestinian population is believed to be 60 percent or more, people took to the streets. Similarly, students demonstrated in the streets of Cairo, calling for an end to the siege. Even in the quiet Gulf nations of Qatar and Bahrain, demonstrations and sit-ins were held after Friday prayers.[14]

What these protestors did not know, however, was that Hamas itself was making conditions harder for Gazans as a means to garner more sympathy. Hamas policemen seized at least one convoy of humanitarian aid, according to the Associated Press.[15] Hamas elicited even more sympathy by staging scenes of darkness for video journalists to capture as part of its campaign to end the political and economic sanctions against the Gaza Strip.[16]

The criticism was not unanimous, however. Jordanian columnist Osama al-Sharif stated his belief that Hamas had become "a liability for all Palestinians" and that its desire to "keep control of Gaza at any cost is dangerous, if not suicidal," particularly since it was Gaza's "citizens who are enduring a huge humanitarian ordeal."[17] Columnist Hussein Shobokshi, in the pages of the London-based Arabic daily *ash-Sharq al-Awsat*, criticized Hamas for "acting in a way that has made it more important than Gaza itself."[18] The paper's editor reportedly stated that Hamas had "committed a stupid act" by firing rockets into Israel. A PA spokesman also said that the crisis was all the result of Hamas's "insistence on creating an Islamic republic in the Gaza Strip."[19] Thus, the sanctions appeared to be working.

Israel waffled, however. As rockets continued to fall, in January 2008, the Olmert government agreed to transfer fuel to Gaza.[20] Weeks later, amid other fuel deliveries, the Olmert cabinet announced that it would again reduce fuel supplies to Gaza in February.[21] Throughout the spring, Israel continued to provide Gaza with fuel, which Hamas often neglected to pass on to the citizens. Generators, hospitals, water pumps, and sewage facilities were denied the fuel necessary to operate. Hamas, however, continued to have enough fuel for vehicles used in strikes against Israel.[22] Thus, Israel undermined its own sanctions strategy, allowing Hamas to maintain its grip on Gaza.

It is important to note that even if Israel held to its own sanctions policies, the government of Egypt ultimately determined their efficacy. The Mubarak regime continued tacitly to allow mass smuggling operations to take place beneath the border separating the Sinai Peninsula from Gaza. Hamas restocked shelves in Gaza Strip stores through these tunnels, thereby undermining the impact of the international sanctions. Indeed, tunnels furnished the Hamas economy in the Gaza Strip with everything from cigarettes and car parts to erectile dysfunction pills and fresh cheese.[23] Hamas effectively took control of the tunnels, which yielded some $140 million per year, charging owners fees of up to $3,000 each day. If owners refused, their tunnels were destroyed.[24] Hamas also padded its pockets by taxing the goods that came in by way of the tunnels.[25]

The Israeli efforts to force Egypt to take stronger action against the tunnels had potentially dangerous consequences. Specifically, Israel did not wish to jeopardize its cold peace with Egypt, which had ensured a tense but important calm in the region since 1978. However, its frustration was boiling over. In some cases, the smuggling of weapons in the tunnels led to the loss of Israeli lives.

According to Israeli officials, the smugglers sometimes paid Egyptian police and border guards with "bribes or other incentives for keeping the tunnels open." Tellingly, when the Israelis destroyed the tunnels with explosives, they witnessed smoke and debris clouds coming out of entrances in areas that were well within the patrol areas of Egypt's border guards.[26]

Cairo initially dismissed those allegations as "old and silly." However, as Israeli protests grew louder, the Mubarak regime complained that it needed more policemen to deploy along the border. Legitimate questions arose over whether an increase in troops might constitute a violation of the Camp David Accords, which stipulated that the border area between Egypt and Israel would not witness a buildup of troops on either side. The discussions quickly stalled.

Frustrated and bloodied, Israel sent videotapes to Washington in December 2007 that clearly showed Egyptian policemen helping smugglers in the tunnels. The hope was that Washington, which approved a sizable foreign aid budget for Egypt every year, might pressure the country to halt the smuggling.[27]

The Israeli plan appeared to pay dividends. The House and Senate agreed in late December on a 2008 foreign aid bill that would withhold about $100 million of the $1.3 billion promised to Egypt unless Secretary of State Condoleezza Rice could certify that Egypt was doing its part to stop the smuggling.[28] After a meeting with the Israeli defense minister, the head of Egypt's *mukhabarat* (intelligence services), Omar Suleiman, announced that the smuggling would end, telling one journalist "You will not hear about it again."[29] Egypt soon reported that it would spend $23 million in American military aid on robots and other technology to help its border patrol detect and destroy the tunnels.[30] In March, Cairo even announced it was establishing a commando unit of elite soldiers to detect and destroy tunnels.[31]

Cairo had a lot to prove. In late January 2008, Egypt had stood by as Hamas gunmen destroyed about two-thirds of the wall separating Gaza from the Sinai Peninsula. As noted previously, hundreds of thousands of Gazans streamed into Egypt, stocking up on food, supplies, and possibly weapons, effectively negating all international sanctions.

Once the Palestinians of Gaza began to stream over the border, Egyptian merchants opened their stores, eager to sell to a population that had been in economic isolation since the Hamas political victory in January 2006. Egyptian police watched Gazans cross the border without checking identification. Only when the Gazans returned would Hamas police check their belongings for drugs or weapons.[32]

Mubarak announced that he ordered his troops to allow Palestinians to cross into Egypt because they were starving. "I told them to let them come in and eat and buy food and then return them later as long as they were not carrying weapons," he said. There was also speculation that the Egyptian president issued this directive as a means to placate the Muslim Brotherhood in Egypt, given their historic ties to Hamas.[33]

The Israeli government was furious. Israeli Foreign Ministry spokesman Arye Mekel stated in a BBC interview that it was "the responsibility of Egypt to ensure that the border operates properly, according to the signed agreements."[34] Finally, after several days of chaos, Egypt's foreign minister, Ahmed Aboul Gheit, announced that Egypt would invite delegations from Hamas and the PA to visit Egypt separately to discuss the border problem, citing "an Egyptian effort to restore the arrangements that existed between Egypt and the Gaza Strip before the Hamas takeover of the sector in last June."[35]

After 12 days of pandemonium, Egypt closed the border. During that time period, Gazans stocked up on provisions and weaponry. According to Israeli security services chief Yuval Diskin, large quantities of long-range rockets, antitank missiles, antiaircraft missiles, and materiel for rocket production were brought into Gaza.[36] Egyptian authorities seized more than $1 million in forged U.S. currency, but it was not known how much more had crossed the border.[37] In February 2008, Rice announced, "We have not been satisfied with Egypt's efforts on the tunnels."[38] Indeed, after the border was sealed, the smuggling operations began anew, pumping weapons and goods into Gaza.

It was clear that any blockade designed to weaken Hamas through financial, and ultimately political, measures was in Egypt's hands. Iran realized this too. The mullahs reached out to Cairo, hoping to send provisions and possibly weapons aboveground through Egypt rather than through the tunnels, which were expensive to dig and difficult to maintain. The height and width of the tunnels also made it difficult to smuggle certain items.

Relations between Iran and Egypt had been icy for nearly 30 years. Tehran had cut ties with Egypt when it recognized the State of Israel. Yet now Iran made contact through its foreign ministry, offering Egypt assistance and funds to help control the border. The controversial Iranian president, Mahmoud Ahmadinejad, reviled in Israel for threatening to wipe the Jewish state "off the map," made a direct call to Husni Mubarak, offering to restore ties between the two countries.[39] Iran's news agency and television confirmed that discussions were ongoing, signaling to its public that ties could be renewed.[40] Iran was lobbying Egypt on behalf of Hamas.

Egypt, however, appeared to have rebuffed its longtime Shi'ite rival. By late February, the Egyptian military began to build a new barrier to withstand the blast of explosives similar to those that tore down the Egypt-Gaza wall in January.[41] The new barrier, built of rock and concrete, also featured watchtowers every 100 yards.[42]

Ironically, the Egyptian government that had once condemned Israel for building a barrier to keep Palestinians out had little choice but to take the same measure. As Aboul Gheit stated, "whoever wishes to build a security fence on his land is free to do that."[43] The government also announced that it would not reopen the border again without the consent of Israel, Western powers, and Fatah.[44]

The Egyptian government made efforts to demonstrate that it was cracking down on tunnel smuggling. Although many tunnels were still operational, Cairo announced in March 2008 that it had discovered some 500 kilograms of explosives as well as 40 land mines in Egyptian territory close to the Gaza Strip. In late May, Egyptian police announced the discovery of a cache containing an additional 500 kilos of explosives that had been hidden in ten sacks along the Gaza border.[45]

Egypt, however, was not necessarily convinced that it would need to isolate Gaza completely. Cairo soon announced that it struck a deal to replace Israel as the Gaza Strip's primary electricity provider. The 150 megawatt project was expected to cost $32 million and be operational within two years.[46]

One year after the Gaza coup, Egypt held the key to enforcing sanctions against Hamas or allowing it to arm.[47] If it helped to isolate Hamas and allowed sanctions to take effect, there was a small chance that Hamas might step down for the greater Palestinian good. If it allowed Hamas to arm, attacks against Israel would increase, creating an impetus for an Israeli invasion. Thus, depending on its policies along a seven-mile border, Egypt could effectively determine whether Israel and Hamas would go to war.

CHAPTER FIFTEEN

THE WINDS OF WAR

On a cool, windy day in February 2008, Israeli officials took nearly 70 foreign ambassadors to its border with the Gaza Strip, hoping that the diplomats might be able to witness firsthand the launching of a Qassam rocket and its trail of smoke. This was an effort to enlist international support for an invasion. Foreign Minister Tzipi Livni explained to the envoys that cross-border rocket fire by Hamas had created an "unbearable" situation that grew worse by the day. "Israel must act in order to reduce these threats," she said.[1]

With few options left, polls in June 2008 indicated that nearly half of all Israeli respondents supported a broad ground operation.[2] As war appeared increasingly likely, Palestinian officials sought to stave off confrontation. Longtime Arafat negotiator Saeb Erakat warned of a "humanitarian disaster."[3] The Israeli novelist and peace activist Amos Oz warned that an invasion would be catastrophic for Israel, too. "Israel would expose itself to far more losses," he said.[4]

Israel, however, appeared to have run out of options. Economic sanctions had not worked. Limited incursions had only kept Hamas in check. At a meeting with Turkish military officials in February, Defense Minister Ehud Barak attempted to explain that Israel did not seek war, but if the Qassam attacks continued, Israel would have little choice but to escalate its response.[5]

Within weeks of the Hamas coup, Israel had carried out limited incursions into Gaza, although it gained little from each operation. The challenges Israel had encountered during the uprisings of 1987 and 2000 were as salient in 2007. Namely, Israel could not attack the Hamas infrastructure in Gaza without creating collateral damage and causing fatalities among the civilian population in this densely populated area. Israel's periodic and strategic counterterrorism operations kept Hamas off balance but certainly did not impact the long-term viability of the group.

Tzipi Livni, a close advisor to Prime Minister Olmert, floated the notion of a Gaza Strip takeover by the North Atlantic Treaty Organization (NATO) during her December 2007 meetings with the NATO Secretary General Jaap de Hoop Scheffer in Belgium.[6] The suggestion was surprising. The PA had supported this idea during the second intifada as a means to control Israeli incursions into the territories.[7] The Israelis had rejected it, fearing that international forces might inhibit full autonomy in their defensive maneuvers in the West Bank and Gaza. After all, UN forces had let Israel down more than once, having failed to protect Israel's right of passage in the Straits of Tehran before the Six-Day War of 1967 and, more recently, having failed to prevent Hizbullah from firing on Israel's north.

With chaos worsening in the territories, the prospect appeared more palatable to Jerusalem. The European Union's Middle East envoy, Marc Otte, indicated that there was "more interest than in the past" in deploying foreign peacekeeping forces, particularly after the 2006 war between Hizbullah and Israel, which had devastated the region. The Israeli military establishment, however, remained opposed to the notion of allowing any other military to defend Israel's borders. Hamas was amassing a more powerful military, and Israel would not trust another military to dismantle it.[8]

Within days of the Hamas takeover in 2007, the Islamist organization had established strategic defensive military positions to punish Israel in the event of an invasion. Hamas's ability to shore up control can be attributed to the relatively small territory involved. (The entire Gaza Strip is about the size of Washington, D.C.) Hamas was also able to gain control thanks to the many mosques, schools, and clubs that the late Ahmed Yassin had established in the preceding decades. In some cases, the Hamas social infrastructure was quickly converted to a military infrastructure.

Israeli security officials subsequently estimated that it would have taken Hamas about a year of smuggling to amass the amount of weaponry it confiscated from the PA forces during the six-day war in Gaza. Hamas, according to reports in October 2007, had also collected an estimated 73 tons of explosives through smuggling operations along the Gaza-Egypt border in the months following the June civil war.[9]

Moreover, when Hamas overran Palestinian Authority (PA) security buildings in June, the spoils of victory included a formidable arsenal of U.S.-supplied weapons. As one Hamas operative gloated, "The U.S. and Israel and other regional powers were generous to provide Fatah security with very good weapons, and now they are in our hands."[10] As previously noted, Hamas had commandeered thousands of assault rifles, large supplies of ammunition, and even rocket-propelled grenades with warheads designed to penetrate armor.[11] This was confirmed during an Israeli incursion into Gaza in December, when a Hamas armor-piercing RPG penetrated an IDF Merkava tank, injuring four soldiers.[12] It was also estimated that Hamas came into possession of large-caliber machine guns and even antiaircraft weapons, such as the shoulder-fired Strela missile. Indeed, Hamas claimed in a December leaflet that its members had fired antiaircraft weapons for the first time at Israeli helicopters.[13]

Armed with more weaponry than it had ever had, plus increased guidance from the Iranians, Hamas began to restructure its fighting force. As one analyst noted, Hamas was soon "capable of controlling domestic challenges and enhancing its capabilities against Israel."[14]

With its new arsenal and training, Hamas established an elaborate bunker system, along with several fortified rocket launching and surveillance positions along the 37-miles of fence that separated Gaza from Israel. To prepare for the next inevitable confrontation, Hamas had studied Israeli military tactics during the IDF's daily operations along the fence.[15] Hamas was able to set up ambushes to attack the IDF units as they entered Gaza for limited operations and even attacked forces on their way out.[16] When Israeli reservists came back from small-scale confrontations with Hamas fighters in November 2007, they told the newspaper *Haaretz*, "The people we killed weren't terrorists, they were soldiers." Indeed, the new Iranian-trained Hamas military was equipped with night-vision goggles and other specialized hardware, making the terrorist group a more formidable foe.[17]

Hamas also stepped up its psychological operations. In response to reports that Israel was mulling an invasion, Syria-based Khaled Meshal threatened that Hamas would harm Corporal Gilad Shalit, the Israeli soldier Hamas kidnapped in June 2006, who was still believed to be in captivity.[18] Hamas leader Mahmoud al-Zahar issued a more direct challenge to Israel. He stated at one Gaza rally, "Whoever enters Gaza will leave it in pieces."[19]

Israel, however, was not easily deterred. The IDF continued to launch operations inside Gaza. In one December raid, the IDF killed eight Hamas operatives after pushing about one mile into Hamas-controlled territory. The operation reportedly focused on a launching area for rockets and mortars that sailed into Israel.[20] In another IDF operation in January, Israeli tanks, bulldozers, and helicopters pushed deep into Gaza again, killing 17 Palestinians, including al-Zahar's son.[21] Incursions continued into spring, as Israel sniped at Hamas installations and operatives, which had the limited effect of only temporarily disrupting Hamas's operations.

Fatah benefited from these incursions to the extent that they weakened Hamas. Yet, when Israel entered Gaza, Fatah often attempted to reassert itself as leaders of the Palestinian cause, threatening to suspend peace talks. Olmert was unmoved. "The more Hamas is hit," he stated, "the greater the chances of reaching a diplomatic agreement and peace."[22]

According to one Israeli government statement issued in late November 2007, "Since June, Palestinians have fired at Israel an average of one Qassam rocket every three hours. More than 200 rockets and mortar shells have been launched since the beginning of November."[23] As if that were not cause enough for a full-scale invasion, reports emerged in December that Hamas had developed the capability of storing Qassam rockets for longer periods of time, which raised the possibility that the group would be able to unleash a barrage of rockets on Israeli civilians. Until this technological breakthrough by Hamas bomb makers, Qassams had to be launched shortly after they were produced due to the volatility of the explosive charge. This short life span was why only a few Qassams at a time usually landed in Israeli territory.[24]

In January, the Hamas Web site boasted that the group had fired 540 rockets and mortars at Israel.[25] Avi Dichter, Israel's internal security minister, expressed serious concerns over whether Hamas might one day develop a longer shelf life and range for the Qassam rocket. He warned of a possible tenfold increase in the number of Israelis who could be exposed to these crude rockets, particularly if Hamas rockets could reach the Israeli town of Ashkelon, north of Gaza on the Mediterranean coast. If so, the number of Israelis potentially threatened by Qassams would jump from 25,000 (in Sderot and the surrounding areas) to 250,000 (to include Ashkelon and its environs). Dichter and other top security officials advocated an extensive operation to destroy the Hamas rocket infrastructure and confiscate Hamas ordnance.[26] When rockets did begin to fall in Ashkelon in early 2008, security officials stepped up their urgent calls for a military intervention.[27]

As the Israeli political leadership struggled with its options, most military analysts reasoned that only a large-scale operation, involving a blitzkrieg on Hamas strongholds, would weaken the group enough to enable Israel to overtake the Gaza Strip. Israel's chief of staff confirmed this when he announced in December that a full-scale invasion of Gaza was almost inevitable. "You cannot defeat a terror organization without eventually taking control of the territory," he said.[28]

With few alternatives, the IDF made plans for an extensive operation inside Gaza. Although details were not revealed, it was believed that any operation would be designed to first gain control over southern Gaza, where the tunnels originating in Egypt emptied and where gunmen roamed the streets with assault rifles and antitank missiles. Common wisdom held that Israel would then march north, taking out Hamas installations and weapons caches along the way.

The call for war, however, subsided amid the fanfare of the Annapolis conference, even as Hamas vowed to increase its attacks against Israel. Defense Minister Barak stressed that he did not want to jeopardize peace talks by launching an Israeli military incursion. Indeed, the former commando seemed to indicate that Israeli casualties were acceptable as long as peace was possible. But after Annapolis had come and gone, as Hamas continued to launch rockets into Israeli airspace, career IDF officials went on record as stating that a military operation in Gaza would be critical to preventing

Hamas from gaining more advanced military capabilities.[29] But in January, after a series of limited incursions into Gaza following Bush's visit to Israel, Olmert announced that it was "highly advisable not to become entangled in operations and costs that are not in proportion to the pressures that we are facing."[30]

There was little doubt, however, among the members of the Knesset—the Israeli parliament—and the military establishment that a full-scale operation was in Israel's best interest. Tzachi Hanegbi, a parliamentarian on Israel's Foreign Affairs and Defense Committee, stated that if Israel waited, it would be "facing Iranian brigades" in Gaza.[31] The question that emerged was whether Israel had the nerve to enter into a protracted confrontation with its longtime Islamist foe.

Iran, the Israelis learned, continued to help Hamas evolve into a stronger, more organized fighting force. After Gaza operations in the spring of 2008, Israeli troops reported that Hamas coordinated its moves by radio, and were equipped with better weaponry.[32] Much of that weaponry was being smuggled from Iran to Gaza by sea, as well as through the tunnels from Egypt.[33]

The Qassam Brigades soon announced that it could hit Israeli helicopters with sophisticated weaponry it had seized from the PA.[34] According to one Hamas commander, the group had been sending hundreds of fighters to Iran and Syria for extensive weapons and tactics training since the Israeli withdrawal in 2005.[35] A report issued in April 2008 by the Intelligence and Terrorism Information Center in Israel also confirmed the growing strength of Hamas. The report noted that Hamas had 20,000 armed operatives, large-scale training operations, better rockets and explosives, and an improved command and control system.[36]

Hamas' strength notwithstanding, the Israelis had little doubt that their advanced weaponry could reduce the Gaza Strip to rubble. But Israel did not wage wars in this way. Rather, the IDF policy was to maintain minimal collateral damage in every military operation, large and small. Yet the Jewish state found itself under attack from Hamas apologists, Palestinian advocates, and human rights groups after smaller operations for using "disproportional force." Jerusalem's war worries were based on the fallout from the international condemnation and isolation that always accompanied Israel's decisions to defend its citizens from attack.

While Israel considered the consequences of an invasion, one nagging question lingered: What would Israel do once it conquered Gaza? Most Israelis would be opposed to reoccupying Gaza and administering the volatile strip. Doing so would almost certainly lead to another popular uprising. But if Israel handed Gaza over to the Fatah-backed PA, there were no guarantees that Fatah would not turn violent again. Moreover, replacing the Hamas government with an Israeli-backed government might arouse popular resentment against the new rulers, particularly given the distrust and hatred for Israel long observed on the Palestinian street.

There were also conflicting reports regarding Fatah's view of a possible Israeli invasion. Some Fatah officials in the West Bank and Gaza Strip vowed to fight alongside Hamas in the event of an Israeli invasion.[37] Other reports, however, indicated that Fatah actually sought such an invasion, as it would almost certainly clear the way for the Palestinian Authority to regain control of the territory it lost in June 2007. In a November speech, Mahmoud Abbas explicitly stated, "We have to bring down this bunch, which took over Gaza with armed force, and is abusing the sufferings and pains of our people."[38]

But even if Israel were to hand over the Gaza Strip to Fatah, as Hamas leader Said Sayyam noted, "In the Gaza Strip all the security services have been dissolved."[39] Sayyam was right. The PA had no infrastructure in the Gaza Strip. Thus, it would not be easy for the PA simply to assume control there. Any period of transition would almost certainly invite violence and chaos.

Nonetheless, talk of a full-scale Israeli invasion continued. Prime Minister Olmert assured the Israeli public that he was "absolutely determined to respond to the challenge of terrorism from Gaza in every possible manner which will be effective. We will not hesitate, we will not stop, we will do what's necessary to be done."[40]

One month later, *Vanity Fair* magazine published an article alleging that President Bush had approved a covert initiative to overthrow the Hamas government. The goal, according to the report, was to empower the PA to reconquer Gaza.[41] The White House never confirmed the report.

Convinced that he could avert what appeared to be an inevitable conflict, former U.S. President Jimmy Carter traveled to the Middle East to hold a controversial meeting with the exiled leader of Hamas, Khaled Meshal. The State Department and the Israeli government openly disapproved of the meeting. Carter, however, insisted that he could persuade Hamas to lay down its weapons. Predictably, his visit accomplished little.[42] Similarly, French officials held meetings with Hamas, but failed to convince the group to renounce violence.[43] The winds of war continued to blow.

CHAPTER SIXTEEN

THE PROSPECTS FOR CHANGE FROM WITHIN

As talk of an Israeli incursion into Gaza dominated headlines through the spring of 2008, it was commonly recognized that violence could be prevented only by Palestinian change from within. The most hopeful and peaceful scenario was one in which Hamas simply handed over the Gaza Strip to the Palestinian Authority (PA) in the name of national unity. Of course, the possibility of Hamas relinquishing control of the Gaza Strip was remote, particularly in light of the group's long history of aggression. Still, as demonstrated by the failed Yemeni accords, even amid the continued violence and war of words, the two factions had been discussing the possibility of reconciliation.

Since the fall of 2007, a flurry of newspaper reports had detailed rumors that Hamas was considering giving back the Gaza Strip to the PA. The Islamist group had endured several months of bloody clashes with both Israel and Fatah in Gaza. Reports also emerged that Hamas leaders were fighting among themselves. In fact, Hamas had arrested several of its own members for allegedly "collaborating" with Arab and Western intelligence agencies. As the internal turmoil unfolded, one member of Hamas reportedly killed a fighter from the venerated Izz al-Din al-Qassam Brigades, the

Hamas military wing. The assassination was thought to have occurred in the context of a power struggle between rival Hamas sub-factions.[1]

As the crisis played out, elements within Hamas reportedly asked for reconciliation talks with Mahmoud Abbas of the PA and even hinted that it would be willing to cede control of its war spoils. "Our administration in Gaza is temporary," Hamas's leader in Gaza, Ismael Haniyeh, reportedly posted on a pro-Hamas Web site (although not the official one).[2] Fatah and Hamas officials also prayed together in the West Bank in early November 2007, in an indication that rapprochement was possible. The official Palestinian television station aired footage of Abbas and three relatively unknown Hamas leaders—Nasser al-Din al-Sha'er, Sheikh Husein Abu Kweik, and Sheikh Ahmed Abu Ruman—praying at a mosque near Abbas's headquarters in Ramallah.[3] Reports also emerged that representatives from the two factions had met in Gaza, Damascus, and Beirut throughout the fall of 2007 in a continuing effort to reconcile their differences.[4] Some pragmatic members of Hamas in the West Bank even went so far as to openly criticize their Gaza Strip brethren over the way in which they mishandled Gaza rule.[5]

Hamas almost certainly understood that its popularity was quickly waning. West Bankers largely viewed the Gaza conquest as an overt aggressive action that divided the Palestinian people. Many Gazans likely welcomed Hamas rule at first, but they gradually viewed the June coup as an event that invited more tragedy to the already poverty-stricken and depressed territory. When Israeli forces entered Gaza in response to Qassam missile attacks, the local residents began to view Hamas as the provocateur; in the past, Hamas typically had been viewed as the doggedly determined resistance group that responded with force to Israeli aggression. By the end of 2007, one poll put the popularity of the Fatah party at 52 percent and Hamas at 40 percent, indicating a sharp swing away from Hamas support.[6]

Growing Iranian influence over Hamas may have played a part in its declining popular support. Arab analysts noted that Iran had gained too much sway over Hamas. Saudi columnist Mshari al-Zaydi went as far as to call Haniyeh a "Sunni Hassan Nasrallah," drawing blunt parallels between the Hamas leader and Hizbullah's oracle, a longtime Lebanese client of Iran.[7] Fatah officials complained that Iran's donor-driven agenda was "encouraging Hamas to create a new organization that would . . . establish

Khaled Meshal as the new face of the Palestinian people, and in the process, further destroy Palestinian unity." Fatah even accused Iran of supplying millions of dollars and weapons to Hamas to prolong the Palestinian civil war.[8]

Fatah leaders also understood that as long as Iran maintained influence over Hamas decision makers, reconciliation would be highly unlikely. To be sure, the Iranians did not fund Hamas for more than two decades to achieve a momentous victory in which Islamists controlled a strategic piece of Middle East real estate, only to relinquish it to Fatah, a secular organization linked to Israel and the United States.

But even as Hamas talked peace with Fatah, the Islamist faction continued to carry out acts of violence against its secular foe in Gaza. In mid-December, at least 3 Fatah mourners were killed and 35 were wounded when a grenade was dropped into a funeral procession. According to Hamas security officials, the grenade had been dropped "accidentally." Abbas, however, was not convinced. "What happened was an assault against our people," he said, declaring three days of mourning. Haniyeh, for his part, called it a "conspiracy to spread chaos."[9]

Despite vows to end the violence, Hamas police kidnapped Omar al-Ghul, an advisor to PA Prime Minister Salaam Fayyad, in Gaza City and held him for six weeks.[10] In fact, between December 28 and December 30, 2007, Hamas police carried out several raids on a Fatah's offices in Gaza, confiscating computers and files and arresting individuals without cause.[11] In January, Hamas gunmen detained the former chief of the PA's security forces, Jamal Kayid, confiscating two cameras, a computer, a cell phone, and even his private car.[12]

Meanwhile, the Hamas Web site continued to print blistering attacks against Fatah for engaging in diplomacy with Israel and the United States. Hamas spokesman Fawzi Barhum accused Abbas of impeding efforts to unify the Palestinians and of supporting Bush's calls for escalated attacks on Hamas and its leaders. He also alleged that Abbas was withholding the salaries of 40,000 civil servants in the Gaza Strip due to their political affiliation. Hamas even boycotted the Palestinian census for a short time, signaling that it did not wish to have Gaza's citizens counted among those from the West Bank. Only months later did Hamas relent, allowing West Bank and Gaza Palestinians to be counted together.[13]

In mid-January 2008, Israeli tanks, bulldozers, and helicopters raided the Gaza Strip in a large-scale operation. Israel Defense Forces troops moved several hundred yards across the border to strike an abandoned house near Gaza City that was used for rocket-launching operations. Fierce firefights broke out, as Israeli tanks and aircraft provided support from afar. According to Hamas, 12 fighters and 3 civilians were killed by late morning and more than 40 Palestinians were wounded. Local hospitals made a public call for blood donations.

Among the dead on the Hamas side was the 24-year-old son of Mahmoud al-Zahar, Hussam. According to press reports, al-Zahar went to the morgue to identify his son, recited the requisite blessings, then went into mourning. The news of Hussam al-Zahar's death spread throughout Gaza, eliciting an outpouring of sympathy. A delegation of senior Fatah officials even visited the home of the Hamas leader.[14] Even more surprising was the fact that Abbas made his "first [phone] call since June" to al-Zahar to express his condolences, according to a Hamas spokesman.[15] In response to Abbas's gesture, Haniyeh invited Abbas to come to the Gaza Strip for a dialogue that could bring an end to the ongoing violence and division. "We hope that this contact will be the lighting of a candle that will guide us to the right path we should be in to end this dispute," said a Haniyeh advisor.[16]

But even as the two sides attempted to draw closer, Hamas forces stormed Fatah's Gaza headquarters, confiscating everything from office equipment to furniture.[17] It was also around this time that Hamas released senior Fatah leader Ibrahim Abu an-Naja after two weeks of captivity, during which Hamas members shaved his head and mustache. In his first public appearance after being freed, the stubbly an-Naja announced that Hamas had to "retract the military coup, and [the] criminals must be punished for what they have done."[18]

Days later, Hamas accused the PA of attempting to assassinate Ismael Haniyeh with "Fatah-affiliated suicide bombers." Fatah denied the accusation, stating that the charge was "an attempt to distract people's attention from the security chaos prevailing in the Gaza Strip."[19] In February, allegations surfaced again that Abbas had plotted to assassinate Haniyeh. Hamas even aired the confessions of suspects. One stated that he had been offered $70,000 to blow himself up at a mosque where Haniyeh was praying. Fatah dismissed the allegations and called Hamas an "outlaw movement."[20] The war of words continued.

Another setback for Palestinian rapprochement came during the aforementioned chaotic breach of the Egypt-Gaza border in January and February 2008, during which a flood of people, cars, motorcycles, and even donkey carts crossed into the Sinai Peninsula while Egyptian border guards watched. When the international community sought to help Egypt reseal the border, tensions arose between Hamas and Fatah over which faction had the right to control it. Hamas announced, "We have our own vision of how the crossing will be run and we will present our vision to our Egyptian brothers."[21] Hamas, in fact, had begun to discuss with Egypt the possibility of establishing financial ties while disengaging completely from Israel—a move that would further assert its independence from the West Bank.[22]

Not surprisingly, the international community envisioned a scenario in which the Fatah-backed PA took control of the Palestinian side of the border. After all, this was the basis for an agreement signed between Israel and the PA in 2005, the Agreement on Movement and Access (AMA), which empowered PA security forces to control the Rafah crossing.[23] Three years later, according to the Palestinian Authority's news service, Abbas won backing for this plan from the United States, Europe, and even Arab foreign ministers.[24] Secretary of State Condoleezza Rice expressed her hope that "a Palestinian Authority presence [would] begin to introduce some order to that border."[25]

There was one problem with this plan: Hamas maintained military control in Gaza, not Fatah. Nonetheless, the embattled PA president stated that by not accepting his plan, Hamas would "be held responsible for the protracted closure of the border crossings."[26]

In the end, surprisingly, Hamas officials stated that Hamas would not object to elite PA presidential guard forces on the border.[27] The rancor, however, remained. Abbas rejected calls for dialogue, stating "Hamas has to go back on its coup d'etat and . . . accept the legitimacy [of the PA], and then the hearts and minds would be open for dialogue."[28] He continued to emphasize that the previous border agreement stipulated PA control.

Hamas was equally intransigent. Mahmoud al-Zahar defiantly stated, "We are the Palestinian Authority. Hamas should govern Gaza and the West Bank." He called Fatah traitors and collaborators, and insisted that the PLO "does not represent a majority."[29]

Through June 2008, the Palestinian press reported that Hamas and Fatah had held several surprise meetings. The meetings typically accomplished little, but they inspired hope among Palestinians.[30] Broadly speaking, the dynamic between Hamas and Fatah could best be described as one of antagonism, interrupted occasionally by fleeting moments in which rapprochement appeared possible.

There was little or no discussion about the possibility of Fatah retaking the Gaza Strip. Due to the fact that Fatah had yet to fully rebuild its army, an Israeli raid was seen as the only likely scenario in which Gaza could be toppled.

There were small signs, however, of a possible Fatah-led uprising against Hamas in the Gaza Strip. In August 2007, just two months after the coup, the Reuters news agency reported that unidentified Palestinians exploded a bomb outside of the presidential compound that had once been inhabited by Mahmoud Abbas. This was the first attack of its kind against Hamas since the group took the Gaza Strip by storm. Fatah did not claim credit for the attack. In fact, no group did.[31]

The *Jerusalem Post* reported in September that there were "increasing indications that Fatah is trying to organize an intifada against Hamas."[32] The combination of "illegal" street protests and planned armed clashes were designed to challenge Hamas rule in a format very familiar to its participants: a Palestinian-style uprising. Only this time, Hamas—the group often at the front lines of the 1987 and 2000 uprisings against Israel—was the target.

In early September, Amnesty International reported that car bombs targeting Hamas members were detonated on two occasions.[33] In October, another car bombing of a Hamas supporter was reported. Shortly thereafter, a spokesperson for the Hamas Interior Ministry confirmed that a series of attacks had taken place against Hamas officials across the Gaza Strip. It was not known whether he was referring to new attacks or to ones that had already been reported.[34]

Hamas even found itself in conflict with PIJ.[35] Although the two groups typically were aligned, tensions were reported immediately after the coup. Part of the problem was that Hamas insisted that it was the only faction allowed to carry weapons in Gaza. PIJ also took issue with Hamas attempts to control certain mosques that were long considered PIJ strongholds. As a result, Hamas forces assaulted PIJ with deadly force, leading to several deaths and numerous injuries.[36] The two Iran-backed organizations, once partners in suicide bombings against Israel, were in conflict.

By November, one columnist for the Saudi *Arab News* noted, "Gazans have had enough of Hamas" and they "no longer fear it." Many began to "accuse Hamas of being in the pay of Iran," which "indicates real hatred." The columnist's conclusion was that Fatah and the rest of the Palestinians would "not be intimidated by Hamas bullets."[37] Later that month, Mohammed Dahlan, the former Fatah strongman in the Gaza Strip, called on Fatah fighters to exact revenge for his ouster. "Victory over those killers will be very soon," he pledged.[38]

In November, an explosion rocked the headquarters of the al-Qassam Brigades in western Gaza City, causing several casualties. The culprits were not identified.[39] Later that month, Fatah held a 250,000-person demonstration commemorating the anniversary of Yasir Arafat's death. Although seven people were killed in an ensuing battle with Hamas, the demonstration was a strong indication that Fatah still had power in Gaza. In other November actions, unknown assailants set fire to an office for social services in a central Gaza refugee camp and others planted an explosive device at a police station in Gaza City, causing minimal damage.[40]

Did Fatah have the strength to mount a sustained campaign against Hamas? According to an assessment by Yuval Diskin, the head of Israel's internal security service, the Palestinians were likely too exhausted to launch an uprising against Israel.[41] It appeared that Fatah was too tired to fight Hamas at this time, as well. This assessment led many analysts to believe that the Gaza Strip would remain under Hamas control unless Israel decided to topple it by force.

Hamas, however, had at least one other domestic weakness. Like Fatah before it, when Hamas conquered the Gaza Strip, the group became a government overnight. Historically, this is a liability for terrorist organizations. It certainly was for Fatah, which suffered from the popular perception among West Bankers and Gazans that the guerrillas turned bureaucrats were corrupt, ossified, and unprepared to govern. Indeed, this factor was one of those that led to Fatah's electoral defeat in January 2006.

Several months into the new Gaza regime, it appeared that Hamas would suffer similar struggles. As Palestinian author Marwan Bishara noted, when Hamas "stepped into Fatah's shoes, it began to lose credibility, becoming hostage to the same dual discourse: good governance to please international donors . . . and the slogans of liberation and Islamism to please the masses."[42]

Specifically, Hamas was forced to reconcile the fact that Gaza's fate was tied to Israel's. Former U.S. Middle East peace negotiator Dennis Ross correctly notes that while "Hamas may not want to deal with Israel, the reality of the situation is that Israel supplies much of the Palestinian electricity and water and collects taxes and customs revenues that have provided much of the money for meeting the costs of the Palestinian administration."[43]

Interestingly, even as Hamas and Israel had been trading blows, *ash-Sharq al-Awsat* reported in November that "Hamas is communicating with Israel via an Arab country that is on friendly terms with Israel."[44] Of course, this was possible, but it also might have been Fatah propaganda. The *Jerusalem Post* had reported similar allegations from PA president Abbas in late October.[45] As Abbas knew, even tacit recognition of the Jewish state that it had vowed to destroy was a huge liability for Hamas. He understood that if the Islamist group shows even minimal signs of cooperation with Israel, hard-line Hamas members, or perhaps even a rival jihadist organization, could emerge and "out-Hamas" the new governing power in Gaza.

The notion that Hamas would not necessarily remain the most radical faction in Gaza was of course a worry to Israel and America, but it was an even greater threat to the Palestinians of Gaza. Such a scenario would begin anew the cycle that had sparked the Fatah-Hamas rivalry two decades earlier. Indeed, Fatah, the terrorist organization that flatly rejected the existence of the State of Israel, became a governing power in 1988 by ultimately recognizing the Jewish state. As soon as the PLO went about the business of state building, Hamas challenged Fatah's credentials as the "liberators of Palestine." Hamas soon became the hard-line terrorist Palestinian organization while Fatah, a terror group turned government, struggled for a new identity.

The Fatah constitution envisions the "[c]omplete liberation of Palestine, and eradication of Zionist economic, political, military, and cultural existence."[46] It calls for steadfastness and Arab unity, insisting that Israel did not have a right to exist on what it saw as Palestinian land. Two decades later, when the Fatah-backed PLO recognized Israel, Hamas published its own covenant, calling for a synthesis of Islamism and Palestinian nationalism. It envisioned Palestine as a state run according to the shari'a and declared that when "enemies usurp some Islamic lands, jihad becomes a duty binding on all Muslims."[47]

If Hamas started to work with Israel—quietly and below the radar to ensure that Gaza starts to function for its people—a new Islamist group would have reason to attack the legitimacy of the Hamas government. The new group could draft a new hard-line covenant that eclipsed the radicalism of Hamas, relegating it to the role of a more "moderate" organization.

What group could fill that role? Historically, no faction can match Hamas or even Fatah in terms of size, firepower, or popularity. But during the battles between Hamas and Fatah in 2007, analysts began to detail the rise of the Islamist group Hizb ut-Tahrir (Liberation Party), which organized a series of demonstrations throughout the West Bank in opposition to the Annapolis peace talks. One analyst documented the group's "slow emergence from eccentric obscurity" among Palestinian factions. Although the group did not maintain an armed wing, it placed significant emphasis on *dawa,* or outreach, much like Yassin's Islamic Center (*mujamma'*) of the 1970s and 1980s, which was the foundation of the Hamas terrorist organization.[48] Other journalists noted that the group was "growing more visible" and "filling a hole left by Hamas in the West Bank."[49]

Nearly one year into the Hamas-Fatah split, Hizb ut-Tahrir had no short-term potential to eclipse either of the warring Palestinian factions. But Palestinian history, as noted throughout this book, has consisted of several tragic cycles. The conditions remain ripe for another faction to emerge from the chaos, much as Hamas did during the intifada of 1987.

CONCLUSION

BETWEEN *FITNA* AND FULFILLMENT

According to a November 2007 poll conducted by a Ramallah polling firm, 83 percent of Gazans believed that the overall state of the Gaza Strip had deteriorated since the Hamas coup. More than two-thirds of Gazans were concerned for their own personal safety as well as the safety of their families and their property. More than half felt that they were unable to voice their opinions freely since the takeover. Finally, 94 percent of all Gazans surveyed believed that the economy had gotten worse since the June civil war.[1]

But the greatest frustration, according to Mustafa Barghouti, a member of the Palestinian Legislative Council, stemmed from "the polarization between Hamas and Fatah, and the silent majority is angry about this meaningless bloodshed."[2] One advisor to Prime Minister Salaam Fayyad likened the struggle for Gaza to "watching two bald men fight over a comb."[3]

Gaza's Palestinians expressed their frustrations in different ways. According to the Maan News Agency, Palestinians youths in both the West Bank and the Gaza Strip were listening to a popular 90-second rap song on their cell phones slamming both Fatah and Hamas for leaving the Palestinian national vision in shambles: "Either you solve it or leave us. . . . Mahmoud Abbas and Ismael Haniyeh, the Palestinian people are suffering from the civil war." The song derided the Palestinian rival parties and says that their dispute was over power, not Palestinian interests. The tune's producer refused to reveal his identity for fear of retribution by both parties, but Palestinians did not seem to mind playing it.[4]

The *Lebanon Daily Star* also ran a story about a satirical play at the Rashad Shawa Cultural Center in Gaza called *al-Watan* (The Nation). The play was said to be a mock trial of both Hamas and Fatah. Both were found "guilty of killing the people and the nation." The "trial" was tagged with the number 48.67.2007, referring to the three seminal dates in the tragic history of the Palestinian people: the 1948 War of Independence for Israel, the 1967 Six-Day War, and the Palestinian Civil War of 2007. As was the case with the cell phone song, some of the actors and producers of the play feared that Hamas, in particular, might seek vengeance.[5]

In an attempt to not exacerbate the *fitna,* perhaps taking their cue from the reports of the human rights groups, Palestinians seemed to blame Hamas and Fatah equally for the abysmal situation. Still, West Bankers and Gazans alike held out hope that the political and military struggle between their people's two largest factions might soon be settled amicably.

It can be argued, however, with a high degree of confidence, that, to the chagrin of the Palestinians, the "other struggle for Palestine" will remain a bloody subplot to the Palestinian-Israeli conflict for years to come. Likely this will be the case even if the West Bank and Gaza Strip politically are reconnected, or if an Arab-Israeli peace deal is negotiated. The basis for this prediction stems primarily from the fact that 44 percent of all countries emerging from civil war relapse into civil war again in five years.[6] Indeed, one year after the Hamas coup, more than 118 Palestinians had been killed in the Gaza Strip at the hands of other Palestinians. Hundreds of others languished in Hamas jails.[7]

One full year after the coup that toppled Gaza, the bad blood between Fatah and Hamas continued, marked by continuing verbal barbs and violent attacks. Many fighters from the Fatah faction, in particular, have sworn revenge against the members of Hamas who shot their limbs at point-blank range to ensure permanent damage or even amputations. As one Fatah amputee stated, "I know the man who did this to me and it is now my life's ambition to do the same to him." Another Fatah man predicted, "Gaza is going to be a hotspot for vengeance. Blood brings blood."[8]

The continuation of internecine violence can also be predicted by the simple fact that Palestinian culture remains violent. Even the "moderate" Palestinian faction, Fatah, continues to call for the destruction of Israel. To mark the forty-third anniversary of the movement in late 2007, Fatah released a poster that portrays all of Israel as Palestine draped in a Palestinian *keffiyeh,* or headscarf.[9] Abbas himself stated in February 2008 that he would not rule out armed "resistance" against Israel, stating that he took pride in the violent past of his organization.[10]

Fatah's radical Islamic splinter faction, the al-Aqsa Martyrs Brigades, is also a continuing indication of the radicalization that pervades the Fatah faction. The Brigades claimed responsibility for rocket attacks on Israel in February 2008, in retribution for the death of senior Hizbullah leader Imad Mughniyeh, even as Fatah negotiators sat with Israelis to discuss peace.[11] The group also issued a leaflet in December 2007 threatening to murder Palestinian Authority Prime Minister Salaam Fayyad for "collaboration" with Israel and America.[12]

All the while, Hamas has carried out its own trademark acts of violence, highlighted by a constant rain of mortar and Qassam missile fire from Gaza into Israeli territory and even a suicide bombing in the town of Dimona in February 2008. Similarly, the Iranian-backed Palestinian Islamic Jihad continues to threaten violence against Israel, cooperating with Hamas in the launching of rockets when convenient. Other lesser-known factions contribute further to the culture of violence that proliferates and spreads throughout the territories.

Adherents to Palestinian nationalism and Islamism alike repeatedly charge that the violence will continue unless there is a just settlement to the Palestinian-Israeli conflict. But it can also be said that the continuation of violence makes a just settlement impossible to achieve. Indeed, without nonviolent brands of Palestinian nationalism, the task of peacemaking becomes all the more challenging.

Dangerous and violent Palestinian ideologies threaten the future of the Palestinians as much as the future of the Israelis. Indeed, when extremists with weapons take the law into their own hands, even when their violence is directed at an outside actor, there is always the risk of detrimental, unintended consequences. As the United States learned in the 1980s, when it funded the mujahideen of Afghanistan to fight the Soviets, those fighters chose to continue their jihad under the banner of al-Qaeda in other countries, such as Algeria and Chechnya, and even launch attacks against the United States. The House of Saud learned a similar lesson in the first years of the twenty-first century when, after years of sponsoring Wahhabism and financing extremism worldwide, a group known as al-Qaeda in the Arabian Peninsula began to launch attacks against the Saudi kingdom.

The lessons from these ill-fated initiatives can be applied to the Palestinian model. Each time the Palestinians launched a round of violence against Israel, whether through uprisings or campaigns of terror, the violence invariably infected the Palestinian population, leading to self-destruction and ultimately civil strife. Should the Palestinians decide not to rectify this problem and continue to reject the path of nonviolence as a solution to the Palestinian-Israeli conflict, the West Bank and Gaza are almost certainly destined to repeat their tragic pasts.

In the spring of 2008, the primary Palestinian factions sent delegations to Egypt to discuss a truce. The talks sputtered, primarily over the fact that Hamas refused to lay down its arms. Predictably, Hamas and Fatah exchanged barbs over the terms of an agreement that would bring an end to the bloodshed.

"Hamas leaders seek martyrdom and would never bargain over the blood of their people like others do," said Hamas spokesman Sami Abu Zuhri, in a clear reference to Fatah.[13]

In early June, one year after the Palestinian Authority fell in Gaza, Abbas made a televised speech, expressing anew his desire for national unity. Analysts immediately noted that his demands for Hamas to rescind control of Gaza were notably missing.[14]

Abbas called for "a national dialogue to implement the Yemeni initiative . . . to end the internal division that harms our people." He stated that if the talks succeeded, he would "call for new legislative and presidential elections."[15]

Days later, it was reported that Hamas and Fatah had completed three days of discussions in Dakar, Senegal. Talk of significant progress was muted, but both sides announced that there would be continued meetings.[16]

The desire for Palestinian unity likely played a role in these new talks, but it soon became apparent that a looming Israeli invasion may have done more to bring the two sides together. According to the London-based Arabic daily *Al-Quds Al-Arabi*, Abbas launched this bid for reconciliation after he was informed of Israeli plans to conquer the Gaza Strip in a large-scale operation.[17] In what appeared to be a last ditch effort to fend off an Israeli invasion that would undoubtedly inflict further hardship on the Gaza population, the Arab League also urged the sides to unify.[18]

Sadly, as conflict threatened, the few but significant Palestinian voices for moderation were drowned out by the drumbeat of war. Indeed, there were several political alternatives to both Hamas and Fatah struggling to be heard.

As described in London's *ash-Sharq al-Awsat* Arabic-language newspaper, Palestinian businessman Munib al-Masri and Palestinian politician Hassan Khreisheh had a new political vision for their people.[19] Al-Masri, a U.S.-educated, 73-year-old billionaire, sought to reach out to the business class of the Palestinian people—the people who wanted to prevent violence in order to protect their investments. Backed by Khreishneh's political savvy, al-Masri inaugurated *Muntada Filastin* (Palestine Forum) by teleconference between Ramallah and Gaza in November. His goal was to make his new group a political party in time for the next elections.[20]

In addition, in March 2007, Mohammed Dajani, the director of the American Studies Institute at the Jerusalem-based al-Quds University, created a party known as *Wassatia*, which means "middle ground" or "moderation." Dajani believed that most Palestinians were burdened by the political visions of factions that did not accurately represent their beliefs. Dajani's party was the only one that did not demand the right of return for all Palestinians displaced by Arab-Israeli wars, a "right" that essentially is a euphemism for the demographic destruction of the State of Israel. *Wassatia* defined itself as an Islamic party but refrained from the fiery rhetoric so common in other Islamic platforms.[21]

Both *Wassatia* and the Palestine Forum were an improvement on the failed Third Way, a party created by Fatah's Salaam Fayyad and noted PLO spokesperson Hanan Ashrawi. Formed in anticipation of the January 2006 elections, this new faction promised to fight the corruption and bad governance that Palestinians almost unanimously associated with Fatah.[22] However, Third Way was full of familiar faces and even more familiar promises. The party received less than 3 percent of the vote in the elections, earning just 2 out of 132 seats in the Palestinian legislature. After the Gaza coup, Abbas named Salaam Fayyad prime minister of the new emergency government, effectively putting Third Way out of business.

To date, neither *Wassatia* nor Palestine Forum has achieved any measure of success in the Palestinian political arena. Hamas and Fatah remain the dominant factions. Indeed, the seemingly endless civil war that continues between Hamas and Fatah in both the West Bank and Gaza Strip leaves little opportunity for new voices.

More to the point, the factional fighting between Hamas and Fatah has overshadowed the very voice of the Palestinian people. Amid their verbal sniping and intermittent clashes, these two warring factions have stopped only occasionally to call for Palestinian independence. Thus, as one analyst for al-Jazeera noted, "The rivalry between Fatah and Hamas had eclipsed demands for putting forward a Palestinian negotiating strategy."[23] The leadership of both Hamas and Fatah have failed to recognize an immutable truth: So long as their internal struggle persists, a negotiated settlement to the Palestinian-Israeli conflict will always be elusive.

The following summer, a series of bombings attributed to Fatah reignited the intra-Palestinian war.[24] While Hamas was often vilified as the aggressor, one frustrated Palestinian quipped, "Hamas is Fatah with beards."[25] In early August 2008, the Hamas-Fatah conflict deteriorated while the shaky ceasefire between Hamas and Israel held. An Israeli invasion of Gaza appeared unavoidable, however, after reports indicated that Hamas was rearming and preparing for confrontation.[26] The future of the Palestinian-Israeli conflict and the Hamas-Fatah conflict hung in the balance.

ABOUT THE AUTHOR

Jonathan Schanzer, the director of policy at the Jewish Policy Center, is an internationally recognized analyst of Middle East affairs and terrorism. He recently served as a counterterrorism analyst for the Office of Intelligence and Analysis at the U.S. Department of the Treasury. Prior to joining the Treasury, he was a research fellow at the Washington Institute for Near East Policy, where he authored the book *Al-Qaeda's Armies: Middle East Affiliate Groups and the Next Generation of Terror* (2004). Mr. Schanzer got his start in the policy world as a research fellow at the Middle East Forum, a Philadelphia-based think tank headed by scholar Daniel Pipes.

The author holds a bachelor's degree from Emory University and a master's degree from the Hebrew University of Jerusalem in Middle Eastern studies. He also studied Arabic at the American University in Cairo in 2001. He is currently a Ph.D. candidate at Kings College, documenting the history of the United States Congress and its efforts to combat terrorism.

Mr. Schanzer has published numerous scholarly journal articles and national newspaper editorials. He has appeared with frequency on American television channels, such as Fox News, as well as Arab television channels, such as al-Jazeera. Mr. Schanzer has traveled widely in Iraq, Yemen, Egypt, Morocco, Kuwait, Qatar, Turkey, Jordan, Israel, and the Palestinian Territories. He speaks Arabic and Hebrew.

NOTES

FOREWORD

1. Asaf Romirowsky and Jonathan Calt Harris, "Arafat Minion as Professor," *Washington Times,* July 9, 2004.
2. For a recent and notable exception, see Hillel Cohen, *Army of Shadows: Palestinian Collaboration with Zionism, 1917–1948* (Los Angeles: University of California Press, 2008).
3. Izz al-Din Al-Qassam Brigades Web site, "In January 2008 Al Qassam Brigades fired 540 rocket and missile and killed two Zionists," February 2, 2008.
4. CNN, "'Dozens Hurt' in Gaza Border Clashes," January 27, 2008.
5. An excellent case study of this phenomenon can be found in Erik R. Nelson and Alan F. H. Wisdom, *Human Rights Advocacy in the Mainline Protestant Churches (2000–2003)* (Washington, D.C.: Institute on Religion & Democracy, 2004).
6. Jonathan Schanzer, "The Challenge of Hamas to Fatah," *Middle East Quarterly* (Spring 2003).
7. Jonathan Schanzer, "Palestinian Uprisings Compared," *Middle East Quarterly* (Summer 2002).
8. Jonathan Schanzer, "A Gaza-West Bank Split? Why the Palestinian Territories Might Become Two Separate States," *Middle East Intelligence Bulletin* (July 2001).

INTRODUCTION

1. Rashid Khalidi, *Palestinian Identity: The Construction of Modern National Consciousness* (New York: Columbia University Press, 1997), p. 193.
2. Reporters Sans Frontieres, "North Korea, Turkmenistan, Eritrea the Worst Violators of Press Freedom," *Annual Worldwide Press Freedom Index 2006,* www.rsf.org/article.php3?id_article=19388.
3. Mahmood Monshipouri, "The PLO Rivalry with Hamas: The Challenge of Peace, Democratization and Islamic Radicalism." *Middle East Policy* 4, No. 3 (1996): 84–105.
4. Don Peretz, *Intifada: The Palestinian Uprising* (Boulder, CO: Westview Press, 1990), pp. 100–101.
5. Martin Kramer, *Ivory Towers on Sand: The Failure of Middle Eastern Studies in America* (Washington, D.C.: Washington Institute for Near East Policy, 2001).
6. Augustus Richard Norton and Sara Roy, "Yes, You Can Work with Hamas," *Christian Science Monitor,* July 17, 2007, www.csmonitor.com/2007/0717/p09s02-coop.html.
7. Maan News Agency, "333 Palestinians Killed in Hamas-Fatah Infighting this Year, B'tselem Says," November 21, 2007, www.maannews.net/en/index.php?opr=ShowDetails&ID=26410.

8. Daniel Pipes, "How Many Islamists?" http://www.danielpipes.org/blog/2005/05/how-many-islamists.html.

9. These thinkers included Sayyid Abul Ala Maududi (1903–1979), Jamal al-Din al-Afghani (1838–1897), Muhammad Abdu' (1865–1905), and Rashid Rida (1865–1935), among others.

10. Hamas charter, Article 15, www.islamonline.net/Arabic/doc/2004/03/article11.SHTML (Arabic), www.yale.edu/lawweb/avalon/mideast/hamas.htm (English).

11. For more, see Elie Kedourie, *Nationalism* (London: Blackwell Publishing, 1993).

12. Wolfgang G. Schwanitz, "Amin al-Hussaini and the Holocaust: What Did the Grand Mufti Know?" *World Politics Review,* May 8, 2008. http://www.worldpoliticsreview.com/article.aspx?id=2082

13. Gilles Kepel, *Jihad: The Trail of Political Islam,* 2nd edition (Cambridge, MA: Harvard University Press, 2002), p. 242.

14. J. Paul De B. Taillon, *Hijacking and Hostages: Government Responses to Terrorism* (Westport, CT: Praeger, 2002), p. 15.

CHAPTER ONE

1. Richard P. Mitchell, *The Society of the Muslim Brothers* (Oxford: Oxford University Press, 1969), pp. 4–5.

2. John Zimmerman, "Sayyid Qutb's Influence on the 11 September Attacks," *Terrorism and Political Violence,* 16, No. 2 (April–June 2004): pp. 222–252.

3. Bat Ye'or, *Islam and Dhimmitude: Where Civilizations Collide* (Cranbury, NJ: Fairleigh Dickinson University Press, 2002).

4. Iyad Barghouti, "Islamist Movements in Historical Palestine," *Islamic Fundamentalism,* ed. Abdel Salam Sidahmed and Anoushiravan Ehteshami (Boulder, CO: Westview Press, 1996), p. 163.

5. Azzam Tamimi, *Hamas: A History from Within* (Northampton, MA: Olive Branch Press, 2007), p. 5.

6. Alan Hart, *Arafat: A Political Biography* (Bloomington: Indiana University Press, 1989), p. 79.

7. Hans Wehr, *A Dictionary of Modern Written Arabic,* 3rd ed., ed. J. Milton Cowan (London: MacDonald & Evans Ltd., 1980), p. 693.

8. Said K. Aburish, *Arafat: From Defender to Dictator* (London: Bloomsbury, 1998), pp. 40–41.

9. Danny Rubinstein, *The Mystery of Arafat* (South Royalton, VT: Steerforth Press, 1995), pp. 52–53.

10. Mark Tessler, *A History of the Israeli-Palestinian Conflict* (Bloomington: Indiana University Press, 1994), p. 377.

11. Ehud Yaari, *Strike Terror: The Story of Fatah* (New York: Sabra Books, 1970), pp. 67–86.

12. Ibid., pp. 98–111.

13. Ibid., p. 111.

14. Charles D. Smith, *Palestine and the Arab-Israeli Conflict* (New York: St. Martin's Press, 1992), p. 196.

15. "Arafat's Notable Words on War and Peace," *Arab News* (Saudi Arabia), November 5, 2004, www.arabnews.com/?page=9&section=0&article=54003&d=5&m=11&y=2004.

16. Tamimi, *Hamas,* pp. 39–40.

17. Ibid., p. 5.

18. David Hirst, "Obituary: Sheikh Ahmed Yassin," *The Guardian*, March 23, 2004, www .guardian.co.uk/israel/Story/0,1175854,00.html.

19. Ziad Abu-Amr, *Islamic Fundamentalism in the West Bank and Gaza: Muslim Brotherhood and Islamic Jihad* (Bloomington: Indiana University Press, 1994), p. xvii.

20. Glenn E. Robinson, *Building a Palestinian State: The Incomplete Revolution* (Bloomington: Indiana University Press, 1997), p. 148.

CHAPTER 2

1. Mark Tessler, *A History of the Israeli-Palestinian Conflict* (Bloomington: Indiana University Press, 1994), pp. 678–679.

2. Ibid., p. 689.

3. Michel Jubran and Laura Drake, "The Islamic Fundamentalist Movement in the West Bank and Gaza Strip," *Middle East Policy*, 2, No. 2 (1993): 7.

4. "December 14 is a Historical Date in the Palestinian Struggle for Freedom," Hamas Web site, December 14, 2007, www.alqassam.ps/english/?action=showdetail&fid=765.

5. Matt Levitt, *Hamas: Politics, Charity and Terrorism in the Service of Jihad* (New Haven, CT: Yale University Press, 2006), p. 24.

6. Gilles Kepel, *Jihad: The Trail of Political Islam,* 2nd ed. (London: I. B. Taurus, 2002), p. 155.

7. Zaki Chehab, *Inside Hamas: The Untold Story of the Militant Islamic Movement* (New York: Nation Books, 2007), p. 30.

8. Ibid., pp. 33–34.

9. Azzam Tamimi, *Hamas: A History from Within.* (Northampton, MA: Olive Branch Press, 2007), p. 189.

10. Chehab, *Inside Hamas,* pp. 33–34.

11. Meir Hatina, *Islam and Salvation in Palestine,* Dayan Center Papers No. 127 (Tel Aviv: Moshe Dayan Center for Middle Eastern and African Studies, 2001), p. 79.

12. Fatah Constitution, www.fateh.net/e_public/constitution.htm (Arabic); www.ipcri.org /files/fatah1964.html (English). See Article 12.

13. Tessler, *A History of the Israeli-Palestinian Conflict*, pp. 692–695.

14. Ziad Abu-Amr, *Islamic Fundamentalism in the West Bank and Gaza: Muslim Brotherhood and Islamic Jihad* (Bloomington: Indiana University Press, 1994), p. 88.

15. Raphael Israeli, *Palestinians Between Nationalism and Islam,* (London: Vallentine and Mitchell, 2008), p.61.

16. Hamas charter, www.islamonline.net/Arabic/doc/2004/03/article11.SHTML (Arabic); www.yale.edu/lawweb/avalon/mideast/hamas.htm (English). See Article 15.

17. Tessler, *A History of the Israeli-Palestinian Conflict*, p. 715.

18. Glenn E. Robinson, *Building a Palestinian State: The Incomplete Revolution* (Bloomington: Indiana University Press, 1997), p. 169.

19. Tessler, *A History of the Israeli-Palestinian Conflict*, p. 722.

20. Abu-Amr, *Islamic Fundamentalism in the West Bank and Gaza,* p. 83.

CHAPTER 3

1. Shaul Mishal and Avraham Sela, *The Palestinian Hamas: Vision, Violence and Coexistence* (New York: Columbia University Press, 2000), p. 21.

2. Youssef Aboul-Enein, "Hamas: A Further Exploration of Jihadist Tactics," *Strategic Insights* 4, No. 9 (September 2005), www.ccc.nps.navy.mil/si/2005/Sep/aboul-eneinSep05.asp.

3. Haim Malka, "Hamas: Resistance and Transformation of Palestinian Society," in *Understanding Islamic Charities*, ed. Jon B. Alterman and Karin Von Hippel (Washington, DC: Center for Strategic and International Studies, 2007), p. 101.

4. Ziad Abu Amr, *Islamic Fundamentalism in the West Bank and Gaza: Muslim Brotherhood and Islamic Jihad* (Bloomington: Indiana University Press, 1994), p. 59.

5. Anat Kurz and Nahman Tal, *Hamas: Radical Islam in a National Struggle*, Jaffe Center for Strategic Studies, Memorandum No. 48 (July 1997), p. 28.

6. Mishal and Sela, *The Palestinian Hamas*, p. 60.

7. This is according to information published on www.palestine-info.net/hamas/index .htm.

8. Zaki Chehab, *Inside Hamas: The Untold Story of the Militant Islamic Movement* (New York: Nation Books, 2007), p. 15.

9. Matthew Levitt, *Hamas: Politics, Charity and Terrorism in the Service of Jihad* (New Haven, CT: Yale University Press, 2006), pp. 75–76.

10. Azzam Tamimi, *Hamas: A History from Within* (Northampton, MA: Olive Branch Press, 2007), p. 63.

11. Ibid., p. 61.

12. Mishal and Sela, *The Palestinian Hamas*, p. 19.

13. Boaz Ganor, "Hamas—The Islamic Resistance Movement in the Territories," *Survey of Arab Affairs*, February 2, 1992, p. 5.

14. Michel Jubran and Laura Drake, "The Islamic Fundamentalist Movement in the West Bank and Gaza Strip," *Middle East Policy* 2, No. 2 (1993): 12.

15. Ze'ev Schiff and Ehud Ya'ari, *Intifada: The Palestinian Uprising—Israel's Third Front* (New York: Simon and Schuster, 1989), p. 239.

16. Mishal and Sela, *The Palestinian Hamas*, p. 58.

17. Yonah Alexander, "Hamas," *Middle East Terrorism: Selected Group Profiles* (Washington, DC: Jewish Institute for National Security Affairs, 1994), p. 21.

18. Testimony of R. James Woolsey, Director of Central Intelligence, Hearing before the Select Committee on Intelligence, U.S. Senate, January 10, 1995.

19. Abu Amr, *Islamic Fundamentalism in the West Bank and Gaza*, pp. 86–87.

CHAPTER 4

1. For more, see "Ezedeen al-Qassam Brigades," Hamas Web site, www.alqassam.ps /english/?action=aboutus.

2. Anat Kurz and Nahman Tal, *Hamas: Radical Islam in a National Struggle*, Jaffe Center for Strategic Studies, Memorandum No. 48 (July 1997): 29.

3. Meir Hatina, *Islam and Salvation in Palestine*, Dayan Center Papers No. 127 (Tel Aviv: Moshe Dayan Center for Middle Eastern and African Studies, 2001), p. 82.

4. Kurz and Tal, *Hamas*, p. 30.

5. Zaki Chehab, *Inside Hamas: The Untold Story of the Militant Islamic Movement* (New York: Nation Books, 2007), p. 105.

6. Palestinian Center for Policy and Survey Research, Public Opinion Poll No. 2, Palestinian Elections, October 5–10, 1993, www.pcpsr.org/survey/cprspolls/94/poll2a.html.

7. Edward Said, *The Politics of Dispossession: The Struggle for Palestinian Self-Determination, 1969–1994* (New York: Vintage Books, 1994), p. 192.

8. Amira Hass, *Drinking the Sea at Gaza: Days and Nights in a Land Under Siege* (New York: Metropolitan Books, 1996), p.75; and Kurz and Tal, *Hamas*, p. 29.

9. Hatina, *Islam and Salvation in Palestine*, p. 83.

10. Congressional Research Services, "Hamas: The Organizations, Goals and Tactics of a Militant Palestinian Organization," October 14, 1993, www.fas.org/irp/crs/931014-hamas.htm.
11. Edgar O'Ballance, *Islamic Fundamentalist Terrorism, 1979–1995: The Iranian Connection* (New York: New York University Press, 1997), p. 133.
12. Azzam Tamimi, *Hamas: A History from Within* (Northampton, MA: Olive Branch Press, 2007), p. 75.
13. Chehab, *Inside Hamas*, pp. 129–130.
14. Anand Gopal, "Mideast: Hamas Flag Goes Up in Lebanon Camps," Inter Press Service, September 5, 2007, http://ipsnews.net/news.asp?idnews=39148.
15. Bernard Rougier, *Everyday Jihad: The Rise of Militant Islam among Palestinians in Lebanon* (Cambridge, MA: Harvard University Press, 2007), p. 155.
16. David Firestone, "Mideast Flare-Up: The Money Trail; F.B.I. Traces Hamas's Plan to Finance Attacks to '93," *New York Times*, December 6, 2001, http://query.nytimes.com/gst/fullpage.html?res=9905E1DA153CF935A35751C1A9679C8B63.
17. Marwan Bishara, "The Undeclared Palestinian Civil War," *Middle East Online* (UK), November 15, 2007, www.middle-east-online.com/english/?id=23095.
18. Mehran Kamrava, "What Stands between the Palestinians and Democracy," *Middle East Quarterly* 6, No. 2 (June 1999), www.meforum.org/article/456.
19. Samih K. Farsoun and Christina E. Zacharia, *Palestine and the Palestinians* (Boulder, CO: Westview Press, 1997), p. 196.
20. Shaul Mishal and Avraham Sela, *The Palestinian Hamas: Vision, Violence and Coexistence* (New York: Columbia University Press, 2000), p. 2.
21. Palestinian Center for Policy and Survey Research, Public Opinion Poll No. 1, "The Palestinian-Israeli Agreement: 'Gaza-Jericho First,'" September 10–11, 1993, www.pcpsr.org/survey/cprspolls/94/poll1.html.
22. Yohanan Ramati, "Islamic Fundamentalism Gaining," *Midstream* 39, No. 2 (February/March 1993): 2.
23. Hazhir Teimourian, "Not Looking Forward to a New Era in Iran," *The World Today* 53, No. 5 (1997): 125.
24. Mohammad Mohaddessin, *Islamic Fundamentalism: The New Global Threat* (Washington, DC: Seven Locks Press, 1993), p. 127.
25. Martin Kramer, "The Moral Logic of Hizbullah," in *The Origins of Terrorism*, ed. Walter Reich (Washington, D.C.: Woodrow Wilson Center Press, 1998), p. 148.
26. Bishara, "The Undeclared Palestinian Civil War."
27. Raphael Israeli, *Palestinians Between Nationalism and Islam* (London: Vallentine Mitchell, 2008), pp. 119–146.
28. Said K. Aburish, *Arafat: From Defender to Dictator* (London: Bloomsbury, 1998), p. 275.
29. Tamimi, *Hamas*, p. 190.
30. Ibid., pp. 82–84.
31. Chehab, *Inside Hamas*, pp. 113–114, 224.
32. "The First Engineer . . . Yahya Ayyash," official Hamas Web site, December 4, 2006, www.alqassam.ps/english/?action=showdetail&fid=39.
33. Tamimi, *Hamas*, p. 89.
34. Ibid., p. 112.
35. Chehab, *Inside Hamas*, p. 115.
36. Ely Karmon, "Hamas' Terrorism Strategy: Operational Limitations and Political Restraints," *Middle East Review of International Affairs* 4, No. 1, March 4, 2000, pp. 1–2, http://meria.idc.ac.il/journal/2000/issue1/jv4n1a7.html.

37. Chehab, *Inside Hamas,* pp. 107–110.
38. Karmon, "Hamas' Terrorism Strategy," p. 5.
39. Matthew Levitt, *Hamas: Politics, Charity and Terrorism in the Service of Jihad* (New Haven, CT: Yale University Press, 2006), p. 115.
40. Bishara, "The Undeclared Palestinian Civil War."
41. P. R. Kumaraswamy, "The Jordan-Hamas Divorce," *Middle East Intelligence Bulletin* 3, No. 8 (August–September 2001), www.meib.org/articles/0108_me1.htm.
42. Reuven Paz, "Hamas's Lessons from Lebanon," *Policywatch,* no. 262, Washington Institute for Near East Policy, May 25, 2000, www.washingtoninstitute.org/templateC05.php ?CID=1953.
43. U.S. Department of State, *Patterns of Global Terrorism 1999* (April 2000), www.state .gov/www/global/terrorism/1999report/appb.htm.
44. Karmon, "Hamas' Terrorism Strategy."

CHAPTER 5

1. Charles Krauthammer, "Arafat's War," *Washington Post,* October 6, 2000.
2. Kenneth Stein, "The Intifadah and the 1936–1939 Uprising: A Comparison," *Journal of Palestine Studies* 76 (1990): 64–85.
3. Baruch Kimmerling and Joel S. Migdal, *Palestinians: The Making of a People* (New York: Free Press, 1993), p. 123.
4. Taysir Nashif, "Palestinian Arab and Jewish Leadership in the Mandate Period," *Journal of Palestine Studies* 6, No. 4 (Summer 1977): 113–121.
5. Yehoshua Porath, "The Political Organization of the Palestinian Arabs under the British Mandate," *Palestinian Arab Politics,* ed. Moshe Maoz (Jerusalem: Academic Press, 1975), p. 17.
6. Kimmerling and Migdal, *Palestinians,* p. 115.
7. Kenneth Stein, "The Intifadah and the Uprising of 1936–1939: A Comparison of the Palestinian Arab Communities," *The Intifadah: Its Impact on Israel, the Arab World and the Superpowers,* ed. Robert O. Freedman (Miami: Florida International University Press, 1991), p. 25.
8. Kimmerling and Migdal, *Palestinians,* p. 115.
9. Charles D. Smith, *Palestine and the Arab-Israeli Conflict* (New York: St. Martin's Press, 1992), p. 101; Porath, "The Political Organization of the Palestinian Arabs under the British Mandate," p. 18.
10. Matthias Küntzel, "National Socialism and Anti-Semitism in the Arab World," *Jewish Political Studies Review* (Spring 2005), www.matthiaskuentzel.de/contents/national-socialism-and-anti-semitism-in-the-arab-world.
11. Kimmerling and Migdal, *Palestinians,* p. 116.
12. Rashid Khalidi, *Palestinian Identity: The Construction of Modern National Consciousness* (New York: Columbia University Press, 1997), p. 115.
13. Ibid., p. 195.
14. Kimmerling and Migdal, *Palestinians,* p. 97.
15. Ibid., quoting W. F. Abboushi.
16. Stein, "The Intifadah and the Uprising of 1936–1939: A Comparison of the Palestinian Arab Communities," p. 19.
17. Edward Said, *The Politics of Dispossession: The Struggle for Palestinian Self-Determination, 1969–1994* (New York: Vintage Books, 1994), p. 197.
18. Ibid., p. 274.

19. Don Peretz, *Intifada: The Palestinian Uprising* (Boulder, CO.: Westview Press, 1990), p. 99.

20. Said, *The Politics of Dispossession,* p. 166.

21. Barry Rubin and Judith Colp Rubin, *Yasir Arafat: A Political Biography* (New York: Oxford University Press, 2003), p. 119.

22. Said K. Aburish, *Arafat: From Defender to Dictator* (London: Bloomsbury, 1998), p. 220.

23. Yizhar Be'er and Saleh 'Abdel-Jawad, *Collaborators in the Occupied Territories: Human Rights Abuses and Violations,* B'Tselem, (January 1994), www.btselem.org/Download /199401_Collaboration_Suspects_Eng.doc, pp. 101–102.

24. Bard E. O'Neill, "The Intifada in the Context of Armed Struggle," *The Intifadah: Its Impact on Israel, the Arab World and the Superpowers,* ed. Robert O. Freedman (Miami: Florida International University Press, 1991), pp. 57–58.

25. David Pollock, "The American Response to the Intifada," *The Intifadah: Its Impact on Israel, the Arab World and the Superpowers,* ed. Robert O. Freedman (Miami: Florida International University Press, 1991), p. 130.

26. Ze'ev Schiff and Ehud Yaari, *Intifada: The Palestinian Uprising—Israel's Third Front* (New York: Simon and Schuster, 1989), p. 148.

27. Associated Press, August 20, 2001, http://detnews.com/2001/nation/0108/21/a07–2734 42.htm.

28. Schiff and Yaari, *Intifada,* pp. 148 and 256.

29. Peretz, *Intifada,* p. 91.

30. Ibid., pp. 96 and 103.

31. Edward Said, "Intifada and Independence," *Social Text,* No. 22 (Spring 1989): 23–39.

32. Peretz, *Intifada,* pp. 84–86.

33. Ibid., p. 84.

34. "Minors Killed Since 9 December 1987," www.btselem.org/English/Statistics/Minors _Killed.asp.

35. Justine McCabe, "Sowing Seeds of War," *Hartford Courant,* January 1, 2000, www .ctgreens.org/articles/sowing_010101.html, citing a 1990 Swedish nongovernmental organization report.

36. Stein, "The Intifadah and the Uprising of 1936–1939: A Comparison," p. 17, quoting Yitzhak Rabin interview, December 15, 1989.

37. Peretz, *Intifada,* pp. 100–101.

38. "Palestinian Speaker Decries Sharon's Visit to Temple Mount," *People's Daily* (China), September 29, 2000, http://english.peopledaily.com.cn/english/200009/29/eng20000929 _51511.html.

39. United Press International, "Was the Intifada Planned?" March 10, 2001.

40. Matthew Levitt, *Targeting Terror: U.S. Policy toward Middle Eastern State Sponsors and Terrorist Organizations, Post-September 11* (Washington, DC: Washington Institute for Near East Policy, 2002), p. 86.

41. Agence France Presse, "Palestinian Death Toll from Intifada Stands at 2,647: Official," August 13, 2003, www.reliefweb.int/rw/rwb.nsf/AllDocsByUNID/1aefb71ae8492212492 56d820011d185.

42. "Minors Killed Since 9 December 1987."

43. Defense for Children International, www.dci-pal.org/english/dcipress/releases/2001 /0024.html.

44. Matthew Levitt, *Hamas: Politics, Charity and Terrorism in the Service of Jihad* (New Haven, CT: Yale University Press, 2006), p. 127, citing Israeli Ministry of Foreign Affairs report.

45. "Palestinian Camps Train Young Guerrillas," *Pittsburgh Post-Gazette*, August 7, 2000.
46. Justus Weiner, "Child Abuse in the Palestinian Authority," *Jerusalem Post*, October 3, 2002.
47. Author's interview with Khairi Abaza, Washington, D.C., January 30, 2008.
48. Ned Parker, "After Year of Intifada, Families Take Law into Their Own Hands," Agence France Presse, October 17, 2001.
49. For a list of collaborator killings, see www.phrmg.org/aqsa/collaborators.htm.
50. CNN, "Three Shot to Death in Palestinian Military Court," February 5, 2002, at www.cnn.com/2002/WORLD/meast/02/05/trial.shooting/index.html.
51. Patrick Graham, "Collaboration Hysteria Sweeps West Bank, Gaza," *National Post* (Canada), September 4, 2001.
52. Matt Rees, "The Enemy Within," *Time*, August 27, 2001.
53. Larry Kaplow, "Aiding the Enemy Brings Harsh Justice," *Austin* (TX) *American States-man*, August 7, 2001.
54. Isabel Kershner, "One Step Away from Chaos," *Jerusalem Report*, April 25, 2001.
55. Salah al-Naimi, "Hamas: The 20-Year Struggle," *ash-Sharq al-Awsat*, December 24, 2007, www.asharqalawsat.com/english/news.asp?section=3&id=11246.
56. Khalil Shikaki, "Palestinians Divided," *Foreign Affairs* (January–February 2002): 89-93.
57. Arieh O'Sullivan, "IDF Warns PA Losing Control of Gaza Strip," *Jerusalem Post*, November 19, 2001.
58. Sandra Cotenta, "Arafat's Regime in Shambles," *Toronto Star*, November 11, 2001.
59. Tom Rose, "Arafat's Naval Adventure," *Weekly Standard*, January 21, 2002.
60. Hasan al-Kashif, cited in Daniel Sobleman, "Palestinian Writer Charges that PA Officials Are Leaving the Country," *Haaretz*, September 5, 2001.
61. Rose, "Arafat's Naval Adventure."
62. Amira Hass, "Hamas Blamed for Attacks against Gaza," *Haaretz*, October 15, 2000.
63. Uriya Shavit and Jalal Bana, "The Secret Exodus—Palestinian Immigration," *Haaretz* (magazine), October 5, 2001.

CHAPTER 6

1. Haim Malka, "Hamas: Resistance and Transformation of Palestinian Society," in *Understanding Islamic Charities*, ed. Jon B. Alterman and Karin Von Hippel (Washington, DC: Center for Strategic and International Studies, 2007), p. 106.
2. Matthew Levitt, *Hamas: Politics, Charity and Terrorism in the Service of Jihad* (New Haven, CT: Yale University Press, 2006), pp. 116–117.
3. Boaz Ganor, "Hamas—The Islamic Resistance Movement in the Territories," *Survey of Arab Affairs*, February 2, 1992, p. 7.
4. Graham Usher, "The Rise of Political Islam in the Occupied Territories, *Middle East International*, No. 453, June 25, 1993, p. 20.
5. Michel Jubran and Laura Drake, "The Islamic Fundamentalist Movement in the West Bank and Gaza Strip," *Middle East Policy* 2, No. 2 (1993): 13.
6. Clyde Haberman, "P.L.O. Moderate Shot Dead, Raising Fears on Pact," *New York Times*, October 22, 1993, http://query.nytimes.com/gst/fullpage.html?res=9F0CE5DF1F31F93 1A15753C1A965958260.
7. Mark Tessler, *A History of the Israeli-Palestinian Conflict* (Bloomington: Indiana University Press, 1994), p. 758.
8. Zaki Chehab, *Inside Hamas: The Untold Story of the Militant Islamic Movement* (New York: Nation Books, 2007), p. 80.

9. "FM Peres Reaction to Afula Attack," Israel Ministry of Foreign Affairs, April 6, 1994, www.mfa.gov.il/MFA/Archive/Speeches/FM%20PERES%20REACTION%20TO%20 AFULA%20ATTACK%20-%2006-Apr–94.

10. Amira Hass, *Drinking the Sea at Gaza: Days and Nights in a Land under Siege* (New York: Metropolitan Books, 1996), p. 77.

11. Clyde Haberman, "Arafat's Forces Arrange a Truce with Militants," *New York Times,* November 20, 1994, http://query.nytimes.com/gst/fullpage.html?res=9505E4DA1131F933 A15752C1A962958260.

12. Hass, *Drinking the Sea at Gaza,* p. 84.

13. "Amnesty International Annual Report 1996," www.amnesty.org/ailib/aireport/ar96 /index.html.

14. Haim Malka, "Hamas," p. 111.

15. Khaled Abu Toameh, "Abbas: Hamas Planning W. Bank Takeover," *Jerusalem Post,* October 28, 2007, www.jpost.com/servlet/Satellite?cid=1192380675509&pagename=JPost %2FJPArticle%2FShowFull.

16. Barry Rubin and Judith Colp Rubin, *Yasir Arafat: A Political Biography* (New York: Oxford University Press, 2003), p. 180.

17. Hass, *Drinking the Sea at Gaza,* p. 76.

18. Chehab, *Inside Hamas,* pp. 6, 113–114, 224.

19. Ali El-Saleh, "Interview with Hamas's Said Siyam," *Ash-Sharq al-Awsat,* November 25, 2007, www.asharqalawsat.com/english/news.asp?section=3&id=10988.

20. "Arafat Arrests Hamas Leaders: Angered Militants Promise to Resume Bombings," CNN news, March 9, 1996. www.cnn.com/WORLD/9603/jerusalem_blast/03–09/index.html.

21. Hass, *Drinking the Sea at Gaza,* p. 91.

22. Lisa Beyer and Aharon Klein, "The West Bank," *Time,* June 15, 1998, www.time.com /time/magazine/article/0,9171,988529,00.html.

23. "Palestinian Authority Arrests Hamas Leader Rantisi," CNN.com, April 9, 1998, www .cnn.com/WORLD/meast/9804/09/hamas.arrest/.

24. Azzam Tamimi, *Hamas: A History from Within* (Northampton, MA: Olive Branch Press, 2007), pp.112–114.

25. Amnesty International, "Palestinian Authority," Annual Report 2000, www.amnestyusa .org/annualreport.php?id=8856D5BB69B57CA1802568E400729F29&c=PSE.

26. Amira Hass, "Top Hamas Officials Still in PA Custody," *Haaretz,* October 15, 2000.

27. Matthew Levitt, *Targeting Terror: U.S. Policy Toward Middle Eastern State Sponsors and Terrorist Organizations, Post-September 11* (Washington, D.C.: Washington Institute for Near East Policy, 2002), p. 88.

28. David Schenker, "Palestinian Fictions—Yasser Arafat Stands Alone as the Undisputed Leader of the Palestinian Authority and the Palestinians," *World and I* (November 2001): 26.

29. Dore Gold, *The Fight for Jerusalem: Radical Islam, the West and the Future of the Holy City* (Washington, DC: Regnery Publishing, 2007), p. 5.

30. Chehab, *Inside Hamas,* p. 134.

31. Daniel Sobelman and Amos Harel, "PA Frees Hamas Prisoners," *Haaretz,* October 6, 2000.

32. Amira Hass, "Hamas Blamed for Attacks against Gaza Liquor Stores," *Haaretz,* October 15, 2000.

33. "Arafat Alarmed by Islamic Unrest," *Middle East Newsline,* January 11, 2002, www .menewsline.com/stories/2002/january/01_11_2.html.

34. Associated Press, "Hamas Rejects Offer to Join Cabinet," June 3, 2002, www.highbeam .com/doc/1P1–53361043.html.

35. "In First, Islamic Opposition Wins Palestinian Majority," *Middle East Newsline,* August 28, 2002.

36. Chehab, *Inside Hamas,* p. 156.

37. IDF spokesman, "Top Hamas Official Brands Marwan Barghouti a Traitor," September 20, 2002, www.idf.il/newsite/english/030.stm.

38. Levitt, *Hamas,* p. 40.

39. Tamimi, *Hamas,* p. 201.

40. Khaled Abu Toameh, "Stepping into Giant Shoes," in *After Arafat? The Future of Palestinian Politics,* ed. Robert Satloff, Washington Institute for Near East Policy, Policy Focus, No. 42 (October 2001): 28.

41. Ely Karmon, "Hamas's Terrorism Strategy: Operational Limitations and Political Restraints," *Middle East Review of International Affairs* (March 2000): 1.

42. WAFA (Palestine News Agency), "President Arafat: We Will Be Steadfast on Our Soil until We Triumph or Martyr," April 3, 2002.

43. WAFA, "President Arafat and PA Leadership Condemn All Terrorist Acts against Civilians," April 13, 2002.

44. "Interviews from Gaza: Palestinian Options under Siege," *Middle East Policy* (December 2002): 118.

45. Wafa Amr, "Arafat's Fatah, Hamas to Meet in Cairo," Reuters, November 8, 2002.

46. Agence France Presse, "Hamas, Fatah to Resume Ceasefire Talks within Days: Palestinians," December 8, 2002.

47. "Members Accused by Hamas of Belonging to Fatah," *Ash-Sharq al-Awsat* (London), December 6, 2002.

48. Lamia Lahoud, "Fatah Threatens Hamas in Leaflet," *Jerusalem Post,* December 11, 2002.

49. Alan Alan, "In Cairo Talks, Islamic Factions Refuse to Stop Resistance," *Jerusalem Times,* December 19, 2002.

50. Associated Press, Ibrahim Barzak, "Hamas Calls for More Attacks on Israel," December 27, 2002.

51. Jihad al-Khazen, "Hamas, Fatah Ready for Increased Cooperation," *al-Hayat* (Arabic), December 27, 2002.

52. "Negotiations between Palestinian Factions Postponed," *Haaretz,* January 3, 2003.

53. Jihad al-Khazen, "Fatah and Hamas," *al-Hayat* (Arabic), January 8, 2003.

54. "Ahmed Yassin: We Went to Cairo to Consolidate National Unity, Not to Wave the White Flag of Surrender at the Jewish Enemy," IDF spokesperson, January 12, 2003, www.kokhavivpublications.com/2003/israel/01/0301122141.html.

55. "Hamas Rejects Calls to Halt Attacks: Egypt-Sponsored Talks Begin," *Dawn* (Pakistan), January 26, 2003, www.dawn.com/2003/01/26/int1.htm.

56. "Palestinian Groups Vow More Suicide Attacks," *Middle East Online* (UK), January 23, 2003, www.middle-east-online.com/english/?id=4109.

57. "PNA: Delay of Inter-Palestinian Talks Not Helpful," *Palestine Media Center,* February 5, 2003, www.palestine-pmc.com/details.asp?cat=1&id=568.

58. Yael Yehoshua, "On the Conflict between Hamas and the Palestinian Authority," MEMRI, Inquiry and Analysis Series, No. 143, July 18, 2003, www.memri.org/bin /articles.cgi?Page=archives&Area=ia&ID=IA14303.

59. Center for Defense Information, "In the Spotlight: Al-Aqsa Martyrs Brigades," June 10, 2002, www.cdi.org/terrorism/aqsa.cfm.

60. Chehab, *Inside Hamas,* pp. 88–89.
61. Matthew Kalman, "Terrorist Says Orders Come from Arafat," *USA Today,* March 14, 2002.
62. Levitt, *Targeting Terror,* p. 103.
63. Intelligence and Terrorism Information Center, "Palestinian Authority Captured Documents," www.terrorism-info.org.il/malam_multimedia/html/final/eng/bu/pa_cd/cd.htm.
64. Tamimi, *Hamas,* p. 187.
65. Malka, "Hamas," p. 109.
66. James Bennet, "Hamas Leader Tells Muslims to Retaliate If U.S. Attacks," *New York Times,* February 8, 2003, http://query.nytimes.com/gst/fullpage.html?res=9C02E3DD 123BF93BA35751C0A9659C8B63.

CHAPTER 7

1. Matthew Levitt, *Hamas: Politics, Charity and Terrorism in the Service of Jihad* (New Haven, CT: Yale University Press, 2006), p. 57.
2. Public Broadcasting System, "Hamas Leader Killed in Israeli Air Strike," March 22, 2004, www.pbs.org/newshour/updates/mideast_03–22–04.html.
3. Gethin Chamberlain, "Israel Has Opened the Gates of Hell," *The Scotsman,* March 23, 2004, http://thescotsman.scotsman.com/ViewArticle.aspx?articleid=2513831.
4. PBS, "Hamas Leader Killed in Israeli Air Strike."
5. Fawaz Gerges, "Hamas Leader Killed," *Washington Post,* March 22, 2004, http://pages.slc .edu/~fgerges/index.php?page=edessayssingle&id=34.
6. Greg Myre, "In Loss of Leaders, Hamas Discovers a Renewed Strength," *New York Times,* April 25, 2004, http://query.nytimes.com/gst/fullpage.html?res=9505E3D9133AF936A1 5757C0A9629C8B63&sec=&spon=&pagewanted=all.
7. Esam Shashaa, ed., "The Assassination of Ismail Abu Shanab," August 21, 2003, www .palestinehistory.com/issues/assassination/abushanab.htm.
8. Reena Ninan, "Dr. Terror: An Interview with Hamas Leader Mahmoud Zahar," Fox News, November 28, 2007, www.foxnews.com/story/0,2933,313645,00.html.
9. Myre, "In Loss of Leaders, Hamas Discovers a Renewed Strength."
10. "Abu Obaida, the English Spokesman, Answers Important Questions about the Brigades," Hamas Web site, December 5, 2007, www.alqassam.ps/english/?action=show inet&inid=17.
11. Levitt, *Hamas,* p. 162.
12. Author's interview with Khairi Abaza, Washington, D.C., January 30, 2008.
13. For more, see "Profile of Khaled Meshal" at www.cfr.org/publication/11111/.
14. Levitt, *Hamas,* p. 174.
15. "Hamas Springs to Iran's Defence," Al-Jazeera, December 17, 2005, http://english .aljazeera.net/English/archive/archive?ArchiveId=17093.
16. Yossi Alpher, "Bankruptcy," Bitterlemons.org, March 29, 2004, www.bitterlemons.org /previous/bl290304ed12.html.
17. Doron Almog, "Lessons of the Gaza Security Fence for the West Bank," *Jerusalem Issue Brief* 4, No. 12, December 23, 2004, www.jcpa.org/brief/brief004–12.htm.
18. Peter Berkowitz. "The Legacy of Ariel Sharon," *Hoover Digest,* No. 1 (Winter 2006), www.hoover.org/publications/digest/2912351.html.
19. David Makovsky, *Engagement through Disengagement: Gaza and the Potential for Renewed Israeli-Palestinian Peacemaking* (Washington, D.C.: Washington Institute for Near East Policy, 2005), p. 115.

20. Jennifer Siegel, "Carter Book Slaps Israel with 'Apartheid' Tag, Provides Ammo to GOP," *The Forward,* October 17, 2006, www.forward.com/articles/carter-book-slaps-israel-with-%E2%80%98apartheid%E2%80%99-tag/.

21. Israeli Ministry of Foreign of Affairs, "Saving Lives: Israel's Anti-Terrorist Fence" (January 2004), www.mfa.gov.il/mfa/mfaarchive/2000_2009/2003/11/saving%20lives-%20israel-s%20anti-terrorist%20fence%20-%20answ.

22. See Makovsky, *Engagement through Disengagement.*

23. Hillel Frisch, *(The) Fence of Offense? Testing the Effectiveness of "The Fence" in Judea and Samaria,* Begin Sadat Center for Strategic Studies, Mideast Security and Policy Studies, No. 75 (October 2007): 15.

24. Israel Ministry of Foreign Affairs, "Israeli Companies Participate in Tender for European Separation Fence," *Israel Line,* August 13, 2004, www.israel-mfa.gov.il/MFA/Archive/Israel+Line/2004/Israel%20Line%2013-Aug–2004.

25. Amnesty International, "Occupied Palestinian Territories Torn Apart by Factional Strife," October 24, 2007, p. 3, http://web.amnesty.org/library/Index/ENGMDE210202007.

26. Matthew Gutman, "In the Last Five Months, We've Had Zero Attacks," *Jerusalem Post,* July 2, 2004.

27. "Saving Lives: Israel's Security Fence," July 26, 2005, http://www.theisraelproject.org/site/apps/nl/content2.asp?c=hsJPK0PIJpH&b=883997&ct=1224111.

28. Frisch, *(The) Fence of Offense?* pp. 22–23.

29. Doron Almog, "Tunnel-Vision in Gaza," *Middle East Quarterly* (Summer 2004), www.meforum.org/article/630.

30. Author's interview with retired Israeli military official, Washington, D.C., October 15, 2003.

31. Kevin Frayer, "Gaza Tunnel Smugglers Grow Under Hamas," Associated Press, August 14, 2007, www.washingtonpost.com/wp-dyn/content/article/2007/08/14/AR2007081400721_2.html.

32. CNN International, "Israel Destroys Palestinian Tunnels into Israel," November 13, 2003, http://edition.cnn.com/TRANSCRIPTS/0311/13/i_ins.00.html.

33. Author's interview with retired Israeli military official.

34. IDF spokesman, "IDF Operation to Uncover Weapon Smuggling Tunnels," October 13, 2003.

35. Levitt, *Hamas,* p. 6.

36. Author's interview with retired Israeli military official.

37. Mitchell Bard, "Will Israel Return to Gaza?" *inFocus Quarterly* (Fall 2007), www.jewishpolicycenter.org/article/60.

38. Text of the speech can be found at "Ariel Sharon Describes 'Disengagement Plan,'" December 18, 2003, www.jewishvirtuallibrary.org/jsource/Peace/sharon_1203.html.

39. Zaki Chehab, *Inside Hamas: The Untold Story of the Militant Islamic Movement* (New York: Nation Books, 2007), p. 52

40. Bard, "Will Israel Return to Gaza?"

41. Khaled Abu Toameh, "PA Official Threatens 'Fallujah-Style' Operation against Hamas," *Jerusalem Post,* January 6, 2005.

42. Al-Jazeera interview transcript from January 7, 2005. Reprinted in Makovsky, *Engagement through Disengagement,* p. 131.

43. Mohammed Yaghi, "Understanding the Hamas Agenda," in *Hamas Triumphant: Implications for Security, Politics, Economy and Strategy,* ed. Robert Satloff, Washington Institute for Near East Policy, Policy Focus No. 3 (February 2006): 11, www.washingtoninstitute.org/templateC04.php?CID=232.

44. Haim Malka, "One Law, One Army: A Strategy for Palestinian Disarmament," *Oxford Journal on Good Governance* 2, No. 2 (August 2005): 44.

45. Christopher Hamilton et al., "Maintaining the Tahdiyya: Hurdles for Hamas's Postelection Military Strategy," in *Hamas Triumphant: Implications for Security, Politics, Economy and Strategy*, ed. Robert Satloff, Washington Institute for Near East Policy, Policy Focus No. 3 (February 2006): 37, www.washingtoninstitute.org/templateC04.php?CID =232.

46. Khalid Amaryeh, "Arafat's Succession Battle Looming," al-Jazeera, December 26, 2003, http://english.aljazeera.net/English/archive/archive?ArchiveId=263.

47. Barry Rubin, "After Arafat," *Middle East Quarterly* (Spring 2004), http://www.meforum .org/article/606.

48. Ehud Ya'ari, "The Morning After," *After Arafat? The Future of Palestinian Politics*, ed. Robert Satloff, Washington Institute for Near East Policy, Policy Focus, No. 42 (October 2001): 7.

49. Deborah Sontag, "There's No Bossing a Democracy, Arafat Learns," *New York Times*, December 13, 1998, http://query.nytimes.com/gst/fullpage.html?res=9802E3DC163DF 930A25751C1A96E958260.

50. Ziv Hellman, "Terminal Situation," *Jerusalem Report*, December 24, 2007, www.jpost .com/servlet/Satellite?cid=1196847301498&pagename=JPost/JPArticle/Printer.

51. Amaryeh, "Arafat's Succession Battle Looming."

52. Haim Malka, "One Law, One Army: A Strategy for Palestinian Disarmament," *Oxford Journal on Good Governance* 2, No. 2 (August 2005): 45.

53. Michael Eisentstadt, *The Palestinians: Between State Failure and Civil War*, Washington Institute for Near East Policy, Policy Focus No. 78 (December 2007): 13, www .washingtoninstitute.org/templateC04.php?CID=285.

54. Chehab, *Inside Hamas*, pp. 2–6.

55. Mark Dubowitz, "Terrorist TV in Eurabia," *inFocus Quarterly* (Winter 2007), www .jewishpolicycenter.org/article/92.

56. Conal Urquhart, "Israel Plunged into Crisis as Sharon Suffers Massive Stroke," *The Guardian*, January 5, 2006, www.guardian.co.uk/israel/Story/0,1678327,00.html.

57. Hussein Agha and Robert Malley, "Hamas Steps into a Complex Landscape," *Boston Globe*, January 24, 2006, www.crisisgroup.org/home/index.cfm?id=3902.

CHAPTER 8

1. CNN News, "Hamas Landslide Shakes Mideast," January 26, 2006, www.cnn.com/2006 /WORLD/meast/01/26/palestinian.election.1604/index.html.

2. Palestinian Central Elections Committee, "The Results of the Legislative Elections 2006" (Arabic), January 29, 2007, www.elections.ps/atemplate.aspx?id=466.

3. Robert Satloff, "A Primer on Hamas: Origins, Tactics, Strategy and Response," in *Hamas Triumphant: Implications for Security, Politics, Economy and Strategy*, ed. Robert Satloff, Washington Institute for Near East Policy, Policy Focus, No. 3 (February 2006): 8, www .washingtoninstitute.org/html/pdf/PF53-Satloff.pdf.

4. Azzam Tamimi, *Hamas: A History from Within* (Northampton, MA: Olive Branch Press, 2007), p. 292.

5. "Profile of Ismael Hanieh," Jerusalem Media and Communication Centre (Ramallah, West Bank), www.jmcc.org/new/06/feb/hanieh.htm.

6. Zaki Chehab, *Inside Hamas: The Untold Story of the Militant Islamic Movement* (New York: Nation Books, 2007), pp. 9–10.

7. Scott Wilson, "Hamas Sweeps Palestinian Elections, Complicating Peace Efforts in Mideast," *Washington Post,* January 27, 2006, www.washingtonpost.com/wp-dyn /content/article/2006/01/26/AR2006012600372.html.

8. "Press Conference of the President," White House Web site, January 26, 2008, www .whitehouse.gov/news/releases/2006/01/print/20060126.html.

9. For more, see www.pcpsr.org.

10. Martin Kramer, "Polls that Hid Hamas," http://sandbox.blog-city.com/hamas_polls _khalil_shikaki.htm.

11. Ibid.

12. Chehab, *Inside Hamas,* p. 3.

13. Sarah El Deeb, "Hamas Claims Majority in Palestinian Election," Associated Press, January 26, 2007, www.chinadaily.com.cn/english/doc/2006–01/26/content_515852.htm.

14. Khalid Amayreh, "Palestinian PM Quits after Poll Upset," Al-Jazeera, January 27, 2006, http://english.aljazeera.net/English/archive/archive?ArchiveId=21245.

15. Palestine Center for Human Rights, "Black Pages in the Absence of Justice: Report on Bloody Fighting in the Gaza Strip from 7 to 14 June 2007" (October 2007): 11–12, www .pchrgaza.org/files/Reports/English/pdf_spec/Gaza%20Conflict%20-%20Eng%209 %20october.pdf.

16. Ibid.

17. Ibrahim Barzak, "Fatah, Hamas Gunmen Clash in Gaza," Associated Press, April 23, 2006, www.washingtonpost.com/wp-dyn/content/article/2006/04/22/AR2006042200481.html.

18. Ibid.

19. Voice of America, "Hamas, Fatah Clash Again in Gaza," May 9, 2006, www.voanews.com /english/archive/2006–05/2006–05–09-voa13.cfm?CFID=260385816&CFTOKEN =12137999.

20. Mohammad Yaghi, "The Growing Anarchy in the Palestinian Territories," Washington Institute for Near East Policy, Policywatch, No. 1103, May 16, 2006, www.washington-institute.org/templateC05.php?CID=2468.

21. Taghreed al-Khodary, "Gaza: Life under Hamas Rule," *Arab Reform Bulletin,* 5, No. 9 (November 2007), www.carnegieendowment.org/files/novemberkhodary1.pdf.

22. Taghreed al-Khodary, "Hamas Police Force Recruits Women in Gaza," *New York Times,* January 18, 2008.

23. Palestine Center for Human Rights, "Black Pages in the Absence of Justice," p. 13.

24. Ibid.

25. "IDF Launches Operation 'Summer Rains,'" (Hebrew), IDF official Web site, June 28, 2008, http://dover.idf.il/IDF/About/history/2000s/2006/062801.htm.

26. Atul Aneja, "Palestinians Flee as Israeli Troops Enter Gaza Strip," *The Hindu* (India), June 29, 2006, www.hindu.com/2006/06/29/stories/2006062904011400.htm.

27. Palestine Center for Human Rights, "Black Pages in the Absence of Justice," pp. 12–15.

28. Al-Jazeera, "Hamas Accuses Fatah over Attack," December 15, 2006, http://english .aljazeera.net/NR/exeres/793DD747-A1B7–4BE3-B120–0CF171612495.htm.

29. Al-Jazeera, "Fragile Ceasefire Holds in Gaza," December 18, 2006, http://english .aljazeera.net/NR/exeres/6F53EE4E-D4C1–46BA-B2E4–4115D2EC9234.htm.

30. Ali El-Saleh, "Interview with Hamas's Said Siyam," *Ash-Sharq al-Awsat,* November 25, 2007, www.asharqalawsat.com/english/news.asp?section=3&id=10988.

31. Michael Eisentstadt, *The Palestinians: Between State Failure and Civil War,* Washington Institute for Near East Policy, Policy Focus, No. 78 (December 2007): 22, www .washingtoninstitute.org/templateC04.php?CID=285.

32. Palestine Center for Human Rights, "Black Pages in the Absence of Justice," pp. 16–19.

33. Alfred B. Prados and Christopher M. Blanchard, "Saudi Arabia: Terrorist Financing Issues," Congressional Research Service, December 8, 2004, www.fas.org/irp/crs/RL32499.pdf.

34. Marwan Bishara, "The Undeclared Palestinian Civil War," *Middle East Online* (UK), November 15, 2007, www.middle-east-online.com/english/?id=23095.

35. Agence France Presse, "Text of Palestinians' Mecca Agreement," February 9, 2007, www.lebanonwire.com/0702MLN/07020923AF.asp.

36. Khaled Abu Toameh, "PA Fears UN May Order All Aid Workers Out of Lawless Gaza," *Jerusalem Post,* April 5, 2007, www.jpost.com/servlet/Satellite?cid=1173879257822&pagename=JPost%2FJPArticle%2FShowFull.

37. "Egypt Quietly Abandons Gaza," *Middle East Newsline,* March 27, 2007, www.menewsline.com/stories/2007/march/03_28_2.html.

38. Mohammed Mar'i, "UNRWA May Stop Aid to Refugees in Gaza, WB," *Arab News* (Saudi), April 8, 2007, www.arabnews.com/?page=4&section=0&article=94691&d=8&m=4&y=2007.

39. Maan News Agency, "Hamas Training Men in Iran, Fatah Training Men in Egypt, *Yedioth Aharanoth* Claims," February 23, 2007, www.maannews.net/en/index.php?opr=ShowDetails&ID=19799.

40. Maan News Agency, "Crime Wave Hits Gaza Streets," April 1, 2007, www.maannews.net/en/index.php?opr=ShowDetails&ID=20825.

41. Steven Erlanger, "Gaza's Reflection in a Foul Threat," *New York Times,* November 6, 2007, www.nytimes.com/2007/11/06/world/middleeast/06cesspool.html.

42. "UN Warns of New Gaza Sewage Flood," http://news.bbc.co.uk/2/hi/middle_east/6503579.stm; and "Gaza Warned of Further Sewer Collapses," *The Age* (Australia), March 28, 2007, www.theage.com.au/news/World/Gaza-warned-of-further-sewer-collapses/2007/03/28/1174761509357.html.

43. Julie Stahl, "Gaza Bible Society Surprised by Bomb Attack," CNS News, April 16, 2007, www.cnsnews.com/ViewForeignBureaus.asp?Page=/ForeignBureaus/archive/200704/INT20070416e.html.

44. Maan News Agency, "Violence Continues in Gaza: Bomb in Beit Hanoun, Road Closed by an Angry Clan, Doctor Abducted and Beaten," March 14, 2007, www.maannews.net/en/index.php?opr=ShowDetails&ID=20324.

45. Reporters without Borders, "Journalists Injured during Gaza Demonstration in Support of Kidnapped British Journalist," April 17, 2007, www.rsf.org/print.php3?id_article=21771.

46. Palestine Center for Human Rights, "Black Pages in the Absence of Justice," pp. 20–22.

CHAPTER 9

1. Palestine Center for Human Rights, "Black Pages in the Absence of Justice: Report on Bloody Fighting in the Gaza Strip from 7 to 14 June 2007" (October 2007), www.pchrgaza.org/files/Reports/English/pdf_spec/Gaza%20Conflict%20-%20Eng%209%20october.pdf.

2. Amnesty International, "Occupied Palestinian Territories Torn Apart by Factional Strife," October 24, 2007, pp. 29–33, http://web.amnesty.org/library/Index/ENGMDE210202007.

3. Palestine Center for Human Rights, "Black Pages in the Absence of Justice."

4. Amnesty International, "Occupied Palestinian Territories Torn Apart by Factional Strife," and Palestine Center for Human Rights, "Black Pages in the Absence of Justice."

5. Shlomo Shamir, "Arabs Thwart PA UN Bid to Condemn Hamas," *Haaretz,* November 19, 2007, http://haaretz.com/hasen/spages/925035.html.

6. Steven Erlanger, "Hamas Seizes Broad Control in Gaza Strip," *New York Times,* June 14, 2007, www.nytimes.com/2007/06/14/world/middleeast/14mideast.html.

7. Cam Simpson and Neil King, Jr, "Hamas to Show an Improved Hand," *Wall Street Journal,* July 30, 2007, http://online.wsj.com/public/article/SB118575064310581669-ttwYG ROTiBzCpFnHeg9hWq1zcc8_20070828.html?mod=tff_main_tff_top.

8. Maan News Agency, "Hamas Has No Intention of Establishing an Islamic State in Gaza, Says Haniyeh," August 20, 2007, www.maannews.net/en/index.php?opr=ShowDetails &ID=24848.

9. Marie Colvin, "Defiant Hamas Rules by Fear in Isolated Gaza," *London Sunday Times,* November 25, 2007, www.timesonline.co.uk/tol/news/world/middle_east/article2937105.ece.

10. "Special Rapporteur on Freedom of Religion or Belief Concludes Visit to Israel and Occupied Palestinian Territory," United Nations Web site, January 28, 2008, www.unog .ch/80256EDD006B9C2E/(httpNewsByYear_en)/982FFB76082F1AB1C12573DE00352 E19?OpenDocument.

11. Palestine Center for Human Rights, "Black Pages in the Absence of Justice."

12. Andrew Lee Butters, "A Sort of Peace in Gaza," *Time,* August 13, 2007, pp. 42–43, www .time.com/time/magazine/article/0,9171,1649291,00.html.

13. "A New and Complicated Palestinian Landscape: An Interview with Ambassador Dennis Ross," *inFocus Quarterly* (Fall 2007), www.jewishpolicycenter.org/article/54.

14. "Ahmad Al-Jabari before Kidnapping Shalit: We Succeeded after Many Tryings," Official Hamas Web site, May 5, 2007, www.alqassam.ps/english/?action=showinet&inid=12.

15. International Press Center (Palestinian), "Two Civilians Killed in Gaza, Several Wounded and Arrested in West Bank," August 23, 2004, www.ipc.gov.ps/ipc_e/ipc_e–1 /e_News/news2004/2004_08/140.html.

16. Amos Harel, "Hamas Losing Grip on Gaza, Fatah Gaining Support," *Haaretz,* November 13, 2007, http://haaretz.com/hasen/spages/923553.html.

17. Judith Sudilovsky, "Rosary Nuns' Compound Ransacked, Looted during Fighting, Catholic Gaza Priest Says," CNS News, June 19, 2007, www.catholic.org/international /international_story.php?id=24449.

18. Khaled Abu Toameh, "Hamas Forced Professor to Convert," *Jerusalem Post,* August 6, 2007, www.jpost.com/servlet/Satellite?cid=1186066387589&pagename=JPost/JPArticle /ShowFull.

19. Khaled Abu Toameh, "Gaza: Christian-Muslim Tensions Heat Up," *Jerusalem Post,* September 25, 2007, www.jpost.com/servlet/Satellite?pagename=JPost/JPArticle/ShowFull &cid=1189411486459.

20. Maan News Agency, "Corpse of Christian Resident of Gaza Discovered," October 7, 2007, www.maannews.net/en/index.php?opr=ShowDetails&ID=25738.

21. Conal Urquhart, "Persona Non Grata in Gaza," *The Guardian,* October 22, 2007, www.guardian.co.uk/international/story/0,2196828,00.html.

22. Ryan Jones, "Gaza Christians Living under Growing Islamic Threat," CNSNews.com, August 16, 2007, www.cnsnews.com/news/viewstory.asp?Page=/ForeignBureaus /archive/200708/INT20070816c.html.

23. Shelley Neese, "Who Will Speak for Gaza's Christians?" *Jerusalem Connection* (September–October 2007): 9.

24. Khaled Abu Toameh, "Muslim Gunmen Target Christian in Gaza," *Jerusalem Post,* December 8, 2007, www.jpost.com/servlet/Satellite?cid=1196847287392&pagename=JPost %2FJPArticle%2FPrinter.

25. Maan News Agency, "Unknown Assailants Blow Up Christian Youth Organization Library in Gaza," February 15, 2008, www.maannews.net/en/index.php?opr=ShowDetails&ID=27804

26. Judith Sudilovsky, "Christians Say Conditions in Gaza Worsen for Them, Moderate Muslims, Catholic News Service, February 19, 2008, www.catholicnews.com/data/stories/cns/0800959.htm

27. Ikhwanweb (Muslim Brotherhood Web site), "Hamas Strongly Condemns the Attack on the YMCA in Gaza," February 15, 2008, www.ikhwanweb.com/Article.asp?ID=15996&SectionID=0

28. Maan News Agency, "Undercover Gunmen Blow up Entrance to Rosary Sister's School in Tal al-Hawa," May 16, 2008, www.maannews.net/en/index.php?opr=ShowDetails&ID=29315.

29. Urquhart, "Persona Non Grata in Gaza."

30. Amnesty International, "Occupied Palestinian Territories Torn Apart by Factional Strife," pp. 16 and 36.

31. Maan News Agency, "Executive Force Leader Admits to Violence and Torture in Gaza," August 19, 2007, www.maannews.net/en/index.php?opr=ShowDetails&ID=24813.

32. Maan News Agency, "Five Fatah Men are Hospitalized in Gaza after Being Kidnapped and Tortured," September 5, 2007, www.maannews.net/en/index.php?opr=ShowDetails&ID=25165.

33. Palestinian Center for Human Rights, "PCHR Calls for Investigation into Methods of Torture Practiced by Palestinian Police in the Gaza Strip," November 19, 2007, www.pchrgaza.org/files/PressR/English/2007/164–2007.html.

34. "Hamas Frees Senior Fatah Sympathizer," *Saudi Gazette,* December 26, 2007, http://saudi-gazette.com.sa/index.php?option=com_content&task=view&id=43387&Itemid=146.

35. Khaled Abu Toameh, "Hamas Detains PA's A-G over Cover-up," *Jerusalem Post,* August 16, 2007, www.jpost.com/servlet/Satellite?cid=1186557465585&pagename=JPost/JPArticle/ShowFull.

36. Taghreed El-Khodary and Isabel Kershner, "Gaza Is Tense as It Tallies Casualties," *New York Times,* January 2, 2008, www.nytimes.com/2008/01/02/world/middleeast/02mideast.html.

37. Palestinian Centre for Human Rights, "PCHR Concerned by Detention of Khan Yunis Governor and Fatah Activists by Gaza Internal Security Apparatus," May 20, 2008, www.pchrgaza.org/files/PressR/English/2008/50–2008.html

38. Maan News Agency, "De Facto Interior Ministry in Gaza Uncovers 'Most Dangerous Network of Collaborators,'" October 24, 2007, www.maannews.net/en/index.php?opr=ShowDetails&ID25987.

39. Palestinian Centre for Human Rights, "PCHR Condemns the Takeover of the Offices of the Financial and Administrative Control Bureau in Gaza," February 19, 2008, www.pchrgaza.org/files/PressR/English/2008/13–2008.html

40. International Middle East Media Center, "Gaza-Based Fatah Main Office Set on Fire," April 5, 2008, www.imemc.org/article/53985

41. Taghreed al-Khodary, "Hamas Police Force Recruits Women in Gaza," *New York Times,* January 18, 2008, www.nytimes.com/2008/01/18/world/middleeast/18gaza.html?partner=rssnyt&emc=rss.

42. Amnesty International, "Occupied Palestinian Territories Torn Apart by Factional Strife," pp. 14–15.

43. Taghreed El-Khodary, "Gaza: Life under Hamas Rule," *Arab Reform Bulletin* 5, No. 9 (November 2007), www.carnegieendowment.org/files/novemberkhodary1.pdf.

44. Colvin, "Defiant Hamas Rules by Fear in Isolated Gaza."

45. *Lebanon Wire,* "Hamas Arrest Abbas-Linked Attorney General after Returning to Gaza," August 16, 2007, www.lebanonwire.com/0708MLN/07081615AP.asp.

46. Al-Jazeera, "Hamas Bans Unregistered Protests," August 13, 2007, http://english .aljazeera.net/NR/exeres/E99185EF–7F95–4360-BFEB–8EC9ED85C8C3.htm.

47. Maan News Agency, "Deposed Palestinian Government Bans Friday Prayers in Public Squares," September 4, 2007, www.maannews.net/en/index.php?opr=ShowDetails&ID =25149.

48. Maan News Agency, "Al-Azhar Scholars Must Intervene in Hamas Fatwa Banning Friday Prayers in Public Squares," September 5, 2007, www.maannews.net/en/index.php ?opr=ShowDetails&ID=25174.

49. Amira Hass, "Like on the First Land Day," *Haaretz,* November 14, 2007, www.haaretz .com/hasen/spages/923917.html.

50. WAFA (Palestine News Agency), "Hamas Militias Attack Friday Prayers, Wounding Scores in Gaza Strip," September 7, 2007, www.wafa.ps/english/body.asp?id=10340.

51. Sarah El Deeb, "Fatah Protest of Hamas Ends in Clashes," Associated Press, August 31, 2007, www.usatoday.com/news/world/2007–08–31–1989026275_x.htm.

52. Amnesty International, "Occupied Palestinian Territories Torn Apart by Factional Strife," pp. 27–28.

53. Maan News Agency, "Hamas Abducts Eight Fatah Members in Gaza," September 1, 2007, www.maannews.net/en/index.php?opr=ShowDetails&ID=25078.

54. Ghassan Bannoura, "Abbas Declares Three Days Mourning for Gaza Dead," International Middle East Media Center (Ramallah), November 13, 2007, www.imemc.org /article/5147.1

55. Paul Martin, "Hamas Carries Out Mass Arrests and Puts Down Gaza Schoolgirl Demo," *Times of London,* November 13, 2007, www.timesonline.co.uk/tol/news/world/middle _east/article2863307.ece.

56. El-Khodary and Kershner, "Gaza Is Tense as It Tallies Casualties."

57. Peter Beaumont, "Gaza's Factions Take Their Fight into the School Playgrounds," *The Observer* (UK), February 10, 2008, www.guardian.co.uk/world/2008/feb/10/israeland-thepalestinians.

58. Kevin Peraino, "Fatah's War on Hamas," *Newsweek,* December 17, 2007, p. 48, www.newsweek.com/id/74459.

59. Taghreed El-Khodary, "Hamas and Fatah Supporters Clash at Gaza University," *New York Times,* April 1, 2008, www.nytimes.com/2008/04/01/world/middleeast/01mideast .html?ref=world

60. Khaled Abu Toameh, "Hamas Sets Up New Security Force," *Jerusalem Post,* July 31, 2007, www.jpost.com/servlet/Satellite?pagename=JPost/JPArticle/ShowFull&cid=11857 89792658.

61. Khaled Abu Toameh, "Palestinian Journalists Say Hamas's Decision to Issue Its Own Press Cards Is 'A Dangerous Step,'" *Jerusalem Post,* October 17, 2007, www.jpost.com /servlet/Satellite?pagename=JPost/JPArticle/ShowFull&cid=1192380585358.

62. Al-Jazeera, "Hamas Bans Unregistered Protests," August 13, 2007, http://english .aljazeera.net/NR/exeres/E99185EF–7F95–4360-BFEB–8EC9ED85C8C3.htm.

63. Sarah El Deeb, "Hamas Widens Gaza Crackdown with New Press Restrictions," Associated Press, November 14, 2007, http://abcnews.go.com/International/wireStory?id=3865380.

64. Associated Press, "Hamas Orders Closure of Newspaper over Caricature," February 10, 2008, www.iht.com/articles/ap/2008/02/10/africa/ME-GEN-Palestinians-Hamas-Newspaper-Ban.php.

65. Khaled Abu Toameh, "Palestinian Journalists Say Hamas's Decision."

66. El Deeb, "Hamas Widens Gaza Crackdown."

67. Maan News Agency, "Union of Palestinian Journalists Claims Hamas Militias Targeting Their Members," November 6, 2007, www.maannews.net/en/index.php?opr=Show-Details&ID=26160.

68. Board of the Foreign Press Association, "Statements 2007," November 14, 2007, www .fpa.org.il/?categoryId=406.

69. Maan News Service, "Hamas-Allied Police Stymie Protest for Press Freedom in Gaza," January 22, 2008, www.maannews.net/en/index.php?opr=ShowDetails&ID=27366.

70. "Palestine Updates: Freedom of the Press," *Arab Reform Bulletin* 5, No. 9 (November 2007). www.carnegieendowment.org/publications/index.cfm?fa=view&id=19783&prog =zgp&proj=zdrl,zme#press

71. Reporters Without Borders, "Palestinian Authority—Annual Report 2007," www.rsf.org /article.php3?id_article=20774.

72. Deutche Presse-Agentur, "Hamas Ministry to Censor Internet Sites in Gaza," May 19, 2008, www.southasianews.com/255554/Hamas-ministry-to-censor-Internet-sites-in-Gaza-.htm

73. Saleh al Naeimi, "Hamas: A Lawless Authority," *ash-Sharq al-Awsat,* August 25, 2007, www.asharqalawsat.com/english/news.asp?section=3&id=10004.

74. Richard Boudreaux, "Israel OKs Gaza Electricity Cutoffs," *Los Angeles Times,* October 26, 2007.

75. Statement issued October 28, 2007, on www.alqassam.ps/english/?action=showdetail &fid=675.

76. al Naeimi, "Hamas: A Lawless Authority."

77. Yaakov Katz, "Israeli Metal Used for Kassam Rockets," *Jerusalem Post,* March 4, 2007. www.jpost.com/servlet/Satellite?pagename=JPost%2FJPArticle%2FShowFull&cid=117 1894568749

78. Avi Issacharoff, "Tough Times in Gaza: No Gas, Coke or Cigarettes," *Haaretz* (English), December 3, 2007, www.haaretz.com/hasen/spages/930339.html.

79. Ali Waked, "Gaza: Smokers Fume over Rising Prices," Ynet News, September 3, 2007, www.ynetnews.com/articles/0,7340,L–3445001,00.html.

80. Scott Wilson, "Sealed Off by Israel, Gaza Reduced to Beggary," *Washington Post,* December 15, 2007, www.washingtonpost.com/wp-dyn/content/story/2007/12/15/ST2007121 500137.html.

81. International Committee of the Red Cross, "The Occupied Palestinian Territories: Dignity Denied," December 13, 2007, www.icrc.org/Web/Eng/siteengo0.nsf/html/Palestine-report–131207/

82. Issacharoff, "Tough Times in Gaza."

83. Sarah El Deeb, "Palestinians Profit from Breach," Associated Press, January 25, 2008, www.wtop.com/?nid=500&sid=1332878; Erica Silverman, "Palestinian Factions to Lobby Cairo," *Washington Times,* January 30, 2008, www.washingtontimes.com/apps /pbcs.dll/article?AID=/20080130/FOREIGN/228603908/1001.

CHAPTER 10

1. Khaled Abu Toameh, "Fatah Leader Wants Probe of Missing $2b," *Jerusalem Post,* January 12, 2008, www.jpost.com/servlet/Satellite?c=JPArticle&cid=1199964904829&page-name=JPost%2FJPArticle%2FShowFull.

2. Khaled Amayreh, "Still in Crisis," *Al-Ahram Weekly,* January 24, 2008, http://weekly .ahram.org.eg/2008/881/re6.htm.

3. Danny Rubinstein, "Deserting a Sinking Ship," *Haaretz,* November 15, 2007, www.haaretz.com/hasen/spages/924657.html.

4. Associated Press, "New Officers' School Part of Abbas' Security Plan, Meant to Keep Hamas in Line," October 30, 2007, www.iht.com/articles/ap/2007/10/30/africa/ME-GEN-Palestinians-Asserting-Control.php?WT.mc_id=rssap_news.

5. Reena Ninan, "Dr. Terror: An Interview with Hamas Leader Mahmoud Zahar," Fox News, November 28, 2007, www.foxnews.com/story/0,2933,313645,00.html.

6. Condoleezza Rice, "Special Briefing by Secretary of State Condoleezza Rice," State Department Briefing, June 18, 2007, www.state.gov/secretary/rm/2007/06/86750.htm.

7. Glenn Kessler, "Aid Request Emphasizes U.S. Support of Palestinian Authority Leadership," *Washington Post,* October 31, 2007, www.washingtonpost.com/wp-dyn/content/article/2007/10/30/AR2007103001944.html.

8. "Donors Pledge US$7.4 Billion Aid to Palestinians," *Business Intelligence Middle East,* December 18, 2007, www.bi-me.com/main.php?id=15926&t=1&c=34&cg=.

9. Nathan J. Brown, "The Road Out of Gaza," Carnegie Endowment for International Peace, Policy Outlook No. 39, February 2008, www.carnegieendowment.org/publications/index.cfm?fa=view&id=19911&prog=zgp&proj=zme.

10. "Donors Give Abbas 7.4bn, Gaza Cries," *Islam Online* (Qatar), December 17, 2007, www.islamonline.net/servlet/Satellite?c=Article_C&cid=1196786387192%20&pagename=Zone-English-News/NWELayout.

11. Yaakov Katz, "PM Approves 25 Armored Vehicles to PA," *Jerusalem Post,* November 21, 2007, www.jpost.com/servlet/Satellite?pagename=JPost%2FJPArticle%2FShowFull&cid=1195546685101.

12. Hilary Leila Krieger and Yaakov Katz, "Barak Fears Hamas W. Bank Takeover," *Jerusalem Post,* March 28, 2008. www.jpost.com/servlet/Satellite?cid=1206632351875&pagename=JPost%2FJPArticle%2FShowFull

13. Charles Levinson, "Fatah Vows to Wipe Hamas from West Bank," *London Sunday Telegraph,* June 24, 2007, www.telegraph.co.uk/news/main.jhtml?xml=/news/2007/06/24/wmid124.xml.

14. Amnesty International, "Occupied Palestinian Territories Torn Apart by Factional Strife," October 24, 2007, p. 40, http://web.amnesty.org/library/Index/ENGMDE21020 2007.

15. Amos Harel and Avi Issacharoff, "Israeli Source: PA Security Forces Have Improved Dramatically in West Bank," *Haaretz,* May 27, 2008, www.haaretz.com/hasen/spages/987445.html.

16. Haim Malka, "Hamas: Resistance and Transformation of Palestinian Society," in *Understanding Islamic Charities,* ed. Jon B. Alterman and Karin Von Hippel (Washington, D.C.: Center for Strategic and International Studies, 2007), p. 105.

17. Liane Sahouri, "Hamas' Midlife Crisis," Maan News Agency, September 29, 2007 www.maannews.net/en/index.php?opr=ShowDetails&ID=25607.

18. Agence France Presse, "Masters of Gaza, Hamas pursued in West Bank," October 2, 2007, http://afp.google.com/article/ALeqM5i-pj6uN-N77-NGm_rGbBRIFoYyQQ.

19. Amnesty International, "Occupied Palestinian Territories Torn Apart by Factional Strife."

20. "Iran President Reaffirms Support to Hamas," *The Peninsula* (Qatar), September 25, 2007, www.thepeninsulaqatar.com/Display_news.asp?section=World_News&subsection=Gulf%2C+Middle+East+%26+Africa&month=September2007&file=World_News20 0709242333.xml.

21. Mohammed Mar'i, "Palestinian Forces Seize Hamas Material in WB Mosque Raids," *Arab News* (UK), October 14, 2007, www.arabnews.com/?article=102457.
22. Harel and Issacharoff, "Israeli Source: PA Security Forces Have Improved Dramatically in West Bank."
23. Joel Greenberg, "In West Bank and Gaza, a Cycle of Retribution Churns," *Chicago Tribune,* October 23, 2007, www.romingerlegal.com/newsviewer.php?ppa=8oplo_%5Cgijjq pjRSecy30qbfen_!.
24. Maan News Agency, "Three Hamas Supporters 'Arrested' in the West Bank," May 17, 2008, www.maannews.net/en/index.php?opr=ShowDetails&ID=29345.
25. Ikhwanweb (Muslim Brotherhood website), "PA Demands Nilesat Stop Carrying Hamas Al-Aqsa TV," July 13, 2007, www.ikhwanweb.com/Article.asp?ID=1149&Section ID=0
26. Maan News Agency, "Hamas: PA Forces Seize Five More Members; Journalists Seized Tuesday Remain in Detention," November 8, 2007, www.maannews.net/en/index.php ?opr=ShowDetails&ID=26190.
27. Maan News Agency, "Release of Executive Ends Maan News Blackout," November 10, 2007, www.maannews.net/en/index.php?oopr=ShowDetails&ID=26212.
28. Ghassan Bannoura, "This Week in Palestine; Week 48, 2007," International Middle East Media Center (Ramallah), November 30, 2007, www.imemc.org/article/51807.
29. Wafa Amr, "Palestinian Government Closes All Alms Committees," Reuters, December 5, 2007, www.reuters.com/article/latestCrisis/idUSL05332330.
30. Khaled Abu Toameh, "PA Releases Three Hamas Prisoners," *Jerusalem Post,* November 25, 2007, www.jpost.com/servlet/Satellite?cid=1195546723448&pagename=JPost%2 FJPArticle%2FShowFull.
31. Amnesty International, "Occupied Palestinian Territories Torn Apart by Factional Strife."
32. Avi Issacharoff and Amos Harel, "U.S. Official Doubts Ability of PA to Police West Bank," *Haaretz,* October 25, 2007, www.haaretz.com/hasen/spages/916805.html.
33. Adam Entous and Wafa Amr, "Cutting Palestinian Forces Poses Challenge for PM," Reuters, October 25, 2007, www.reuters.com/article/worldNews/idUSL2226586720071 025; and Khaled Abu Toameh, "PA to Fire 30,000 Policemen from the West Bank Security Forces," *Jerusalem Post,* October 27, 2007, www.jpost.com/servlet/Satellite?cid= 1192380666649&pagename=JPost%2FJPArticle%2FShowFull.
34. Michael Eisentstadt, *The Palestinians: Between State Failure and Civil War,* Washington Institute for Near East Policy, Policy Focus, No. 78 (December 2007): 24, www.washingtoninstitute.org/templateC04.php?CID=285.
35. Ali Daraghmeh and Diaa Hadid, "Abbas Picks West Bank's Most Chaotic City to Prove He Can Rule, Implement Peace with Israelis," Associated Press, October 25, 2007, www.nctimes.com/articles/2007/10/26/news/nation/14_16_1710_25_07.txt.
36. Muin Shadid, "Palestinians Expand Security Drive with New Forces," Reuters, December 4, 2007, www.reuters.com/article/worldNews/idUSL0457902720071204.
37. Adam Entous and Wael al-Ahmed, "Palestinians Begin Rebuilding Symbols of Authority," Reuters, November 15, 2007, www.reuters.com/article/topNews/idUSL1458505820 071115.
38. "Abbas Cracks Down on Hamas Charities," *Gulf News* (Dubai), December 4, 2007, http://archive.gulfnews.com/articles/07/12/04/10172355.html.
39. Avi Issacharoff, "PA to Launch Welfare Network in Hopes of Countering Hamas," *Haaretz,* March 21, 2008, www.haaretz/com/hasen/spages/966723.html

40. *Jerusalem Post,* "IDF W. Bank Chief: Hamas Could Take Over in Days," February 26, 20008. www.jpost.com/servlet/Satellite?cid=1203847473168&pagename=JPost%2FJPArticle%2F Printer

41. Amir Rappaport, "Abbas' West Bank Rule an Optical Illusion," *Maariv* (Hebrew), December 4, 2007.

42. Reuters, "Palestinian Court Sentences Collaborator to Death," April 28, 2008, www .reuters.com/article/worldNews/idUSL2878800920080428

43. Yaakov Katz, "APCs Are the Least of Israel's Problems," *Jerusalem Post,* November 22, 2007, www.jpost.com/servlet/Satellite?cid=1195546693991&pagename=JPost%2FJP Article%2FPrinter.

44. Avi Issacharaoff and Barak Ravid, "Shin Bet: PA Has Arrested 250 Hamas Operatives," *Haaretz,* January 6, 2008, www.haaretz.com/hasen/spages/9442101.html.

45. Khaled Abu Toameh, "Abbas: Hamas Planning to Overthrow West Bank Gov't," *Jerusalem Post,* October 28, 2007, www.jpost.com/servlet/Satellite?cid=1192380675509 &pagename=JPost%2FJPArticle%2FShowFull.

46. Al-Aqsa Voice (Hamas Radio Arabic Web site), "Abbas' Security Apparatus Arrests 4 Hamas Members in the West Bank," February 22, 2008. http://alaqsavoice.ps/arabic /index.php?action=detail&id=13752

47. Ali Waked, "Hamas: Palestinian Authority Worse Than Israel," Ynet News, February 23, 2008. www.ynetnews.com/articles/0,7340,L–3510244,00.html

48. Associated Press, "Hezbollah Becomes More Visible in W. Bank," March 15, 2008, www .haaretz.com/hasen/spages/964234.html

49. David R. Sands, "Abbas Aide Warns Government May 'Disappear,'" *Washington Times,* April 26, 2008, www.washingtontimes.com/article/20080426/FOREIGN/904114643/1003

50. Griff Witte and Ellen Knickmeyer, "Palestinian Recruits Hit Streets Unprepared," *Washington Post,* May 3, 2008, www.washingtonpost.com/wp-dyn/content/article/2008/05 /02/AR2008050204001_pf.html

51. Yaakov Katz, "Israel Rejects Request for PA Body Armor," *Jerusalem Post,* May 15, 2008, www.jpost.com/servlet/Satellite?cid=1210668639064&pagename=JPost%2FJPArticle %2FShowFull

52. Maan News Agency, "Fatah Claims Hamas Attacked Nakba Rally in Jabalia," May 15, 2008, www.maannews.net/en/index.php?opr=ShowDetails&ID=29303.

53. Khaled Abu Toameh, "Palestinian Affairs: Abbas's Latest Headaches," *Jerusalem Post,* March 27, 2008, www.jpost.com/servlet/Satellite?cid=1206632349492&pagename =JPost%2FJPArticle%2FShowFull

54. Maan News Agency, "PA Justice Minister Refutes Hamas Accusation of Selling Land to Foreigners," February 20, 2008, www.maannews.net/en/index.php?opr=ShowDetails &ID=27889.

CHAPTER 11

1. "Abu Mazen: Hamas Affords al-Qaeda a Foothold in Gaza," *Al-Arabiya* (Arabic), July 10, 2007, www.alarabiya.net/articles/2007/07/10/36407.html.

2. al-Jazeera, "Bin Laden Warns against US Plots," December 29, 2007, http://english .aljazeera.net/NR/exeres/E9AFE383-A4AE–41BE–99F0–8C1074A5A9C5.htm.

3. Christopher Hamilton et al., "Maintaining the Tahdiyya: Hurdles for Hamas's Post-Election Military Strategy," in *Hamas Triumphant: Implications for Security, Politics, Economy and Strategy,* ed. Robert Satloff, Washington Institute for Near East Policy,

Policy Focus No. 3 (February 2006): 39, www.washingtoninstitute.org/templateC04.php
?CID=232.

4. "Hamas Identifies with and Supports Chechen and International Islamic Terrorism on
CDs Found in the Palestinian Authority–Administered Territories." IDF document,
www1.idf.il/SIP_STORAGE/DOVER/files/3/33853.pdf.

5. Dore Gold, *The Fight for Jerusalem: Radical Islam, the West and the Future of the Holy
City* (Washington, DC: Regnery Publishing, 2007), p. 202.

6. Habib Trebelsi, "Zawahiri Blasts Hamas over Unity Government," March 12, 2007, *Middle East Online* (UK), www.middle-east-online.com/english/?id=19947.

7. Marie Colvin, "Al-Qaeda Goes Recruiting in Festering Gaza," *London Sunday Times,*
April 9, 2006, www.timesonline.co.uk/article/0,2089–2125228,00.html.

8. Al-Jazeera, "Al-Qaeda Deputy Backs Hamas," June 25, 2007, http://english.aljazeera.net
/NR/exeres/CC39A8CD-DC4D–4ABC–994E-A3FAB150695F.htm.

9. Carolyn Fluehr-Lobban and Richard Lobban, "The Sudan Since 1989: National Islamic
Front Rule," *Arab Studies Quarterly* (Spring 2001).

10. Dore Gold, "Ties between al Qaeda and Hamas in Mideast Are Long and Frequent," *San
Francisco Chronicle,* March 5, 2006, www.sfgate.com/cgi-bin/article.cgi?file=/chronicle
/archive/2006/03/05/INGERHG75F1.DTL.

11. Dana Priest and Douglas Farah, "Terror Alliance Has U.S. Worried; Hezbollah, Al Qaeda
Seen Joining Forces," *Washington Post,* June 30, 2002.

12. "Hizb Chief Appears in Public," *The Hindu* (India), March 27, 2006, www.hindu.com
/2006/03/27/stories/2006032700391300.htm.

13. U.S. Department of the Treasury, "United States Designates bin Laden Loyalist," February 24, 2004, www.ustreas.gov/press/releases/js1190.htm.

14. "Bin Laden Loyalist, Wanted by the U.S. Yemenite Sheikh Abd Al-Majid Al-Zindani, in
Support of Palestinian Suicide Bombers at a Hamas Fundraiser Live on Al-Jazeera,"
Middle East Media Research Institute, No. 129, March 29, 2006, http://memri.org/bin
/articles.cgi?Page=archives&Area=sd&ID=SP112906.

15. Affidavit in Support of Arrest Warrant, "United States of America against Mohammed
Ali Hasan al-Moayad," January 5, 2003, pp. 22–23, http://news.findlaw.com/hdocs/docs
/terrorism/usalmoayad10503aff.pdf.

16. U.S. Department of the Treasury, "Recent OFAC Actions," October 12, 2001, www.treas
.gov/offices/enforcement/ofac/actions/20011012.shtml.

17. Matthew Levitt, "The Role of Charities and NGOs in the Financing of Terrorist Activities," U.S. Senate Committee on Banking, Housing and Urban Affairs, August 1, 2002,
http://banking.senate.gov/02_08hrg/080102/levitt.htm.

18. Juan Zarate, Testimony, House Financial Subcommittee, Oversight and Investigations, February 12, 2002, p. 10, http://financialservices.house.gov/media/pdf/021202
jz.pdf.

19. Victor Comras, "Al-Qaeda Finances and Funding to Affiliated Groups," *Strategic Insights*
4, No. 1 (January 2005), www.ccc.nps.navy.mil/si/2005/Jan/comrasJan05.asp.

20. Dore Gold, "Terrorism Financing: Origination, Organization, and Prevention," Committee on Governmental Affairs, U.S. Senate, July 31, 2003, http://hsgac.senate.gov
/_files/sprt108245terror_finance.pdf.

21. "Palestinian Jailed over al-Qaeda links," BBC.com, February 3, 2003, http://news.bbc.co
.uk/1/hi/world/middle_east/2721665.stm.

22. Matt Rees and Jamil Hamad, "Hamas Goes Global," *Time,* May 26, 2003, www.time.com
/time/magazine/article/0,9171,1101030526–452768,00.html.

23. Yaakov Amidror and David Keyes, "Will a Gaza 'Hamas-stan' Become a Future al-Qaeda Sanctuary?" *Jerusalem Issue Brief* 43, No. 7, November 8, 2004, www.jcpa.org/brief/brief 004–7.htm

24. Gold, *The Fight for Jerusalem*, p. 247.

25. Global Terror Alert, "Al-Qaida's Jihad in Palestine," October 6, 2005, www.globalterror-alert.com/pdf/1005/qaidapalestine1005.pdf.

26. Michael Eisenstadt, "Regional Security Implications of the Hamas Electoral Victory," in *Hamas Triumphant: Implications for Security, Politics, Economy and Strategy*, ed. Robert Satloff, Washington Institute for Near East Policy, Policy Focus, No. 3 (February 2006): 37, www.washingtoninstitute.org/templateC04.php?CID=232.

27. "Israeli Security Apparatus Is Able to Arrest Purported Leaders that Are Members in al-Qaeda," *al-Hayat al-Jadida* (Arabic), (undated), www.alhayat-j.com/details.php?opt=3&id=21445.

28. "Al-Qaeda Militants Ransack Gaza School: Director," *Middle East Times*, January 12, 2008, www.metimes.com/Politics/2008/01/12/alqaeda_militants_ransack_gaza_school_director/afp/.

29. Jonathan Dahoah-Halevi, "The Growing Hamas-Al Qaeda Connection," *Jerusalem Center for Public Affairs* 7, No. 1, May 17, 2007, www.jcpa.org/JCPA/Templates/ShowPage .asp?DBID=1&LNGID=1&TMID=111&FID=283&PID=0&IID=1574.

30. Ahmed al-Khatib, Mohamed Abou Zeid-Arish, Maher Ismael, and Salah el-Bolok, "2000 Egyptians Request to Join the Resistance; Hamas Returns Them to Egypt," *Al-Masry Al-Youm* (Egypt), February 6, 2008. www.almasry-alyoum/article.aspx?ArticleID=92673.

31. Ali El-Saleh, "Egypt: Security Detains Egyptians Suspected of Entering Gaza to Attack Israel," *Al-Sharq Al-Awsat* (UK), February 9, 2008, aawsat.com/english/news.asp?section=1&id=11729

32. Sheera Claire Frenkel, "Yadlin: Al-Qaida Entered Gaza During Breach," *Jerusalem Post*, February 26, 2008, www.jpost.com/servlet/Satellite?cid=1203847472236&pagename =JPost/JPArticle/ShowFull

33. U.S. Department of State, "Patterns of Global Terrorism 2003," Appendix B, April 29, 2004, www.state.gov/s/ct/rls/crt/2003/31711.htm.

34. Hashem Kassem, "Understanding the Significance of Ain al-Hilweh," *East West Record* (2003), www.eastwestrecord.com/Get_Articles.asp?ArticleID=480.

35. Mshari Al-Zaydi, "Nahr al Bared Up in Flames," *Ash-Sharq Al-Awsat* (UK), May 23, 2007, www.aawsat.com/english/news.asp?section=2&id=9051.

36. "Fatah al-Islam in Gaza," *Turkish Weekly*, December 26, 2007, www.turkishweekly.net /news.php?id=51159.

37. Zaki Chehab, *Inside Hamas: The Untold Story of the Militant Islamic Movement* (New York: Nation Books, 2007), pp. 140–142.

38. Testimony of David Aufhauser, "The Hamas Asset Freeze and Other Government Efforts to Stop Terrorist Funding," U.S. House of Representatives, Committee on Financial Services, Subcommittee on Oversight and Investigation, September 24, 2003, http://commdocs.house.gov/committees/bank/hba92334.000/hba92334_0.HTM.

39. Alfred B. Prados and Christopher M. Blanchard, "Saudi Arabia: Terrorist Financing Issues," Congressional Research Service, December 8, 2004, www.fas.org/irp/crs/RL32499.pdf.

40. Ibid.

41. Chehab, *Inside Hamas*, p. 139.

42. Charmaine Seitz, "Palestinian Politics a Battleground," Al-Jazeera, December 22, 2006, http://english.aljazeera.net/NR/exeres/3B03DA8A–8950–485F–84DA-E56B5F3B95B6 .htm.

43. "Testimony of Secretary of State Condoleezza Rice before the House Committee on Foreign Affairs," U.S. House of Representatives, October 24, 2007, http://foreignaffairs .house.gov/110/ric102407.htm.

44. Jonathan Schanzer, "Saddam's Ambassador to al Qaeda," *Weekly Standard,* March 1, 2004, www.weeklystandard.com/Content/Public/Articles/000/000/003/768rwsbj.asp.

45. Dan Eggen and Walter Pincus, "New Links between Iran, Al Qaeda Cited," *Washington Post,* July 22, 2004, www.washingtonpost.com/wp-dyn/articles/A4191–2004Jul21.html.

46. Al-Jazeera, "New Bin Laden Tape Warns Israel," May 16, 2008, http://english .aljazeera.net/NR/exeres/6912B81B-AB7B–4B30–8D26–03E8C259A15B.htm

47. Salah Nasrawi, "Al-Qaida's No. 2 Urges Holy War Over Gaza Strip," AP, June 4, 2008, http://gaza-strip-news.newslib.com/story/378–3241729/

CHAPTER 12

1. International Crisis Group, "Inside Gaza: The Challenge of Clans and Families," *Middle East Report,* No. 71, December 20, 2007, p. 1, www.crisisgroup.org/home/index.cfm?id =5234&l=1.

2. Kimary Shahin, "Notes on Palestinian Arabic with Speech Samples," Birzeit University (October 1999).

3. Marianne Heiberg and Geir Ovensen, "Palestinian Society in Gaza, West Bank and Arab Jerusalem: A Survey of Living Conditions," Fafo Report No. 151, http://almashriq.hiof .no/general/300/320/327/fafo/reports/FAFO151/10_1.html.

4. International Crisis Group, "Inside Gaza," p. 2.

5. Meir Litvak, *The Islamization of the Palestinian Identity: The Case of Hamas* (Tel Aviv: Moshe Dayan Center for Middle Eastern and African Studies, 1996), p. 6.

6. Anat Kurz and Nahman Tal, *Hamas: Radical Islam in a National Struggle.* Jaffe Center for Strategic Studies, Memorandum No. 48 (July 1997): 19.

7. Justus Reid Weiner and Diane Morrison, *Linking the Gaza Strip with the West Bank: Implications of a Palestinian Corridor across Israel* (Jerusalem: Jerusalem Center for Public Affairs, 2008), pp. 9, 22–23, www.jcpa.org/JCPA/Templates/showpage.asp?DBID=1 &LNGID=1&TMID=103&FID=448&PID=0&IID=1810.

8. Jamal Halaby, "Jordan Denies Wanting West Bank Back," Associated Press, February 27, 2008. http://abcnews.go.com/International/wireStory?id=4355313

9. See the UNRWA Web site for updated statistics: www.un.org/unrwa/publications/index .html.

10. World Bank, "Poverty in the West Bank and Gaza" (January 2001), http://lnweb18 .worldbank.org/mna/mena.nsf/Attachments/Poverty+Report+WBG/$File/poverty +report.pdf.

11. Khalil Shiqaqi, *The West Bank and Gaza Strip: Future Political and Administrative Relations* (Arabic) (Jerusalem: PASSIA, 1994), pp. 83 and 78.

12. Ibid., pp. 79–80.

13. Ibid., pp. 83–84.

14. Ibid., pp. 88–89.

15. *Haaretz,* February 16, 2001.

16. Ehud Ya'ari, "The Morning After," in *After Arafat? The Future of Palestinian Politics,* ed. Robert Satloff, Washington Institute for Near East Policy, Policy Focus, No. 42 (October 2001): 10.

17. David Schenker, *Palestinian Democracy & Governance* (Washington, DC: Washington Institute for Near East Policy, 2000), p. 105.

18. Daniel Sobelman, "PA's Rajoub: Dahlan Is Undermining My Authority in West Bank," *Haaretz*, November 5, 2002, www.haaretz.co.il/hasen/pages/ShArt.jhtml?itemNo =162311&contrassID=1&subContrassID=0&sbSubContrassID=0.

19. Frank Bruni, "Arafat Picks Security Adviser He Had Shunned," *New York Times*, August 26, 2003, http://query.nytimes.com/gst/fullpage.html?res=9C01E0D81239F935A1575B C0A9659C8B63.

20. International Crisis Group, "Inside Gaza," executive summary, pp. 3 and 5.

21. Ibid., p. 18.

22. Amira Hass, "Hamas Tightens Control on State Institutions in Gaza," *Haaretz*, December 11, 2007, www.haaretz.com/hasen/spages/933389.html.

23. "Hamas MPs Challenge Abbas with Parliament Session in Gaza," *Daily Star* (Lebanon), November 8, 2007, www.dailystar.com.lb/article.asp?edition_id=10&categ_id=2&article _id=86615.

24. Ali Waked, "PA May Hold Election by Year's End, Source Says," Ynet News, April 2, 2008, www.ynetnews.com/articles/0,7340,L–3526848,00.html

25. Karin Laub, "Economic Woes Behind New Unrest in Gaza," Associated Press, November 13, 2007, www.guardian.co.uk/worldlatest/story/0,–7074416,00.html.

26. Amos Harel and Avi Issacharoff, "Hamas Outmaneuvers Israel with Three Quick Moves," *Haaretz*, January 25, 2008, www.haaretz.com/hasen/spages/948098.html.

27. Khaled Abu Toameh, "Egypt Nixes Hamas Call for Alliance," *Jerusalem Post*, February 4, 2008, www.jpost.com/servlet/Satellite?cid=1202064573300&pagename=JPost%2FJPArticle %2FShowFull.

28. Roee Nahmias, "Hamas Considering Economic Disengagement from Israel," Ynet News, February 2, 2008, www.ynetnews.com/articles/0,7340,L–3501759,00.html.

29. Amnesty International, "Egypt Blocks Gazans' Access to the Outside World," January 31, 2008, www.amnesty.org/en/news-and-updates/news/egypt-blocks-gazans-access-outside-world–20080131.

30. Martin Kramer, "Gaza into Egypt," *Sandbox*, January 25, 2008. http://sandbox.blog-city .com/gaza_into_egypt.htm.

31. Barak Ravid, "J'lem Said to Favor Hamas Bid to Cut Israel-Gaza Ties," *Haaretz*, February 2, 2008, www.haaretz.com/hasen/spages/950393.html.

32. Rushdi Abu Alouf and Richard Boudreaux, "Gaza Border Breached; Thousands Flood into Egypt," *Los Angeles Times*, January 23, 2008, www.latimes.com/news/nationworld /world/middleeast/la-fg-gaza23jan23,1,6332024.story.

33. Associated Press, "1 Dead in Palestinian-Egyptian Clashes," February 4, 2008, www.jpost .com/servlet/Satellite?c=JPArticle&cid=1202064579870&pagename=JPost%2FJPArticle %2FShowFull.

34. *Al-Gumhouriya*, January 27, 2008. Translation courtesy of MEMRI at: http://memri.org /bin/articles.cgi?Page=archives&Area=sd&ID=SP183708.

35. Will Rasmussen, "Gaza Border Breach Fuels Anger over Food Shortages," Reuters, January 28, 2008, www.reuters.com/article/idUSL28733455.

36. Sarah El Deeb, "Palestinians Profit from Breach," Associated Press, January 25, 2008, www.wtopnews.com/?nid=500&sid=1332878.

37. Maan News Agency, "9,000 Gazans Still at Large in Egyptian Cities," February 8, 2008, www.maannews.net/en/index.php?opr=ShowDetails&ID=27670; and "Egypt Deports 3,000 Palestinians to the Gaza Strip," February 11, 2008, www.maannews.net/en/index .php?opr=ShowDetails&ID=27790.

38. Amos Harel and Avi Issacharoff, "The Gaza Border Is Closed, but the Bomb Is Ticking," *Haaretz*, February 4, 2008, www.haaretz.com/hasen/spages/950759.html.

39. Omar Sinan, "Gazans Want to Get Deeper into Egypt," Associated Press, January 30, 2008, www.guardian.co.uk/worldlatest/story/0,–7269062,00.html.

40. Barak Ravid, Yoav Stern and Avi Issacharoff, "Mubarak: Gaza Tensions Brings Iran Threat Closer," *Haaretz*, March 25, 2008, www.haaretz.com/hasen/spages/968428.html

41. Maan News Agency, "Palestinians Held By Egypt Threaten Suicide," February 17, 2008, www.maannews.net/en/index.php?opr=ShowDetails&ID27840

42. Associated Press, "Official: Egypt Released 21 Detained Palestinians, Some were Members of Hamas," February 25, 2008, www.iht.com/articles/ap/2008/02/25/africa/ME-GEN-Egypt-Palestinians.php

43. "Egypt Warns Palestinians Not to Breach Gaza Border," *Al-Manar* (Hizbullah television Web site), February 7, 2008. www.almanar.com.lb/NewsSite/NewsDetails.aspx?id=35125.

44. International Crisis Group, "Inside Gaza," executive summary.

45. Ahmed Yousef, "Hamas Doesn't Want a Separate Gaza," *The Daily Star* (Lebanon), February 18, 2008, www.dailystar.com.lb/article.asp?edition_id=10&categ_id=5&article_id=89035

CHAPTER 13

1. White House Press Release, "President Bush Discusses the Middle East," June 16, 2007, www.whitehouse.gov/news/releases/2007/07/20070716–7.html.

2. Condoleezza Rice, "Roundtable Interview with Print Journalists," U.S. Department of State, November 21, 2007, www.state.gov/secretary/rm/2007/11/95545.htm.

3. "The Palestinian Factions: Abbas Has No Right to Give Up One Inch of Palestine," Official Hamas Web site, November 27, 2007, www.alqssa,m.ps/english/?action=showmimp&fid=735.

4. Isabel Kershner and Taghreed El-Khodary, "Hamas Urges Taking Hard Line against Israel," *New York Times*, November 27, 2007, www.nytimes.com/2007/11/27/world/middleeast/27mideast.html?partner=rssnyt&emc=rss.

5. "Celebrating Anniversary, Hamas Warns of Intifada," *Ash-Sharq al-Awsat* (UK), December 15, 2007, www.asharq-e.com/news.asp?section=1&id=11165.

6. Maan News Service, "Hamas Kidnaps Five Fatah Members," November 25, 2007, www.maannews.net/en/index.php?opr=ShowDetails&ID=26465.

7. Kershner and El-Khodary, "Hamas Urges Taking Hard Line against Israel."

8. "Weapons to Abbas Militia Is an Authorization to Right Resistance and Zionist Gift to Ramallah Gang," November 21, 2007, www.alqassam.ps/english/?action=showsta&sid=755.

9. Khalid Amayreh, "Timeline of Jewish Terrorists Designs Against the Aqsa Mosque," Palestinian Information Center, Official Hamas Web site, February 15, 2007, www.palestine-info.co.uk/en/default.aspx?xyz=U6Qq7k%2bcOd87MDI46m9rUxJEpMO%2bi1s74zx3uR44pF3wFg6AZmzH6V2IYdBu9tPXItdfyy%2fGIkZaadbHDQ7hcVaB1%2bC4jZWx00%2frKczdRUABmKguIlRnKnYKm4o3GDHdMf%2beTIJniwE%3d.

10. Aaron Klein, "Hamas Broadcasts from Temple Mount," Ynet News, December 19, 2007, www.ynetnews.com/articles/0,7340,L–3484659,00.html.

11. http://alaqsavoice.ps/arabic/index.php?action=index.

12. "Statehood Bush Promised," Hamas Web site, November 28, 2007, www.alqassam.ps/english/?action=showdetail&fid=736.

13. "We Won't Waive an Inch of Palestinian Lands," Hamas Web site, December 9, 2007, www.alqassam.ps/english/?action=showdetail&fid=758.

14. Wisam Afifa, "New Round of Talks Expected Between Fatah and Hamas Movements," International Middle East Media Center (Beit Sahour, West Bank), December 11, 2007, www.imemc.org/article/51963.

15. Maan News Agency, "Mash'al: Hamas Ready to Form Central Government in West Bank and Gaza Strip," December 11, 2007, www.maannews.net/en/index.php?opr=Show-Details&ID=26733.

16. Isabel Kershner, "Abbas's Premier Tells Israel to Reopen Gaza," *New York Times,* December 14, 2007, www.nytimes.com/2007/12/14/world/middleeast/14mideast.html.

17. "Hamas Ready for Unconditional Talks with Abbas," *Middle East Online,* January 5, 2007, www.middle-east-online.com/english/?id=23771.

18. Al-Jazeera "Palestinian Rivals Reach Agreement," March 23, 2008, http://english .aljazeera.net/NR/exeres/029A76B6–0DA9–4CCE–8F3A–8EBB6E1204A0.htm

19. Maan News Agency, "Hamas and Fatah at Odds over Interpretation of Yemeni-Brokered Agreement," March 24, 2008, www.maannews.net/en/index.php?opr=ShowDetails&ID =28438

20. Karin Laub, "Disarray Snags Palestinian Unity Effort," Associated Press, March 24, 2008, http://abcnews.go.com/International/wireStory?id=4514607

21. Janine Zacharia, "Abbas Rejects Offer from Hamas to Visit Gaza Strip," Bloomberg News, April 1, 2008, www2.nysun.com/foreign/abbas-rejects-offer-from-hamas-to-visit-gaza-strip/

22. An-Najah University, "Results of Palestinian Public Opinion Poll (34)," May 19, 2008, www2.najah.edu/nnu_portal/index.php?news_id=1163

23. Al-Jazeera, "Hamas Leader Renews Truce Offer," December 19, 2007, http://english .aljazeera.net/NR/exeres/93CE99EF-F349–4BCE-A8A4-BCC5FBD35F49.htm.

24. Khalid Amayreh, "Draft of a Proposed Ceasefire Agreement between Israel and Hamas Being Studied," Palestinian Information Center, Official Hamas Web site, January 28, 2008, www.palestine-info.co.uk/en/default.aspx?xyz=U6Qq7k%2bcOd87MDI46m9rU xJEpMO%2bi1s7rOCXKz9%2fLgZY2xGA2T9I%2fWpGYll7cL1KrefSBIC%2bXovwN %2fq%2f1FRwDJDuJpg%2bS%2fSpiZfVmZkPhHLD0MTU%2bnInDh%2byQix7yEb %2fB%2fovoV07iN0%3d.

25. Seth Wikas, "The Hamas Ceasefire: Historical Background, Future Foretold?" Washington Institute for Near East Policy, PeaceWatch, No. 357, January 3, 2002, www .washingtoninstitute.org/templateC05.php?CID=2048.

26. Gil Hoffman and Herb Keinon, "Ministers Split on 'Hudna' Offer," *Jerusalem Post,* December 19, 2007, www.jpost.com/servlet/Satellite?cid=1196847381433&pagename =JPost%2FJPArticle%2FShowFull.

27. Amos Harel, "Hamas Policy: Escalation to Force Israel into Cease-Fire in Gaza," *Haaretz,* January 18, 2008, www.haaretz.com/hasen/spages/946028.html.

28. Al-Jazeera, "Israel Weighs Response to Rockets," February 10, 2007, http://english .aljazeera.net/NR/exeres/E5B3A58B–00E7–47F1-A443–94F2A9DC950B.htm.

29. "Ahmed Yousuf: Open Letter to Condoleezza Rice," December 6, 2007, www .palestinechronicle.com/story–120607142819.htm.

30. Avi Issacharoff, "On 20th Anniversary, Hamas Vows Never to Recognize Israel," *Haaretz,* December 16, 2007, www.haaretz.com/hasen/spages/934774.html.

31. "Hamas Calls Bush Visit 'Unwelcome,'" *Al-Jazeera Magazine,* January 5, 2008, http: //english.aljazeera.com/news/newsfull.php?newid=75539.

32. Nidal al-Mughrabi, "Thousands Protest in Gaza against 'Vampire' Bush," Reuters, January 9, 2008, http://uk.reuters.com/article/UKNews1/idUKL0930149920080109.

33. Maan News Agency, "Haniyeh: We Will Not Accept a Dwarfed Palestinian State," January 12, 2008, www.maannews.net/en/index.php?opr=ShowDetails&ID=27171.

34. "Bush Promises 'Unacceptable' for Next Generations of Palestinians," *al-Manar* (Hizbullah television Web site), January 12, 2008, www.almanar.com.lb/NewsSite /NewsDetails.aspx?id=33225.

35. Agence France Presse, "US Admits Mideast Peace Deal Hangs on the Fate of Gaza," January 13, 2008, http://afp.google.com/article/ALeqM5jkhAUi-cSpOQHP9bqWNz-nWpCyzQ.

CHAPTER 14

1. Al-Jazeera, "Abbas: Hamas Must Talk Peace," February 22, 2006, http://english .aljazeera.net/English/archive/archive?ArchiveId=18826.
2. Al-Jazeera, "Israel Imposes Sanctions on PA," February 24, 2006, http://english .aljazeera.net/English/archive/archive?ArchiveId=18694.
3. Al-Jazeera, "Hamas: Take Us Off Terror List," February 19, 2006, http://english .aljazeera.net/English/archive/archive?ArchiveId=18773.
4. Al-Jazeera, "Hamas Secures More Iranian Funding," March 6, 2007, http://english .aljazeera.net/NR/exeres/2A62C583-E1C7–454E-B0B3–16DB56E3C4FD.htm.
5. Wafa Amr, "U.S. to Lift Sanctions on New Abbas government," Reuters, June 17, 2007, www.reuters.com/article/newsOne/idUSL8196756120070617?pageNumber=1&virtual BrandChannel=0.
6. B'Tselem: The Israeli Center for Human Rights in the Occupied Territories, "Israeli and Palestinian Organizations Petition High Court to Resume Fuel Supply to Gaza," January 21, 2008, www.btselem.org/english/Gaza_Strip/20080121_Increase_of_sanction_on _Gaza.asp.
7. International Committee of the Red Cross, "The Occupied Palestinian Territories: Dignity Denied," December 13, 2007, www.icrc.org/Web/Eng/siteeng0.nsf/html/palestine-report–131207.
8. Adalah: The Legal Center for Arab Minority Rights in Israel, "Supreme Court Petition Challenging the Israeli Government's Decision to Cut Fuel and Electricity to Gaza," January 26, 2008, www.adalah.org/eng/pressreleases/pr.php?file=08_01_26.
9. Sarah El Deeb, "Israeli Court Orders Delay in Electricity Cut to Gaza," Associated Press, November 30, 2007, www.iht.com/articles/ap/2007/11/30/africa/ME-GEN-Israel-Palestinians.php.
10. Maan News Agency, "Palestinian Health Ministry Accuses Hamas of Looting Gaza Strip Hospital's Reserve Fuel," December 6, 2007, www.maannews.net/en/index.php?opr =ShowDetails&ID=26661. This continued through the spring of 2008. See Agence France Press, "Hamas Blocked Fuel for Gaza Hospitals," April 27, 2008, http://afp.google .com/article/ALeqM5jgtcs9jOvynI_-yTmGNq9lEy15ew
11. Ibrahim Barzak, "Gazans Facing 8-Hour Daily Power Outages Because of Israeli Fuel Cutbacks," Associated Press, January 6, 2008, www.iht.com/articles/ap/2008/01/06 /africa/ME-GEN-Israel-Palestinians.php.
12. Maan News Agency, "Gaza's Power Plant Shuts Down as Israel Blocks Fuel and Food Shipments for Third Day," January 20, 2008, www.maannews.net/en/index.php?opr =ShowDetails&ID=27329.
13. International Committee of the Red Cross, "Convention (IV) relative to the Protection of Civilian Persons in Time of War," www.icrc.org/ihl.nsf/385ec082b509e76c412567390 03e636d/6756482d86146898c125641e004aa3c5
14. Saed Bannoura, "Dozens of Protests Held Worldwide Calling for an End to Gaza Siege," International Middle East Media Center, February 24, 2008, www.imemc.org/article/53026
15. Associated Press, "Hamas Seizes Aid Meant for Red Crescent," February 7, 2008, www .ynet.co.il/english/articles/0,7340,L–3504227,00.html.
16. Khaled Abu Toameh, "Palestinian Journalists: Hamas Staged Blackouts," *Jerusalem Post*, January 23, 2008, www.jpost.com/servlet/Satellite?c=JPArticle&cid=1201070777685 &pagename=JPost%2FJPArticle%2FShowFull.

17. Osama al-Sharif, "Hamas Must Stand Down," *Arab News* (Saudi Arabia), February 13, 2008, www.arabnews.com/?page=7&section=0&article=106722&d=13&m=2&y=2008.

18. Hussein Shobokshi, "Hamas First and Foremost," *ash-Sharq al-Awsat,* February 10, 2008, www.asharq-e.com/news.asp?section=2&id=11736.

19. Khaled Abu Toameh, "Arab Editor Blames Hamas for Gaza Crisis," *Jerusalem Post,* January 21, 2008, www.jpost.com/servlet/Satellite?cid=1200572510762&pagename=JPost %2FJPArticle%2FShowFull.

20. Aviram Zino, "Barak Authorizes Increasing Shipments of Diesel Fuel to Gaza," Ynet News, January 10, 2008, www.ynetnews.com/articles/0,7340,L–3492928,00.html.

21. "Gaza Power Reductions to Begin Thursday," *Jerusalem Post,* February 6, 2008, www .jpost.com/servlet/Satellite?pagename=JPost%2FJPArticle%2FShowFull&cid=1202246 332374.

22. Barak Ravid and Avi Issacharoff, "Israel and PA: Hamas Seizing Half of All Fuel Sent to Gaza Strip," *Haaretz,* April 11, 2008, www.haaretz.com/hasen/spages/974043.html

23. Dan Murphy, "Gaza Tunnel Smugglers Stay Busy," *Christian Science Monitor,* January 14, 2008, www.csmonitor.com/2008/0114/p06s02-wome.html.

24. Israel Ministry of Foreign Affairs, "Terror in Gaza: Ten Months Since the Hamas Takeover," April 30, 2008, www.mfa.gov.il/MFA/Terrorism-+Obstacle+to+Peace /Palestinian+terror+since+2000/Terror+in+Gaza-+Two+months+since+the+Hamas +takeover+16-Aug–2007.htm

25. Erica Silverman, "Goods Smuggled in Gaza Tunnels, Taxed by Hamas," *Washington Times,* January 9, 2008, www.washingtontimes.com/article/20080109/FOREIGN/7940 77501,

26. Author's interview with senior Israeli official, November 2007, Tel Aviv.

27. Yaakov Katz, Herb Keinon, and Hilary Leila Krieger, "Israel Sends US Videos of Egypt Helping Hamas," *Jerusalem Post,* December 18, 2007, www.jpost.com/servlet/Satellite ?c=JPArticle&cid=1196847366227&pagename=JPost%2FJPArticle%2FShowFull.

28. Dina Ezzat, "Another Summer Cloud," *Al-Ahram Weekly* (Egypt), No. 850, June 21–27, 2007, http://weekly.ahram.org.eg/2007/850/eg2.htm.

29. Yaakov Katz, "Suleiman: Egypt to End Smuggling," *Jerusalem Post,* December 26, 2007, www.jpost.com/servlet/Satellite?cid=1198517213296&pagename=JPost%2FJPArticle %2FShowFull.

30. Ellen Knickmeyer, "Egypt to Bolster Gaza Border," *Washington Post,* January 7, 2008, www.washingtonpost.com/wp-dyn/content/article/2008/01/06/AR2008010602055.html

31. Yaakov Katz, "Egypt Launching Tunnel Detection Unit," *Jerusalem Post,* March 31, 2008, www.jpost.com/servlet/Satellite?pagename=JPost%2FJPArticle%2FShowFull&cid=120 6632370621

32. Amira Hass, "Gaza Source: Hamas Planned Border Wall Blast for Months," *Haaretz,* January 24, 2008, www.haaretz.com/hasen/spages/947775.html.

33. Al-Jazeera, "Blockaded Gazans Pour into Egypt," January 24, 2008, http://english .aljazeera.net/NR/exeres/2CE3A5EC–9904–4A84-B0E1–2588EBD7429F.htm.

34. BBC News, "Gazans Flood through Egypt Border," January 23, 2008, http://news.bbc.co .uk/2/hi/middle_east/7204029.stm.

35. Maan News Agency, "Hamas and PA Delegations Summoned to Egypt to Discuss Rafah Border Situation," January 26, 2008, www.maannews.net/en/index.php?opr=Show-Details&ID=27447.

36. Avi Issacharoff, Yuva Azoulay and Amos Harel, "Shin Bet: Militants Smuggled Advanced Arms into Gaza Strip," *Haaretz,* February 4, 2008, http://haaretz.com/hasen/spages /950571.html.

37. Maan News Agency, "1 Million Forged US Dollars from Gaza Reportedly Seized in Egypt," February 7, 2008, www.maannews.net/en/index.php?opr=ShowDetails&ID =27653.

38. Agence France Presse, "US 'Not Satisfied' with Egyptian Efforts to Scrap Tunnels," February 13, 2008, http://news.yahoo.com/s/afp/20080213/pl_afp/usmideastpalestinian gazaegypt.

39. "Iran Advances to Help Egypt on Rafah," *Al-Alam* (Iran), January 27, 2008, www.alalam .ir/English/en-NewsPage.asp?newsid=032030120080128100513.

40. IRNA (Iran News Agency), "Iran, Egypt Discuss Keeping Gaza Supply Route Open," January 28, 2008, www2.irna.com/en/news/view/menu–234/08012896191222103.htm. "Press TV (Iran Television Web site), Ahmadinejad's Egypt Visit Not on Agenda," February 5, 2008, www.presstv.ir/detail.aspx?id=41779&sectionid=351020101.

41. Abdel-Rahman Hussein, "Hamas Fires at Egyptian Builders to Prevent New Wall," *Daily News Egypt,* February 13, 2008, www.dailystaregypt.com/article.aspx?ArticleID=11870

42. Ashraf Sweilam, "Egypt Walls Up Gaza Border," Associated Press, March 6, 2008, http://apnews.myway.com/article/20080307/D8V8ARO80.html

43. David Schenker, "Egypt Builds a Wall," *Weekly Standard,* April 28, 2008, www.weekly-standard.com/Content/Public/Articles/000/000/015/010aplyi.asp

44. Reuters, "Egypt: No Gaza Border Deal Without Consent of Israel, PA," February 17, 2008, www.haaretz.com/hasen/spages/955034.html

45. Associated Press, "Egyptian Police Uncover 500kg TNT Near Rafah," May 27, 2008, www.ynetnews.com/articles/0,7340,L–3548630,00.html

46. Agence France Press, "Palestinian Authority Approves Gaza-Egypt Powerline," April 29, 2008, www.naharnet.com/domino/tn/NewsDesk.nsf/MiddleEast/43845B114F760B4FC 22574390054D1E6?OpenDocument

47. Fathia al-Dakhakhni, "Omar Suleiman Will Visit Israel in Days to Discuss the Crisis of 'Crossing and Prisoners'," *Al-Masry Al-Youm* (Arabic), February 7, 2008, www.almasry-alyoum.com/article.aspx?ArticleID=92728.

CHAPTER 15

1. Adam Entous, "Israel Seeks International Backing for Gaza Campaign," Reuters, February 13, 2008, www.reuters.com/article/worldNews/idUSL1222044720080213.

2. Independent Media Review Analysis, "Polls: Public Supports Large Military Operation Over Ceasefire 44%:33%" June 12, 2008, www.imra.org.il/story.php3?id=39608

3. Rami Almeghari, "Negotiator Eriqat Warns of Israeli Invasion of Gaza, Denies Talks on Jerusalem Delayed," International Middle East Media Center (Ramallah), February 13, 2008, www.imemc.org/article/52748.

4. Agence France Presse, "Amos Oz Warns 'Catastrophe' of Gaza Invasion," February 12, 2008, http://afp.google.com/article/ALeqM5houoWAjq3S1WtciX_0Omsf_pfqfg.

5. Amos Harel, "Barak Says Ministerial Calls for Action in Gaza are Dangerous," *Haaretz,* February 13, 2008, www.haaretz.com/hasen/spages/953688.html.

6. Herb Keinon, "Livni to Push for Int'l Force in Gaza," *Jerusalem Post,* December 7, 2007.

7. Michael Eisentstadt, *The Palestinians: Between State Failure and Civil War,* Washington Institute for Near East Policy, Policy Focus, No. 78 (December 2007): 36, www .washingtoninstitute.org/templateC04.php?CID=285.

8. Herb Keinon, "Otte to Post: Int'l Force for Gaza Could be Set up Quickly," *Jerusalem Post,* December 19, 2007, www.jpost.com/servlet/Satellite?cid=1196847385402&pagename=JPost%2FJPArticle%2FShowFull.

9. Amos Harel and Avi Issacharoff, "Government Concerned over Egypt-Hamas Ties," *Haaretz,* October 23, 2007, www.haaretz/com/hasen/spages/916111.html.

10. Fox News, "Hamas Militants Train for Attack on Israel," December 6, 2007, www .foxnews.com/story/0,2933,315–488,00.html.

11. Nick Francona, "Hamas's Military Capabilities after the Gaza Takeover," Washington Institute for Near East Policy, Policywatch, No. 1278, August 27, 2007, www.washington-institute.org/templateC05.php?CID=2654.

12. *Jerusalem Post,* "RPG Penetrated IDF Tank in Gaza Strip," December 12, 2007, www .jpost.com/servlet/Satellite?cid=1196847322860&pagename=JPost%2FJPArticle%2F ShowFull.

13. Roee Nahmias, "Hamas Says Fired Anti-Aircraft Guns at Israeli Helicopters," YNet News, December 21, 2007, www.ynetnews.com/articles/0,7340,L–3485211,00.html.

14. Francona, "Hamas's Military Capabilities after the Gaza Takeover."

15. Yaakov Katz, "Hamas Establishing Bunker System Along Gaza Fence," *Jerusalem Post,* October 29, 2007, www.jpost.com/servlet/Satellite?pagename=JPost%2FJPArticle%2F ShowFull&cid=1192380683478.

16. Amos Harel, "IDF's Tactical Upper Hand over Hamas in Gaza Is Diminishing," *Haaretz,* October 30, 2007, www.haaretz.com/hasen/spages/918243.html

17. Amos Harel, "Reservists: Hamas Fights Like an Army," *Haaretz,* November 7, 2007, www.haaretz.com/hasen/spages/921630.html.

18. *Jerusalem Post,* "Hamas Will Harm Schalit If IDF Carries Out Gaza Incursion," December 14, 2007, www.jpost.com/servlet/Satellite?cid=1196847338287&pagename=JPost %2FJPArticle%2FShowFull.

19. Mark Weiss, "Whoever Enters Will Leave in Pieces," *Jerusalem Post,* November 8, 2007, www.jpost.com/servlet/Satellite?cid=1192380775988&pagename=JPost%2FJPArticle %2FShowFull.

20. Yuval Azulay, "8 Palestinians Killed, 4 IDF Soldiers Hurt in Gaza Raids," *Haaretz,* December 11, 2007, www.haaretz.com/hasen.spages/933219.html.

21. Al-Jazeera, "Palestinians Killed in Israeli Raid," January 15, 2008, http://english .aljazeera.net/NR/exeres/114A4248-B3E6–400C–9B59–13295A1C9600.htm.

22. Isabel Kershner, "Abbas Puts Peace Talks on Hold as Israel Continues Military Offensive in Gaza," *New York Times,* March 3, 2008, www.nytimes.com/2008/03/03/world /middleeast/03mideast.html?fta=y

23. IDF Spokesperson Announcement, "IDF Targets Hamas Post in Southern Gaza," November 28, 2007, www.mfa.gov.il/MFA/Terrorism-+Obstacle+to+Peace/Terrorism+and +Islamic+Fundamentalism-/IDF%20targets%20Hamas%20post%20in%20southern %20Gaza%20%2028-Nov–2007.

24. Amos Harel, "Defense Officials Concerned as Hamas Upgrades Qassam Arsenal," *Haaretz,* December 7, 2007, www.haaretz.com/hasen/spages/932106.html.

25. "In January 2008: Al Qassam Brigades Fired 540 Rocket and Missile and Killed Two Zionists," Official Hamas Web site, February 2, 2008, www.alqassam.ps/english/?action =showdetail&fid=837.

26. Roni Sofer, "Dichter: 250,000 Under Qassam Threat if We Don't Act," Ynet News, December 9, 2007, www.ynetenews.com/articles/0,7340,L–3480533,00.html.

27. Isabel Kershner, "Hamas Rocket Kills Israeli," *International Herald Tribune,* February 28, 2008, www.iht.com/articles/2008/02/28/africa/28mideast.php

28. Roee Nahmias, "Army Chief: Gaza Operation Unavoidable," Ynet News, December 12, 2007, www.ynetnews.com/articles/0,7340,L–3481991,00.html.

29. Hanan Greenberg, "Defense Officials Predict Limited Conflict in Gaza after Summit," Ynet News, November 18, 2007, www.ynetnews.com/articles/0,7340,L–3472673,00.html.

30. Shahar Ilan, "Olmert Rules Out Gaza Ground Operation," *Haaretz,* January 14, 2008, www.haaretz.com/hasen/spages/944665.html.

31. Aaron Lerner, "MK Hanegbi: Invasion of Gaza Inevitable," Independent Media Review and Analysis (IMRA), January 17, 2008.

32. Amos Harel, "IDF: Officers: We Faced Fierce But Unorganized Resistance in Gaza," *Haaretz,* March 5, 2008, www.haaretz.com/hasen/spages/960855.html

33. Yaakov Katz and Herb Keinon, "Iran Smuggling Arms to Gaza by Sea," *Jerusalem Post,* April 17, 2008, www.jpost.com/servlet/Satellite?pagename=JPost%2FJPArticle%2F ShowFull&cid=1208422633228

34. Al-Qassam Brigades Web Site, "Al-Qassam Briages Hit a Zionist Helicopter by Heavy Machine Guns and the Enemy Admitted," March 15, 2008, www.alqassam.ps/english /index.php?action=showsta&sid=1030

35. Marie Colvin, "Hamas Wages Iran's Proxy War on Israel," *The Times* (UK), March 9, 2008, www.timesonline.co.uk/tol/news/world/middle_east/article3512014.ece

36. Intelligence and Terrorism Information Center (Israel), "Hamas's Military Buildup in the Gaza Strip," April 8, 2008, www.terrorism-info.org.il/malam_multimedia/English /eng_n/pdf/hamas_080408.pdf

37. Khaled Abu Toameh, "Exclusive: Fatah, Hamas May Join Ranks," *Jerusalem Post,* November 29, 2007, www.jpost.com/servlet/Satellite?pagename=JPost%2FJPArticle%2F ShowFull&cid=1195546765575.

38. Al-Jazeera, "Abbas Calls for Hamas Overthrow," November 15, 2007, http://english .aljazeera.net/NR/exeres/A63A98CF-BEB2–4142–8D68–786D283A2936.htm.

39. Ali El-Saleh, "Interview with Hamas's Said Siyam," *Ash-Sharq al-Awsat* (London), November 25, 2007, www.asharqalawsat.com/english/news.asp?section=3&id=10988.

40. *Ash-Sharq Al-Awsat,* "Olmert: Israel Will Fight Gaza Terrorism by All 'Effective Means'," February 12, 2008, www.asharqalawsat.com/english/news.asp?section=1&id=11754.

41. David Rose, "The Gaza Bombshell," *Vanity Fair,* April 2008, www.vanityfair.com /politics/features/2008/04/gaza200804

42. *Washington Post,* "Carter Urged to Shun Hamas," April 11, 2008, www.washington-post.com/wp-dyn/content/article/2008/04/10/AR2008041003640.html

43. Molly Moore, "France Discloses 'Contacts' with Hamas," *Washington Post,* May 20, 2008, www.washingtonpost.com/wp-dyn/content/article/2008/05/19/AR2008051901586 .html?hpid=moreheadlines

CHAPTER 16

1. Khaled Abu Toameh, "Hamas Shaken by Collaborator Suspicions," *Jerusalem Post,* December 27, 2007, www.jpost.com/servlet/Satellite?cid=1198517230494&pagename =JPost%2FJPArticle%2FShowFull.

2. Palestine Media Center, "Hamas Plans Fatah Talks, Says Gaza Rule Temporary," PLO Web site, October 11, 2007, www.palestine-pmc.com/details.asp?cat=1&id=1112.

3. Xinhua (China), "Abbas, Hamas Leaders Pray Together in W. Bank," November 2, 2007, http://news.xinhuanet.com/english/2007–11/02/content_7000416.htm.

4. "Mashaal: Hamas Ready to Cede Control," *Jerusalem Post,* December 12, 2007, www.jpost .com/servlet/Satellite?pagename=JPost%2FJPArticle%2FShowFull&cid=1196847305632.

5. Khaled Abu Toameh, "Infighting Dragging Hamas Down," *Jerusalem Post,* November 5, 2007, www.jpost.com/servlet/Satellite?pagename=JPost%2FJPArticle%2FShowFull&cid =1192380734763.

6. Palestinian Center for Policy and Survey Research, Palestinian Opinion Poll No. 28, June 9, 2008, www.pcpsr.org/survey/polls/2008/p28epressrelease.html

7. Mshari al-Zaydi, "For Lebanon's Sake," *Al-Sharq al-Awsat* (UK), July 20, 2006, http://aawsat.com/english/news.asp?section=2&id=5692.

8. Khaled Abu Toameh, "Syria, Iran Trying to Overthrow Abbas and Fatah," *Jerusalem Post*, January 15, 2008, www.jpost.com/servlet/Satellite?pagename=JPost%2FJPArticle%2FShowFull&cid=1200308086914.

9. Nidal al-Mughrabi, "Gaza Tensions Flare after Abduction and Funeral Blast," *The Peninsula* (Qatar), December 15, 2007, www.thepeninsulaqatar.com/Display_news.asp?section=World_News&subsection=Gulf%2C+Middle+East+%26+Africa&month=December2007&file=World_News2007121515133.xml.

10. Adel Zaanoun, "Hamas Frees Palestinian PM Aide Amid Exchange Mediation," *Middle East Times*, February 1, 2008, www.metimes.com/Politics/2008/02/01/hamas_frees_pm_aide_amid_palestinian_exchange_mediation/afp/.

11. Palestinian Centre for Human Rights, "PCHR Calls for Stopping attacks against Offices of Fatah Movement and Affiliated Institutions in Gaza," December 30, 2007, www.pchrgaza.ps/files/PressR/English/2007/178–2007.html.

12. Maan News Agency, "Hamas-Allied Police Detain Former Gaza Security Chief," January 15, 2007, www.maannews.net/en/index.php?opr=ShowDetails&ID=27210.

13. See Palestinian Bureau of Statistics, Press Release, December 12, 2007, www.pcbs.gov.ps/census2007/DesktopDefault.aspx?tabID=4081&lang=ar-JO.

14. Maan News Service, "Fatah Delegation Visits Home of Bereaved Hamas Leader Az-Zahhar," January 17, 2008, www.maannews.net/en/index.php?opr=ShowDetails&ID=27275.

15. Press TV (Iran), "Abbas Condoles Hamas Leader," January 17, 2007, www.presstv.ir/detail.aspx?id=39139&sectionid=351020202.

16. Maan News Agency, "Haniyeh's Political Advisor Invites Abbas to Visit Gaza Strip," January 17, 2008, www.maannews.net/en/index.php?opr=ShowDetails&ID=27283.

17. Maan News Agency, "Fatah Reopens Its Gaza Headquarters 24 Hours After Hamas-Allied Police Raid," January 16, 2008, www.maannews.net/en/index.php?opr=ShowDetails&ID=27254.

18. Maan News Agency, "First Public Appearance of Fatah Leader since His Abduction in Gaza," January 16, 2008, www.maannews.net/en/index.php?opr=ShowDetails&ID=27252.

19. Maan News Agency, "Fatah Denies Hamas Accusations of Plot to Assassinate Haniyeh," January 19, 2008, www.maannews.net/en/index.php?opr=ShowDetails&ID=27314.

20. *Ash-Sharq al-Awsat*, "Hamas: Abbas Aides Plotted Assassination," February 17, 2008, www.asharqalawsat.com/english/news.asp?section=1&id=11806

21. James Hider and David Charter, "Palestinians Clash over Control of Border," *The Times* (UK), January 28, 2008, www.timesonline.co.uk/tol/news/world/middle_east/article3261643.ece.

22. Nicola Lombardozzi and Alix Van Buren, "Israel Will Not Offload Gaza on to Us," *La Repubblica* (Italy), January 31, 2008 [BBC Translation Service], http://fiservsw.portalvault.com/Default.aspx?pageMode=control&pageModeType=NewsArticleControl&pageModeParam=&storyId=114149151.

23. "PA to Assume Control of Rafah," *Jerusalem Post*, January 27, 2008, www.jpost.com/servlet/Satellite?cid=1201367876198&pagename=JPost%2FJPArticle%2FShowFull.

24. WAFA (Palestine News Agency), "Abbas Wins International Support for PNA Running Egypt-Gaza Border," January 29, 2008, www.wafa.ps/english/body.asp?id=11065.

25. Condoleezza Rice, Press Briefing, U.S. Department of State, January 28, 2008, www.state.gov/secretary/rm/2008/01/99762.htm.

26. "Abbas Sets Conditions for Gaza Talks with Hamas," *Ash-Sharq al-Awsat* (UK), January 30, 2008. www.asharq-e.com/news.asp?section=1&id=11631

27. "New Reality, Old Dilemma," *Al-Ahram Weekly* (Egypt), No. 882, January 31–February 6, 2008, http://weekly.ahram.org.eg/2008/882/fr1.htm.

28. "Gaza Deal Elusive," *Saudi Gazette,* January 31, 2008, www.saudigazette.com.sa/index.php?option=com_content&task=view&id=45941&Itemid=99999999.

29. "A Hamas Hardliner," *The Economist,* January 31, 2008, www.economist.com/world/africa/displaystory.cfm?story_id=10609550.

30. Maan News Agency, "Abbas Meets with Hamas Leaders," May 27, 2008, www.maannews.net/en/index.php?opr=ShowDetails&ID=29515.

31. Khaled Neimat, "Abbas to Meet with Bakhit Today," *Jordan Times,* August 9, 2007, www.jordanembassyus.org/08092007002.html.

32. Khaled Abu Toameh, "Increased Signs of Anti-Hamas 'Intifada' in Gaza," *Jerusalem Post,* September 2, 2007, www.jpost.com/servlet/Satellite?cid=1188392519220&pagename=JPost%2FJPArticle%2FShowFull.

33. Amnesty International, "Occupied Palestinian Territories Torn Apart by Factional Strife," October 24, 2007, p. 35. http://web.amnesty.org/library/Index/ENGMDE21020 2007.

34. Maan News Agency, "Man Injured in Gaza Strip Car Bomb, Hamas Blames Fatah," October 11, 2007, www.maannews.net/en/index.php?opr=ShowDetails&ID=25801.

35. Palestinian Centre for Human Rights, "Palestinian Killed in a Training Accident and Another Killed, 10 Injured in Renewed Clashes Between Islamic Jihad and Hamas in Rafah," October 22, 2007, www.pchrgaza.org/files/weapon/english/2007/report105.html.

36. Al-Jazeera television transcript, "Al-Jazirah: PIJ, HAMAS Officials Comment on Recent Armed Clashes, Ceasefire" Foreign Broadcast Information Service translation, October 22, 2007, http://techweb.rfa.org/pipermail/fbis/2007-October/180329.html.

37. "Black Mark on Hamas," *Arab News* (Saudi Arabia), November 13, 2007, www.arabnews.com/?page=7&section=0&article=103491&d=13&m=11&y=2007.

38. Maan News Agency, "Seven Dead, 55 Injured as Hamas Forces Fire on Massive Rally Honoring Arafat," November 12, 2007, www.maannews.net/en/index.php?opr=ShowDetails&ID=26245.

39. Maan News Agency, "Explosion Rocks Hamas' al-Qassam Brigades Headquarters in Gaza City," November 5, 2007, www.maannews.net/en/index.php?opr=ShowDetails&ID=26146.

40. Palestinian Centre for Human Rights, "Security and Weapon Chaos Continues in the Gaza Strip," November 25, 2007, www.pchrgaza.org/files/weapon/english/weapon_update.htm.

41. Shahar Ilan, "Shin Bet Chief: Palestinians Too 'Exhausted' for New Intifada," *Haaretz,* October 29, 2007, www.haaretz.com/hasen/spages/918163.html.

42. Marwan Bishara, "The Undeclared Palestinian Civil War," *Middle East Online* (UK), November 15, 2007, www.middle-east-online.com/english/?id=23095.

43. Dennis Ross "From Washington to Hamas: Change or Fail," in *Hamas Triumphant: Implications for Security, Politics, Economy and Strategy,* ed. Robert Satloff, Washington Institute for Near East Policy, Policy Focus, No. 3 (February 2006): 48, www.washingtoninstitute.org/templateC04.php?CID=232.

44. Kifah Zaboun, "Fatah and Hamas: The Division Continues . . ." *Ash-Sharq al-Awsat* (UK), November 5, 2007, www.asharqalawsat.com/english/news.asp?section=3&id=10781.

45. Khaled Abu Toameh, "Abbas: Hamas Planning to Overthrow West Bank Gov't," *Jerusalem Post*, October 28, 2007, www.jpost.com/servlet/Satellite?cid=1192380675509 &pagename=JPost%2FJPArticle%2FShowFull.

46. Fatah Constitution, www.fateh.net/e_public/constitution.htm (Arabic); www.ipcri.org /files/fatah1964.html (English).

47. Hamas charter, www.islamonline.net/Arabic/doc/2004/03/article11.SHTML (Arabic); www.yale.edu/lawweb/avalon/mideast/hamas.htm (English).

48. Jonathan Spyer, "A Rising Force," *Haaretz*, December 8, 2007, www.haaretz.com/hasen /spages/932087.html.

49. Ilene R. Prusher, "Palestinian Group Sounds Like Al-Qaeda but Forgoes Violence," *Christian Science Monitor*, January 22, 2008, www.csmonitor.com/2008/0122/p01s03- wome.html.

CONCLUSION

1. Near East Consulting, "Gaza Monitor," Bulletin No. 4, November 20, 2007, www .neareastconsulting.com/surveys/gaza/p211.

2. Salma Waheedi, "Interview with Dr. Mustafa Barghouti, Member of the Palestinian Leg- islative Council and Leader of the Independent Palestine Bloc," *Arab Reform Bulletin* 5, No. 9 (November 2007).

3. Taghreed El-Khodary, "Gaza: Life under Hamas Rule," *Arab Reform Bulletin* 5, No. 9 (November 2007), www.carnegieendowment.org/files/novemberkhodary1.pdf.

4. Maan News Agency, "Palestinian Youths Listen to Song Mocking Fatah and Hamas on Their Mobile Phones," July 7, 2007, www.maannews.net/en/index.php?opr=Show- Details&ID=23724.

5. "Hamas and Fatah in the Dock for 'Audacious' New Drama in Gaza City," *Lebanon Daily Star*, August 18, 2007, www.dailystar.com.lb/article.asp?edition_id=1&categ_id=4 &Article_id=84603.

6. Paul Collier et al., *Breaking the Conflict Trap: Civil War and Development Policy*, vol. 1 (Washington, DC: World Bank, 2003), p. 83.

7. Avi Issacharoff, "A Year After Gaza Takeover, Hamas Shows No Sign of Ending Vio- lence," *Haaretz*, June 13, 2008, www.haaretz.com/hasen/spages/992551.html.

8. Martin Chulov, "Palestinian Victims of Hamas Swear Revenge," *The Australian*, May 17, 2008, www.theaustralian.news.com.au/story/0,25197,23710388–2703,00.html.

9. "Poster Commemorating the 43rd Anniversary of the Fatah Movement," Official Fatah Information Web site (Arabic), December 22, 2007, www.palvoice.com/index.php?id =5852.

10. *Jerusalem Post*, "Abbas: 'Resistance' Not Ruled Out," February 28, 2008, www.jpost .com/servlet/Satellite?pagename=JPost%2FJPArticle%2FShowFull&cid=1204127196532.

11. Mel Frykberg, "Missile Barrages Traumatize Israeli Town," *Middle East Times* (Egypt), February 14, 2008, www.metimes.com/International/2008/02/14/missile_barrages _traumatize_israeli_town/3372/.

12. Al-Zaytouna Center for Studies and Consultations, "Palestine Now: Al-Aqsa Martyrs Brigades Demands of Its Members n the West Bank: Liquidate Fayyad Immediately" (Arabic), December 30, 2007, www.alzaytouna.net/arabic/?c=929&a=54485.

13. Nidal al-Mughrabi, "Hamas Disputes Abbas Comments on Truce Deal Terms," Reuters, March 11, 2008, www.reuters.com/article/latestCrisis/idUSL11323208.

14. Isabel Kershner, "Palestinian Leader Urges Talks with Hamas," *New York Times*, June 5, 2008, www.nytimes.com/2008/06/05/world/middleeast/05mideast.html

15. Ynet News, "Abbas To Hamas: Let's Talk," June 4, 2008, www.ynetnews.com/articles/0,73 40,L–3552088,00.html.

16. Maan News Agency, "Hamas and Fatah Hold Talks in Senegal, Agree to Further Meetings," June 8, 2008, www.maannews.net/en/index.php?opr=ShowDetails&ID=29803.

17. Ynet News, "Report: Abbas Informed of Israel's Plan to Retake Gaza," www.ynetnews .com/articles/0,7340,L–3552955,00.html.

18. Maan News Agency, "Egyptian Ambassador to Meet Hamas Members in Further Sign of Thaw Between Hamas and Fatah," June 7, 2008, www.maannews.net/en/index.php?opr =ShowDetails&ID=29786.

19. Kifah Zaboun, "Fatah and Hamas: The Division Continues . . ." *Ash-Sharq al-Awsat,* November 5, 2007, www.asharqalawsat.com/english/news.asp?section=3&id=10781.

20. WAFA (Palestine News Agency), "Palestinian Forum Holds Constitutional Meeting in Ramallah, Gaza," November 15, 2007, www.zibb.com/article/2205279/Palestinian +Forum+holds+constitutional+meeting+in+Ramallah+Gaza.

21. Sheera Claire Frenkel, "Another Way," *Jerusalem Post,* January 7, 2008, www.jpost .com/servlet/Satellite?cid=1198517318293&pagename=JPost%2FJPArticle%2FShowFull.

22. Al-Mubadara: Palestinian National Initiative, "Independent Palestine—the 'Third Way'—Announces List of Candidates for Legislative Elections," December 15, 2005, http://almubadara.org/new_web/articles/IP%20Annouces%20List%2015–12–05.htm.

23. Lamis Andoni, "Palestinians Yearn for Unity," al-Jazeera, January 15, 2008, http://english .aljazeera.net/NR/exeres/DE0324CB–885B–4C31-A8E9–872E999501C0.htm.

24. Palestinian Centre For Human Rights, "PCHR Condemns Gaza Beach Crime and the Response of the Government," July 26, 2008, www.pchrgaza.org/files/PressR/English/ 2008/69–2008.html

25. Ethan Bronner, "A Year Reshapes Hamas and Gaza," *New York Times,* June 15, 2008, www.nytimes.com/2008/06/15/world/middleeast/15gaza.html

26. Amnon Meranda, "Hamas Using Truce to Plant Mines in Gaza," Ynet News, July 21, 2008, www.ynetnews.com/articles/0,7340,L–3571546,00.html

INDEX